EurographicSeminars

Tutorials and Perspectives in Computer Graphics

Edited by G. Enderle and D. A. Duce

Data Structures for Raster Graphics

Proceedings of a Workshop
held at Steensel, The Netherlands, June 24–28, 1985

Edited by
L.R.A. Kessener F.J. Peters M.L.P. van Lierop

With 80 Figures

Springer-Verlag
Berlin Heidelberg New York Tokyo

Eurographic Seminars
Edited by G. Enderle and D. A. Duce
for EUROGRAPHICS –
The European Association for Computer Graphics
P.O. Box 16
CH-1288 Aire-la-Ville

Editors

Laurens R. A. Kessener
University of Technology Eindhoven
Computing Centre
P.O. Box 513
NL-5600 MB Eindhoven

Frans J. Peters
PHILIPS Corporate ISA CAD Centre,
P.O. Box 218
NL-5600 MD Eindhoven

Marloes L. P. van Lierop
University of Technology Eindhoven
Department of Mathematics
and Computing Science
P.O. Box 513
NL-5600 MB Eindhoven

ISBN-13: 978-3-642-71073-5 e-ISBN-13: 978-3-642-71071-1
DOI: 10.1007/978-3-642-71071-1

Library of Congress Cataloging in Publication Data.
Data structures for raster graphics. (EurographicSeminars) "Bibliography on quadtrees and related hierarchical data structures, [by] Hanan Samet": p. 1. Data structures (Computer science) – Congresses. 2. Computer graphics – Congresses. I. Kessener, L. R. A. (Laurens R. A.), 1944- . II. Peters, F. J. III. Lierop, M. L. P. van (Marloes L. P. van), 1955- . IV. Series: Eurographic seminars. QA76.9.D35D38 1986 006.6 86-1805
ISBN-13: 978-3-642-71073-5 (U.S.)

Softcover reprint of the hardcover 1st edition 1986

2145/3145-543210

Preface

Raster graphics differs from the more traditional vector or line graphics in the sense that images are not made up from line segments but from discrete elements orderly arranged in a two-dimensional rectangular region. There are two reasons for the growing popularity of raster graphics or bit-mapped displays:

1) the possibilities they offer to show extremely realistic pictures

2) the dropping prices of those displays and associated processors and memories.

With the rise of raster graphics, all kinds of new techniques, methods, algorithms and data representations are associated -such as ray tracing, raster operations, and quadtrees- bringing with them a lot of fruitful research.

As stated above raster graphics allows to create extremely realistic (synthesized) pictures. There are important applications in such diverse areas as industrial design, flight simulation, education, image processing and animation. Unfortunately many applications are hampered by the fact that with the present state of the art they require an excessive amount of computing resources. Hence it is worthwhile to investigate methods and techniques which may be of help in reducing computer costs associated with raster graphics applications. Since the choice of data srtuctures influences the efficiency of algorithms in a crucial way, a workshop was set up in order to bring together a (limited) number of experienced researchers to discuss this topic. The workshop was held from 24 to 28 June 1985 at Steensel, a tiny village in the neighbourhood of Eindhoven, the Netherlands. The workshop was funded by the Department of Mathematics and Computing Science of the Eindhoven University and the Netherlands Foundation for Pure Research (ZWO). This volume consists of the papers presented at the workshop covering a wide range of subjects.

Franklin's paper discusses fundamental problems with raster graphics algorithms. Due to round-of errors, operations on values of type real do not satisfy the distributivity, associativity and commutativity property of arithmetics. Hence, computers do not satisfy the intuition of graphics experts. Computational errors lead to graphics errors. But even worse, due to the bumpiness of integers, integer problems are intrinsically more difficult than problems with real valued numbers. That exactly is the reason why raster graphics is much more difficult than vector graphics.

Quadtrees have emerged as a convenient method to encode raster graphics images. From Samet's bibliography on quadtrees and related hierarchical data structures it can be seen that they arouse a large number of papers. Inevitably, this volume contains also some papers on this subject, such as a paper on linear quadtrees to store vector data by Samet, Shaffer and Webber. This paper presents a new data structure called segment quadtree with applications to a geographic database.

In Oliver's paper hardware realisation of display algorithms for quadtrees and octrees are discussed. Octrees, which are similar to quadtrees, are used to encode 3-D objects. For interactive use images have to be displayed in the shortest possible time: this implies the use of special hardware. Accordingly, the fast display of quadtrees and octrees depends on scan-conversion algorithms which are simple enough to be implemented in hardware. Three hardware systems for the display of quadtrees are described. Quadtrees containing no less than 30 000 leaves can be displayed in real time. For realistic pictures, however, this is not yet sufficient.

Van Lierop describes two algorithms and implicit data structures to display 3-D scenes, composed of polygons, on a raster device. Both algorithms are based on the so-called painter's technique and are investigated to be used in interactive applications.

Ray tracing is a very elegant method that has provided some of the finest examples of image synthesis in raster graphics. Ray tracing effectively models optical effects, such as mirroring reflections, cast shadows and transparency with refraction. Long processing times are the price for this sophistication. Hence it is worthwhile to study algorithms and data structures to improve the efficiency of ray tracing. Jansen gives an overview of data structures and algorithms to decrease ray tracing time.

The Programmer's Hierarchical Interactive Graphics System (PHIGS) is a proposed graphics programming standard under development by the American National Standards Institute (ANSI). This standard provides facilities for the development of interactive 3-D graphics applications. Any implementation of PHIGS should strive toward the ultimate goal of providing real time support for the full functionality. Abi-Ezzi and Milicia point out in their paper that that goal is impossible to achieve using current, readily available graphics hardware. This is due to the inherent complexity of 3-D interactive graphics. One possible solution is the development of a 'PHIGS machine'.

In recent years several graphical standards (GKS, PHIGS, CORE) have been proposed. These standards provide primitives which can utilize the facilities of raster displays. However, these standards are not particularly well suited to raster graphics and exclude functions for shading, texturing and other advanced raster graphics techniques. Teunissen and van den Bos propose a hierarchical model based upon a number of 2-D, 1-D and 0-D pattern primitives. ten Hagen and Trienekens present a structured representation for area oriented picture elements in order to allow both efficient interaction and scan conversion.

Leray presents the CUBI-7 system for 3-D animation. On conventional systems (like VAX 11/750) the computing costs for the production of one second of animated film vary from $ 2000 to $ 3000. In order to decrease those costs, the CUBI-7 system is designed.

Finally, using Bresenham's algorithm as an example, van Overveld shows how modern programming techniques may lead to efficient and elegant programs, which enjoy our confidence to be correct.

Rens R.A. Kessener
Frans J. Peters
Marloes L.P. van Lierop

Table of Contents

Problems with raster graphics algorithms 1
Wm. Randolph Franklin

Display algorithms for quadtrees and octtrees and their hardware realisation 9
Martin A. Oliver

Intermediate data structures for display algorithms 39
Marloes L.P. van Lierop

Data structures for ray tracing 57
Frederik W. Jansen

An approach for a PHIGS machine 75
Salim S. Abi-Ezzi and Michael A. Milicia

Using linear quadtrees to store vector data 91
Hanan Samet, Clifford A. Shaffer, and Robert E. Webber

A model for raster graphics language primitives 125
Wim J.M. Teunissen and Jan van den Bos

Pattern representation 143
Paul J.W. ten Hagen and Toos Trienekens

A 3D animation system 165
Pascal Leray

Applications of the method of invariants in computer graphics 173
Kees van Overveld

Bibliography on quadtrees and related hierarchical data structures 181
Hanan Samet

Problems with raster graphics algorithms *

Wm. Randolph Franklin

Electrical, Computer, and Systems Engineering Dept.
Rensselaer Polytechnic Institute
Troy, NY, 12180, USA

ABSTRACT

Assorted unusual problems with raster graphics digitization or scan conversion algorithms, where the implementation is much harder than the concept, are considered. They include digitizing a line that is on a plane so that the line is always visible, and digitizing a subset of a line correctly. Raster graphics is harder than vector graphics, in a deep sense.

1. Floating point problems

Before we consider raster algorithms in particular, a review of general arithmetic problems on computers is in order, since many graphics difficulties have an underlying algebraic aspect.

Many raster graphics problems arise from computer floating point numbers. In fact, it is to avoid these complexities that integers are sometimes used. Floating point numbers are a model of the real number field which is defined by certain axioms, (Spiegel, 1963). In fact, for almost every real number axiom, there is a computer implementation for which it is violated:

Distributivity $A \times (B + C) = A \times B + A \times C$

For a violation of this rule, consider a decimal floating number system which stores one decimal digit for each number. Calculations are performed exactly and then rounded to one digit. Thus 9 and 10 are exactly representable in this system, but 11 is not. Because of rounding, $2 \times 4 = 10$ but $2 \times 8 = 20$. Let $A = 2$, $B = 6$, and $C = 2$. In this number system, distributivity is not satisfied, since $A \times (B + C) = 20$, but $A \times B + A \times C = 10$.

Associativity $(A + B) + C = A + (B + C)$

* This research is based upon work supported by the National Science Foundation under Grant No. ECS-8351942, and by the Schlumberger-Doll Research Lab, Ridgefield Conn.

This is violated on any machine with fewer than 30 significant digits if A = 1.E30, B = −1.E30, C = 1.

Commutativity A + B = B + A

This can be violated on systems which can hold temporary numbers in registers at a higher precision than they can be stored in memory, and further allow a register - memory operation if the register is the first operand. When the second operand is stored in memory, it will lose precision. Four different machines with overlength floating point registers that violate commutativity are given in (Malcolm, 1972) and (Gentleman and Marovich, 1974).

Reciprocal $\underline{E}(Y : X \times Y = 1)$.

For example, in the APL system at RPI, there is no multiplicative inverse for 3 since $1 - 3 \times (1/3) = 1.388E-17$.

These problems can be reduced by using a properly designed floating point standard, but cannot be entirely removed. The IEEE standard, designed by numerical analysts, is the best. In contrast, those systems dating from the 1960s can be quite poor.

2. Raster coordinate standards

Two different coordinate systems are possible:

- having the coordinate system pass between the pixels, which are considered to be little squares and
- having it pass through the centers of the pixels, which are considered to be points.

These two standards are of equal power, but are incompatible in various *off by one* ways:

- Between X = 1 and X = 10, there are 9 pixels by the first standard, but 10 pixels by according to the second.
- If we define a circle such as $x^2 + y^2 = 4$, then the number of pixels inside it depends on the standard.
- These differences are also reminiscent of the different methods of antialiasing. For example, if a pixel is a point then any object smaller than the pixel spacing will be invisible. Thus if pixels are points, we must filter and bandwidth-limit the objects. On the other hand, if pixels are squares (or more complicated convolution functions) then the objects need not be pre-filtered.

We will switch between the two standards as appropriate.

3. Why raster is harder than vector

Many people assume that raster graphics is easier than vector graphics since we are working with simple integers, perhaps from 0 to 1023, rather than with an infinite number of real numbers. This first impression is false, as consideration of the following problems may show:

- drawing a slanted line, and
- filling a polygon

Drawing a vector line is trivial, but a raster line requires a scan conversion algorithm. Filling a vector polygon requires only intersecting the crosshatch lines with the edges. However a raster polygon raises questions such as 4-connectedness versus 8-connectedness, and how to find a seed in each component of the polygon.

People feel that raster graphics should be simple because integers are simpler than real numbers. This is also false. Consider the problem intuitively. One can describe integer problems, that were posed several centuries ago, and are to date unsolved, to an intelligent primary school student. Take Goldbach's conjecture, or Fermat's Last Theorem, for example. Goldbach's conjecture is that every even number is the sum of two primes. There are no comparable problems in the real numbers where there is such a large gap between a problem's statement and its solution.

The comparative difficulty of the integers has a deep foundation in first order logic. Consider the set of all formulae with variables in some domain, and using the universal and existential quantifiers ($\underline{A}$ and $\underline{E}$). We are also allowed certain primitive functions, such as addition. For example, the following formula says that every number has a half:

$$\underline{A}(x : \underline{E}(y : y + y = x)) \tag{1}$$

Now if our domain is the integers with addition and the successor function, we have Presburger arithmetic. There is a decision procedure for automatically proving the truth or falsity of any such formula, (Yasuhara, 1971), in double exponential time. However, if we also allow multiplication, then there is no such decision procedure, and some formulae are undecidable. Since Goldbach's conjecture could be expressed with addition and multiplication, if a decision procedure existed, then the theorem would be trivial.

However, if the variables are real numbers, then all formulae with addition and multiplication are solvable using Tarski's decision procedure, in double exponential time. Further, formulae with just addition can be proved much more quickly over the reals, in single exponential time, than over the integers. Although every integer solution is also a real solution, it is not contradictory for the integer formulae to be slower to solve. The truth of a formula depends on the domain of the variables. The above formula (1) is false over the integers but true over the reals. The really difficult cases, such as Fermat's Last Theorem, have a continuum of real solutions but only a few integer solutions, if any. Further, in this logic, there is no way to write a formula which selects the integers only. To do so would require a primitive floor function or remainder function which is not provided.
Thus, in a deep sense, bumpy integers are harder than smooth reals.

4. Simple Z-buffer drawing

The goal of any algorithm should be to produce the intuitively correct result for a user who is unaware of the algorithm's internals. For example, if object A is in front of object B in real life, then A should be in front of B in the Z-buffer. Many of these problems arise in attempting to form a three dimensional generalization of the two dimensional Bresenham line drawing algorithm.

4.1. Digitizing a line into a Z-buffer

In two dimensions, the obvious way to scan convert or digitize a line is to mark all pixels within distance 0.5 of the line. However, in three dimensions, consider the line

$$L : x = 3y, z = 9y$$

It is easy to give pixel (0,0) the value $z = 0$. However, what about pixel (1,0)? Since this point is not exactly on the line, we cannot substitute into the equation to get z. Various solutions are possible:

- Drop a perpendicular from (1,0) to the closest point on the line, (0.9, 0.3), and use that z-value, $z = 2.7$.

- Since the line's slope is less than one, we can run a vertical line straight up to L, at (1,1/3) and use the corresponding $z = 3$.

- If we know that L is on some relevant plane, such as $2x + 3y - z = 0$, then we can substitute (1,0) into this to get $z = 2$. The problem with this is that L may be at the common intersection of several planes.

- If instead we consider the pixel to be a square, around the point, then we can put bounds on z as L passes through the square. Here the square's lower left and upper right corners are at (0.5, —0.5) and (1.5, 0.5) respectively. Line L enters the square on the left with $z = 1.5$ and leaves on the right with $z = 4.5$. This is some help if we are working with interval arithmetic, but doesn't help us get one particular number for the Z-buffer. Sometimes there are particular reasons for using the minimum or maximum z, as we shall see.

Thus in three dimensions, unlike 2-D, there is no single obvious way to digitize lines.

4.2. Digitizing a plane into a Z-buffer

Determining what z to assign for each pixel covered by a plane is easy if the pixels are considered to be points. However, if the pixels are to be squares, then the plane covers a range of z-values, from which we might choose the min or max perhaps.

4.3. Two crossing lines

Consider two lines, L_1 and L_2, in three dimensions. If L_1 crosses in front of L_2, as seen by the viewer, then we might expect that if L_1 and L_2 cause the same pixel to be marked in the frame buffer, then that pixel's final colour should be that of L_1. This is impossible in general.

For example, consider the following two lines:

$$L_1 : x = 1, z = 6y + 2$$
$$L_2 : x = 3y, z = 9y$$

In continuous space, they cross at the point (1, 1/3), where $z_1 = 4 > z_2 = 3$. However, they overlap at the pixel (1,0), where, using the second digitizing method described above, $z_1 = 2 < z_2 = 3$. Thus although L_2 is really closer than L_1, it appears farther in the Z-buffer.

The situation gets worse. Consider a set of lines, M_i, covering every pixel, and a single line, L:

$$L : x = 1, z = 6y + 2$$
$$M_i : y = x/3 + i, z = 3x + 6i$$

Now L crosses M_i at $(1, i + 1/3)$, where $z_L = 6i + 4 > z_M = 6i + 3$. However in the raster domain, they cross at pixel (1,i), where $z_L = 6i + 2 < z_M = 6i + 3$. This means that although L is behind all of the M_i in the continuous domain, it is completely visible in the Z-buffer.

Next let us fit a plane through all the M_i, we get

$$M : x + 6y - z = 0$$

The plane M is in front of L everywhere in the buffer, so there is a difference whether we use a plane or a set of lines in the plane.

4.4. Line and plane

Another principle that users might want is that if we have a plane and a line on it, then the line should be visible in front of the plane in every pixel that it covers in the Z-buffer. Many of the digitization methods for lines described above will have an undesirable effect: the line will be in front of the plane for several pixels, and then behind it for several pixels. This is a supreme jaggy effect.

One simple solution is to digitize the lines and planes thus:

- Consider the pixels to be squares, and the lines and planes mark any pixel whose square they pass through.
- When a line passes through a pixel, choose the minimum z-value that the line has anywhere in the pixel.
- When a plane passes through a pixel, choose the maximum z-value that the plane has anywhere in the pixel.

With this standard, any line that is exactly on a plane will appear in front of it in the Z-buffer. However, lines that are slightly behind the plane may also appear in front at certain pixels. This is unavoidable. This method was designed assuming that slightly behind lines are less common than lines on the plane.

4.5. Line and point

Alternatively, we may have lines and points that we may wish to insert into the Z-buffer such that if a point is on a line, then it overrides the line at that pixel. One method that works is this:

- Consider the pixels as squares again.
- If a point is in a certain pixel then use the point's z-value to mark that pixel.
- If a line passes through a certain pixel, then use that line's *maximum* z-value, not the minimum as before.

Now a point on (or even slightly behind) a line will appear in front of the line in the Z-buffer. The problem with this method is that it is incompatible with line and plane method in the previous section. It is an open question whether points, lines, and planes can all be painted into a Z-buffer, with the points in front of the lines that they are on, and the lines in front of the planes that contain them.

5. The subset line problem

Even in two dimensional raster graphics it is difficult to determine an unambiguous part of a line to erase it. This problem can be formalized thus:

- We wish a line digitization algorithm to have the following property:
- Assume that we have digitized a line, L, between two pixels A and B, that is we have determined a set of pixels, **S**, in between A and B that are to be marked to signify the line.
- Assume that we pick two pixels, C and D, from **S** and digitize a line, M, between them by setting the pixels in the set **T**.
- Then, since M is clearly ideally a subset of L, we want our digitization algorithm to cause **T** to be a subset of **S**. The problem is not trivial since we must digitize M without any knowledge of L. Thus for all lines L whose set of pixels, **S**, contains C and D, we require that **T** contains **S**.

It is easy to show that the Bresenham algorithm doesn't satisfy this property. In fact the following stronger property holds.

Let a *translation invariant* digitization algorithm be one which just depends on the difference between the line's endpoints and not on their absolute coordinates. Then no translation invariant algorithm has the subset line property unless it is undesirable in certain other ways.

It is easy to get a digitization algorithm with the subset line property if we relax the constraint that the pixels marked be within one half pixel of the actual continuous line. For example, we could draw a line from A(x1,y1) to B(x2,y2) by going horizontally from A to (x2,y1) and then vertically to B. However this is not a useful digitization.

Although there are some preliminary results, this is still an open problem: it is not even known whether a good algorithm exists, let alone how complicated it might be. It is conceivable that the simplest good algorithm might have to explicitly store the digitizations of all 1000^4 lines on a 1000 by 1000 screen, and use table lookup. Such a solution would be of theoretical interest only.

6. Summary

The study of low level raster algorithms is important because first, theoretical gaps in them will cause problems in any higher algorithms that use them, and second, until the simple algorithms are understood, there is no reasonable hope of a detailed understanding of more complex algorithms. We have seen how some problems, such as handling crossing lines and planes, have no perfect solution, and how other problems, such as the subset raster line problem, remain open.

References

(Gentleman and Marovich, 1974)
W.M. Gentleman and S.B. Marovich. "More on Algorithms That Reveal Properties of Floating Point Arithmetic Units", *Comm. ACM 17*, (5), (May 1974), pp. 276–277.

(Malcolm, 1972)
M.A. Malcolm, "Algorithms to Reveal Properties of Floating Point Arithmetic:, *Comm. ACM 15*, (11), (November 1972), pp. 949-951.

(Spiegel, 1963)
M.R. Spiegel, *Theory and Problems of Advanced Calculus*, Schaum's Outline Series, McGraw-Hill, New York, (1963).

(Yasuhara, 1971)
A. Yasuhara, *Recursive Function Theory and Logic*, Academic Press, New York, (1971).

Display algorithms for quadtrees and octtrees and their hardware realisation

M. A. Oliver

Computing Laboratory, The University
Canterbury, Kent, England CT2 7NF

ABSTRACT

For interactive use images have to be displayed in the shortest possible time: this implies the use of special hardware. Accordingly, the fast display of quadtrees and octtrees depends on scan conversion algorithms which are simple enough to be implemented in hardware. Three hardware systems for the display of quadtrees are described; the algorithms which underlie the hardware implementations are described together with the data structures on which they work. Several algorithms for the display of octtrees are described together with hardware possibilities.

1. Introduction

In a recent paper Samet [12] has described a family of algorithms for the scan conversion of quadtrees. They put out the image row by row in scan order without the use of a frame buffer; the only extra memory requirement over that required for the quadtree is that for a single line buffer, i.e. one row of pixels. The design of these algorithms has been primarily concerned with considerations of space. The quadtree representation used is a linked list in which each node in the tree is stored as a record which contains six fields: five fields contain pointers to the father and four sons of the node; one field contains the colour of the node (black or white for a leaf, grey for an interior node).

In the present paper speed of execution is taken to be paramount and the use of memòry is very much a secondary consideration. Nevertheless, the data structures used for the representation of the quadtree are considerably more compact than those generally used in work on quadtrees. The goal is to be able to refresh the image directly from a quadtree data structure. The feasibility of this goal depends on the image size (number of pixels) and whether or not one is willing to restrict the complexity of the image. There are some constraints in the problem which suggests that without some form of parallel processing the goal is unattainable. There is just too much data to read in the time available in the case of an image for which every leaf is a pixel. Such an image can be very 'simple': e.g. a monochrome image of horizontal bands, each band consists of a sequence of scan-lines coloured

0, 1, 2, ... up to the maximum intensity.

In the first part of this paper three machines which accept quadtrees for display are described together with the algorithms on which they operate. Milford and Willis [6] have built a hardware decoder for quadtrees which converts a quadtree into a display list of quadrants stored in scan order; the video generator then scans this store repeatedly to refresh the image. A simplification of a machine called DisArray, built by Ian Page [11], gives an example of how parallel processing can be used to help display a quadtree. A machine which is at present being built, Aura, is designed to implement in hardware an algorithm due to Stewart [13].

In the rest of the paper algorithms for the display of octtrees are described and the octtree machine of Meagher [5] is mentioned.

2. Quadtree scan conversion algorithms

2.1. The data structures

In the algorithms to be described here two data structures are used for the representation of quadtrees: the linear list and the *one-to-four* linked list. All the algorithms can be modified for the conventional linked list representations. However, the latter consume somewhat more memory and also require an additional administrative effort to update. A sample image is given in figure 1.

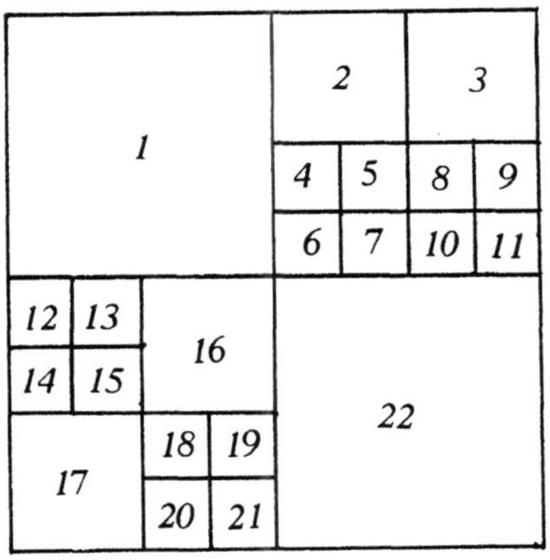

Figure 1. A sample quadtree image

The linear list

This consists of a linear list of the quadtree nodes in the order of some tree traversal. The usual order of traversal is depth first with the quadrants in the order NW, NE, SW, SE and the child nodes, if any, immediately follow their parent. Leaf nodes are represented by their colour values whereas parent nodes are represented by a special value. Parent nodes can be given a colour value (say, the average of the values of their children) together with a flag (say the most significant bit set to one for a parent, zero for a leaf) to show their parenthood. The linear quadtree code (with 29 nodes) for the sample image is given in figure 2, where R indicates a parent node. It is simply the list of node colour values in the order of a depth first traversal over the quadtree. The linear list quadtree is the most compact direct representation of a quadtree.

R 1 R 2 3 R 4 5 6 7
R 8 9 10 11 R R 12 13 14
15 16 17 R 18 19 20 21 22

Figure 2. Linear list code for sample image

Unlike linked list representations, the linear list representation does not allow any flexibility in the choice of tree traversal. The sextree algorithm which is described below gets around this problem by the generation of a larger data structure, a sextree, on which the required traversals can be made. The disadvantage of this approach is that a new data structure has to be constructed for the particular purpose in hand.

The one-to-four data structure

Stewart [13] has proposed a quite new linked list representation: the *one-to-four* linked list. The *one-to-four* linked list representation stands between the usual linked list representations where four (or more, as in [12]) pointers are assigned to each node and the linear linked list in which there are no pointers. The *one-to-four* representation has enough flexibility of traversal to compete with the more common, and more memory consuming, linked list representations and has fewer overheads.

The basic building block of the *one-to-four* data structure is a record with five fields: the first field is a pointer to the records of all the children; the other four fields are the node descriptors of the children in the order NW, NE, SW, SE. The four records for the children are held consecutively in memory so that the pointer points to the group of four records. This is shown in figure 3. The node descriptor holds the colour and type of the node. There is one pointer for every four (interior or exterior) node values and hence the name.

With the *one-to-four* data structure used as just described it is apparent that memory is wasted, see figure 4. The only function of the empty records is to ensure that the filled records are correctly placed for their offset value. There are several techniques which can be used to avoid the necessity for this padding. A convenient technique is to include in the record the four offsets of the filled records of the children, then the unfilled records can be omitted. One convenient format is for two words of memory to be used for one record, see figure 5; the data structure with this format is shown in figure 6. With a 16-bit address space the system can deal with quadtrees of up to 256K nodes. The 'extra' eight bits can be used to

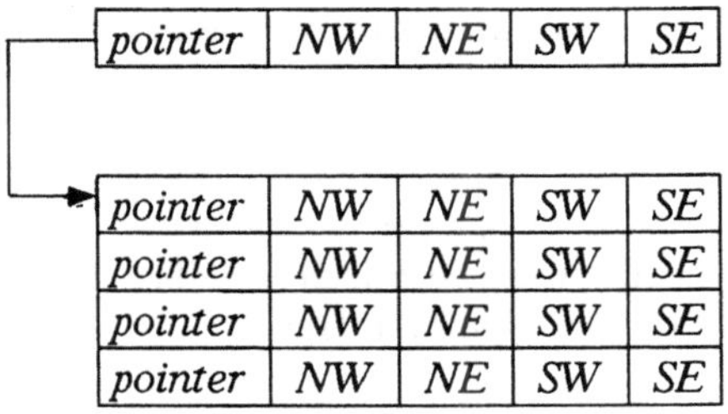

Figure 3. Basic record structure of the one-to-four data structure

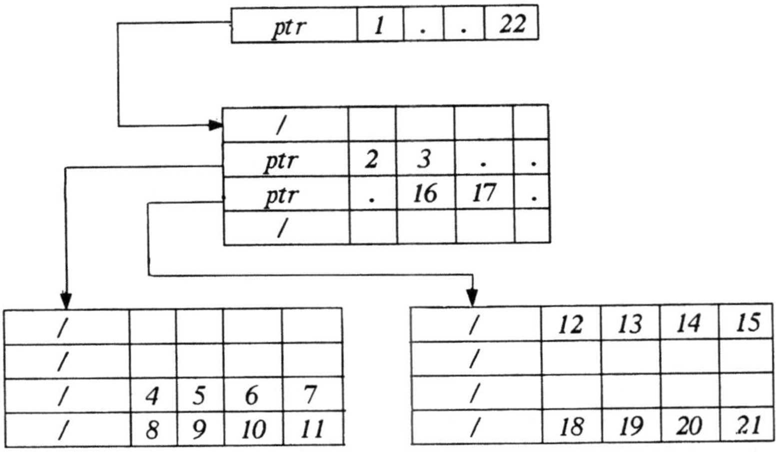

Figure 4. Full one-to-four data structure for sample image

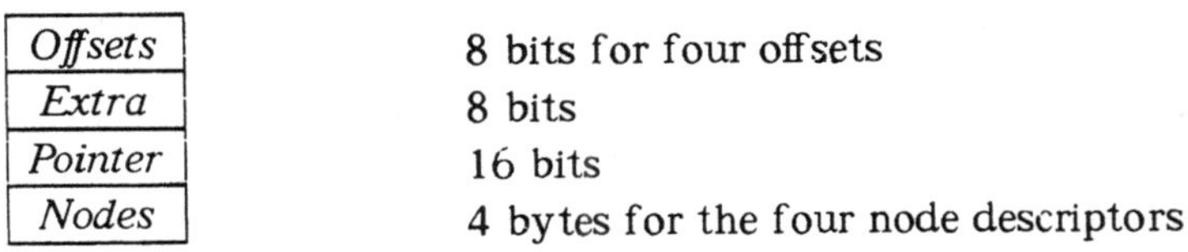

Figure 5. Record for compact form of one-to-four

indicate the node type so that the node descriptors can be used for colour, or to extend the pointer, or for the node depth, or for other information.

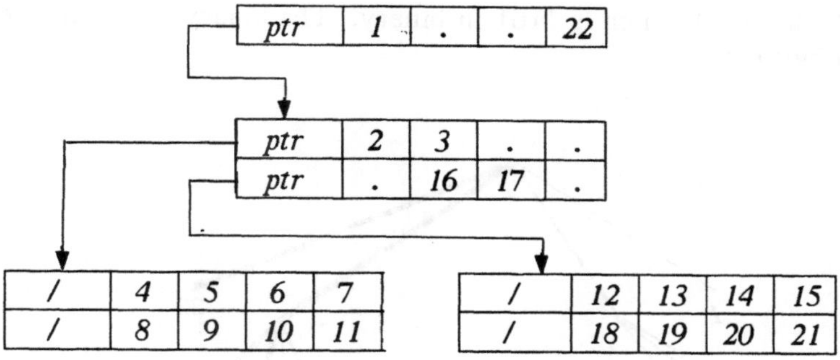

Figure 6. Compact one-to-four data structure for sample image

2.2. Scan conversion with sextree

The basis of the scan conversion

A full description of this algorithm together with code is given in Oliver, King, and Wiseman [10]. Consider the quadtree which represents an image. If a scan-line, which is one pixel thick, passes through the quadrant represented by a parent node then it passes through either both of the quadrants represented by the first and second child nodes (the North quadrants viz. nodes 0 and 1) or those quadrants represented by the third and fourth child nodes (the South quadrants viz. nodes 2 and 3).

Accordingly, at each level in the quadtree either the left pair of nodes (the North quadrants) or the right pair (the South quadrants) is taken. Denote left (North) by 0 and right (South) by 1. There are N levels in the tree so write these N digits from left to right in the order first level to Nth level. This list of binary digits is stored in a variable *route*: it defines the route through the quadtree that defines a scan-line binary tree.

A depth first walk over the scan-line binary tree gives the leaves touched by the scan-line in scan-line order. Thus run-length code for this scan-line is generated if the side length and colour of each leaf is emitted as it is reached on the walk. If the scan-lines are numbered from 0 (top line) to 2^N-1 (bottom line) then the value of the variable *route* as a binary number is just the ordinal number of the scan-line.

Suppose that the image space for the image shown in figure 1 is 16×16 pixels in size; so the smallest square in the image contains four pixels. As an example consider the fourteenth scan-line on the image; the run-length code for this line is

4 17 2 18 2 19 8 22

which is a sequence of pairs of length and colour values. The line number, i.e.

route , is 13 (decimal) which is 1101 in binary. The binary tree which is generated is shown in figure 7.

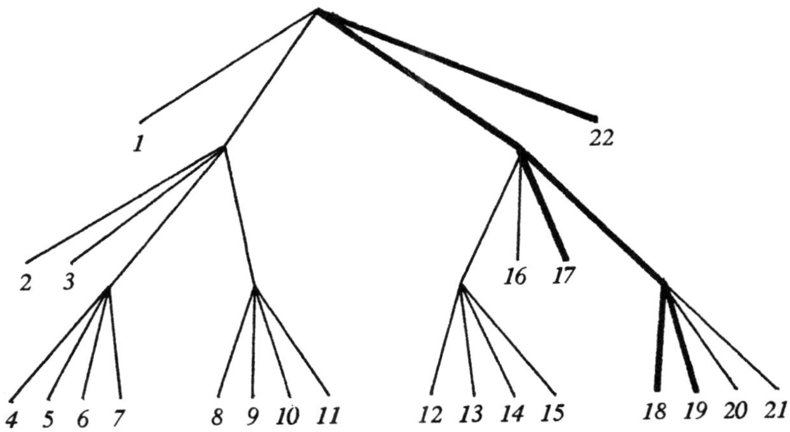

Figure 7. A scan-line binary tree on the quadtree of figure 1

The size and colour of the leaves touched in a depth first walk over the scan-line binary tree do indeed give the run-length code given above. Notice that the value of *route* and the scan-line depend on the size of the image space.

The algorithm

Now the problem is: how can we pick our way over the quadtree in such a manner that in effect we walk depth first over the selected scan-line binary tree? For data structures other than the linear quadtree the pointer structures can be used to step over the quadtree.

With a linear quadtree the trick is to rewrite the quadtree as a sextree. Two new children (leaves) are given to each parent node. The correspondence between the children of a quadtree parent and the children of the parent to which it corresponds in the associated sextree is given in figure 8.

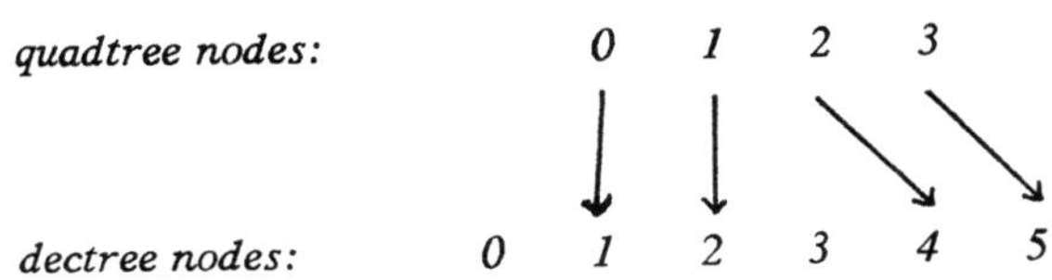

Figure 8. Relation between quadtree and sextree nodes

In the sextree the first node (node 0) is a leaf the value of which is the offset of the fourth node (node 3); the fourth node (node 3) is a leaf the value of which is the offset of the last leaf in the branch at the sixth node (node 5).

In a walk over the sextree either the North nodes or the South nodes can be stepped over with the aid of the offsets that have been introduced into node 0 and node 3 respectively. The values in the offset nodes, i.e. nodes 0 and 3, allow for incrementing the offset before evaluation of the node colour in the walk over the sextree. The values of the bits of the binary number *route* are the information required to specify left or right at any level on the walk.

The linear sextree code (with 43 nodes) that corresponds to the sample quadtree shown in figure 1 is given in figure 9.

R	24	*1*	*R*	9	*2*	*3*	22	*R*	14
4	*5*	15	*6*	*7*	*R*	21	*8*	*9*	22
10	*11*	43	*R*	35	*R*	31	*12*	*13*	32
14	*15*	*16*	42	*17*	*R*	41	*18*	*19*	42
20	*21*	*22*							

Figure 9. Linear sextree code

This code should be compared with the linear quadtree code for the sample quadtree which is given in figure 2. The non-italic numbers are the offset values in the first and fourth children.

Each scan-line is produced by a call of the procedure which walks over the sextree with the scan-line number *route*. Accordingly, a simple for-loop generates the complete frame.

2.3. Scan conversion of *one-to-four*

BCPL code for the algorithm will be found in Stewart [13]. The walk over the binary subtree which generates the run-length code for a scan-line is achieved by stepping over the quadtree with the aid of the pointers in the *one-to-four*. The variable *route* determines whether the North children or the South children are wanted as before.

There are greater overheads in the walk over the *one-to-four*, but not having to generate the sextree more than compensates for this. Also, the space taken up by the *one-to-four* is less than that of the quadtree together with its associated sextree. Another advantage of the *one-to-four* is that a small modification of the algorithm allows the quadrants to be visited in any order: in this way rotations and reflections can be done at the same time as the scan conversion.

In Stewart's BCPL implementation of this algorithm the *one-to-four* to run-length is roughly 10% faster than the sextree algorithm; if the sextree construction time is discounted the reverse is true.

2.4. Scan conversion with each leaf touched once only

In the sextree scan conversion algorithm, or its variants, each scan-line is obtained from a complete walk over a binary subtree. This means that leaves are visited 'leaf size' times in the course of the scan conversion of an image. This amounts to a lot of multiple memory reads.

The *one-to-four* has enough traversal flexibility to enable the leaves to be visited just once: in fact, no node need be visited more than once. (Code is given in Stewart [13]).

The algorithm

A store is maintained of pointers to the ancestors of the leaves touched by the current scan-line. This is called the 'ancestor tree'. The storage structure is a triangular array which is depicted in figure 10.

leaf side exponent	*pointers at each level*
8	*0*
7	*0 1*
6	*0 1 2 3*
5	*0 1 2 3 4 5 6 7*
4	*0 1 2 .... 14 15*
3	*0 1 2 .... 30 31*
2	*0 1 2 .... 62 63*
1	*0 1 2 .... 126 127*
0	*0 1 2 .... 254 255*

Figure 10. Ancestor store

Given the x-coordinate of a pixel the pointer to its ancestor at any level in the quadtree can be found. A similar structure records whether or not the southern leaves have been visited.

There are two scan-line buffers which contain three fields for each pixel: colour, size, duration. The 'duration' gives the number of scan-lines which the leaf covers below the current one. One buffer holds the data for the current scan-line and the other buffer is for the next scan-line.

The first scan-line initialises the ancestor trees and one of the scan-line buffers. When the first scan-line has been scanned the first line buffer contains for each pixel its colour value, leaf size, and duration; the durations for this first scan-line will be equal to the size less one. No run-length code has been emitted at this stage.

For all subsequent scan-lines, except the last, the procedure is the same: the three fields are copied from the old line buffer to the new line buffer, unless the duration of the leaf is zero, and as this is done run-length code is emitted. If the duration of the leaf is zero then the leaf is replaced with the aid of the ancestor trees.

There is a high probability that if one leaf is finished with then there will be a sequence of leaves which are finished with. For example, when in the quadtree in figure 1 the leaf 6 is finished with the leaves 7, 10, and 11 are also finished on this line: the quadrant 22 is read into the line buffer for the next line. All the leaves in this sequence can be written into the line buffer for the next scan-line at the same time. It is done as follows.

(i) The pointer in the record of the expired leaf is found in the ancestor tree and inspected to see if the southern half has been read i.e. its sibling which is directly south of it.

(ii) If its southern half has not been read it is read now; otherwise the ancestor tree is climbed until a record is found with its southern child unread.

(iii) The southern child so found is marked as read.

(iv) The binary subtree of northern children which has as its root this southern child is traversed. In this traversal the values of the southern children are read into the line buffer and the pointers are stored in the ancestor tree where they are flagged appropriately.

When the end of the scan-line is reached the roles of the line buffers are swapped.

For the last scan-line the line buffer is simply read for its run-length code.

2.5. Interruptible breadth first display

It is easy to scan the *one-to-four* quadtree data structure breadth first. Accordingly, it is a straightforward matter to modify the scan conversion algorithm of §2.4 so that it converts the quadtree at a specified depth i.e. resolution. This is the basis of another strategy for quadtree display given by Stewart [13].

In the time taken to video scan a single line the next line must be made up ready to scan. The line can be made up first at a low resolution in a line buffer (choose the highest resolution at which a line is guaranteed to be completely made up), then at the next highest resolution in another buffer, then the next, and so on until time runs out. In order to do this there is a set of pairs of line buffers: one pair for each resolution. When time runs out the highest resolution line buffer is read for video.

If a scan-line is only partly finished when the interrupt occurs the ancestor tree is corrupted. The novelty in this algorithm is the way in which corrupted data structures are dealt with.

The image which results contains scan-lines at different resolutions. If the run-length code is written to a frame buffer then after the first pass the image contains scan-lines at different resolutions; in subsequent frames the lines at low resolution could be filled in.

3. Hardware for quadtree display

3.1. The Quad Encoded Display Machine

This machine was purpose built to display quadtrees and is described in Milford and Willis [6]. The application program is run on a host computer and a quadtree is sent to the Quad Encoded Display Machine for display. The host is connected to the display by a conventional serial line which operates at 19200 baud. The machine is managed by a Motorola 68000 16-bit processor.

As the quadtree data is received by the machine, in the form of a breadth-first linear quadtree, it is converted into a linked list and written into the main memory of the display. The main memory is intended to hold several images. A quadtree for display is taken from main memory and converted into a quad list as it is inserted into the picture buffer. The quad-list is simply the list of quadtree leaves in scan order and scan order is the order in which the leaves are first touched as the raster is scanned line by line.

The machine displays images on an interlaced raster of 512 × 512 pixels at 50 Hz. An important feature of the display is that the displayed image is refreshed from the quad-list in the picture buffer. The picture decoder cannot be defeated by image complexity; it can refresh as large a quad-list (for a 512 × 512 image) as the picture buffer can hold. The overall structure of the machine is shown in figure 11.

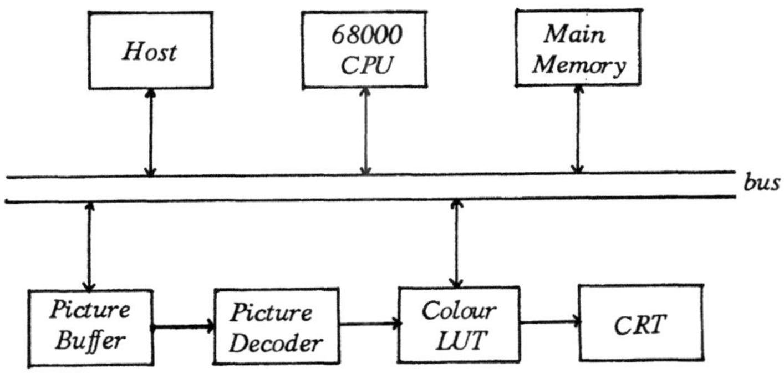

Figure 11. Quad Encoded Display

Scan ordered leaves

A straightforward modification of any of the scan conversion algorithms described above will generate the scan ordered list of quadrants. Two static variables *maxleaf* and *minleaf size* are needed.

As the binary subtree is traversed the size of any leaf which is touched is inspected. The variable *minleaf size* is used to hold the size of the smallest leaf touched by the scan-line. When the scan-line is finished *minleaf size* is added to the scan-line number. In this way the identical scan-lines are skipped.

A leaf is only put out if it has not been previously touched. The variable *maxleaf* is given the size of the largest new leaf which can be touched on the current scan-line. The value of the largest possible new leaf on a scan-line depends on the scan-line number in an obvious way.

Actually there is a modification to scan order for leaves which are pixels; the reason for this modification and its description is given below. A brief description of how the image is refreshed from the picture buffer follows.

The refresh cycle

Every item in the quad list is accessed once and only once in every field scan.

There are two identical line buffers of fast memory each with 512 pixel locations. Each line buffer holds a 12-bit pixel colour code and a 5-bit height code for each of the 512 pixels on the current scan-line.

The two line buffers allow for double buffering: the next scan-line is constructed in one buffer as the current scan-line is read for video from the other buffer; when the end of the line is reached the roles of the buffers is exchanged. A scan-line must be completed in the time which it takes to read a line at video speed; the worst case is a line of pixels.

Scan-lines are numbered from zero. If the odd field is being refreshed then it is possible that a large number of pixels (all on the interlaced even scan-line) would have to be read before the current scan-line is reached (with the corresponding pixels). This problem is solved by a modification of the quad-list order from the simple scan order: put each group of four pixels with a common parent node into the quad list in the order NW, SW, NE, SE as shown in the example in figure 12. This ensures that any group of four consecutive pixels will have two on the scan-line.

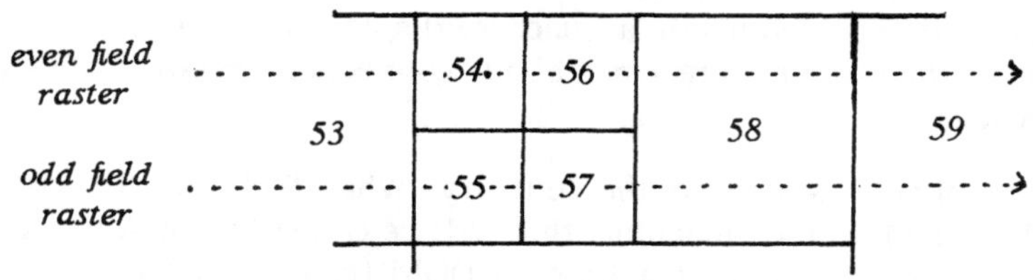

Figure 12. Order of pixel quads in quad list

The buffer memory has an access time of 200 *ns* and the required pixel period (for an image with 512×512 pixels) is 70 *ns*. Clearly some degree of parallelism is necessary for memory read: eight quads are read from the picture buffer in parallel into the decoder in each read cycle. At worst four pixel values for the current scan-line will be read in 200 *ns*; since the pixel period is 70 *ns* all is well.

A width code determines the number of pixel places which are filled in the line buffer by the pixel colour and its height code.

A height code determines the number of scan-lines for which a particular line buffer entry remains valid. When it is zero a new entry is obtained.

Remarks

There are three delays from the time when a quadtree is sent to the machine for display to the time when the image is refreshed from the picture buffer.

(i) The delay due to the 19200 baud link with the host.

(ii) The delay due to the conversion of the linear quadtree to the linked list quadtree in the main memory; this is completely masked by (i).

(iii) The delay due to the main memory to picture buffer transfer in which the quad-list is generated. This program can convert the quadtree at the rate of 40 leaves per *ms*.

If the mode of operation is one where the system is loaded with a set of images which are then examined within the display machine the delay in loading might be acceptable. For other modes of operation the delay would be irritating and, for large quadtrees, very serious.

3.2. DisArray as a quadtree display machine

DisArray is a 16 × 16 RasterOp processor which has been designed, and a prototype built, by Ian Page [11]. The Processing Elements (PE) and their memory are closely coupled which results in high speed; high throughput is due to the parallelism. The machine is easily programmed to display quadtrees and also to perform more general manipulations of quadtrees.

DisArray is an example of an SIMD bit serial machine. The design of DisArray can be simplified considerably if a quadtree display machine is all that is required: in particular the (four) nearest neighbour connections between PE's on the array are not needed.

Unless explicitly stated to the contrary, what follows will always refer to the hypothetical simplified machine: this will be called the DisArray Quadtree Machine (DQM). It is believed that a 16 × 16 DQM (constructed with similar technology) could run about twenty times faster than DisArray. A brief description of this machine follows; for details of the complete DisArray Machine see [11].

The Array Processor

The DisArray Quadtree Machine (DQM) has an array of 16 × 16 PE's which are each simple 1-bit processors with individual 16K×1-bit local memories. As a whole the array deals with square words of 256-bits known as planes. All PE's execute the same instruction simultaneously on their local data. Thus the DQM is

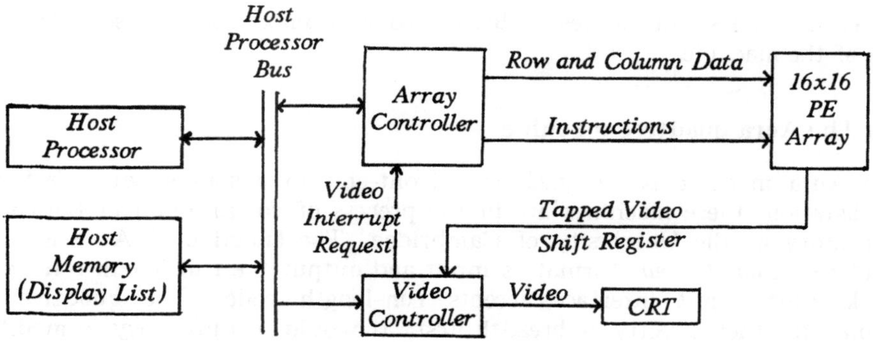

Figure 13. The DisArray Quadtree Machine organisation

a simple example of a SIMD bit serial machine. There is a 16-bit data bus between the host and the array memory.

Row and column masks (16 bits each) are used to define a rectangular region of the array. With the aid of this mask an arbitrary function can be applied to any defined rectangular region of the array. A single 1-bit register (the Q-register) holds the result of computations.

The basic array cycle

An array instruction consists of a read/modify/write operation on a single plane in memory. The instruction performs the following function:

(i) Read the contents of a 256-bit plane from (the PE) memory.

(ii) Examine the state of the row and column input lines for the masking information: the logical AND of these inputs is generated to select a rectangle.

(iii) Apply a Boolean operation between the contents of the plane and the Q-register in the selected rectangle and applies a different Boolean operation outside that rectangle.

(iv) Write the array contents back to the same location selected in (i).

The DQM display algorithm

The Host processor runs the application program which produces the quadtree data structure that is to be displayed. The quadtree is read into the Array Control Unit (by DMA) as required by the driver program.

For an image space of 512×512 pixels the 16×16 pixel plane corresponds to a leaf on the quadtree at depth 5. Accordingly, leaves at depth 5 or greater can be inserted into memory with equal efficiency and the vast majority of leaves fall into this class. The procedure to deal with a leaf at depth 4 or less is simple since it is tiled by a complete plane. Nevertheless, it may be worthwhile to expand all leaves at depth 4 or less into leaves at depth 5 so as to maximise the use of the parallelism of the machine.

3.3. The Aura quadtree machine

The Aura machine is designed as a front-end to a sophisticated fast graphics workstation; these machines are in the process of construction in the computing laboratory at the University of Cambridge. The function of Aura is to take a quadtree in *one-to-four* format as input and output the run-length code, since the workstation input interface accepts run-length code. The quadtree can be displayed either directly or breadth first. It would be quite easy to modify Aura to put out video directly and so transform it into a special purpose quadtree display device.

The primary reason for the choice of data structure is that the amount of data to be read is kept to a minimum and a reasonably high degree of flexibility is retained for the implementation of other algorithms if and when needed.

The Aura hardware

The algorithm implemented is Ian Stewart's second algorithm which is described in §2.4. The hardware organisation mirrors the structure of the scan conversion algorithm. The application program runs on a host computer and creates a *one-to-four* quadtree ready for display. Quadtree node values (colours or pointers) are read from the main memory of the host when they are needed.

The basic organisation of the machine is shown in figure 14.

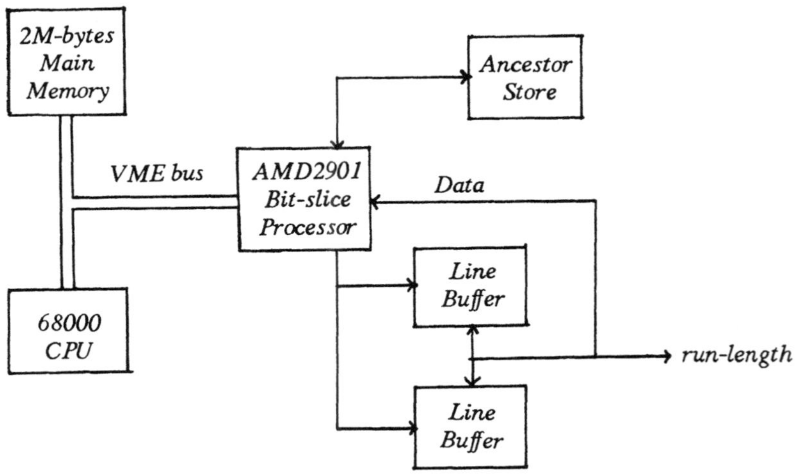

Figure 14. The organisation of the Aura hardware

The display software runs on the AMD2901 bit-slice processor (16-bits are used).

The other components are an 'ancestor' memory and double line buffers. The line buffers exchange roles after each scan-line is output.

4. Browsing high definition images

Willis and Milford [15] have proposed a way in which a large image which is represented by a quadtree can be browsed by panning and zooming with a window on the image space.

Zooming is quantised by the depth structure of the quadtree and has to be done by halving or doubling the window size. To zoom smoothly is a far from simple anti-alias problem.

For a quadtree data structure translation is quantised by the pixel size and so can be done 'smoothly'. It is easy to do this simply by a walk over the quadtree for the whole image with the required window. However, Willis and Milford [15] argue that this is an inefficient way in which to generate the image and they reorganise their data for more efficient image generation. Their method quantises translation in steps of 64 pixels, so smooth translation is not achieved.

The penalty incurred in a walk over a large quadtree in order to display an arbitrary window on the image may not be very high. After all what the walk over a quadtree achieves is a two dimensional binary search of a region and that is a good way to proceed if the unwanted branches are stepped over. The display needs nine levels (for a 512×512 display surface) and at its root level (in the large quadtree) at most four branches will contain leaves to be displayed, e.g. if the root is at level three only four of the 64 branches at this level will be traversed.

4.1. On the Quad Encoded Machine

A quadtree of depth 12 (which corresponds to an image space of size 4096×4096 pixels) is to be displayed on a display surface of 512×512 pixels. The quadtree is modified by the replacement of the *top* six levels by a 4096 way branch at the root; any leaf above the sixth level is tiled by the appropriate number of leaves. Thus the maximum sized leaf in the quadtree is 64×64 pixels.

If the window is placed over the entire image space then the quadtree is only inspected to depth nine and the display shows a 512×512 anti-aliased overview of the quadtree image. The window size can be successively halved three times before the quadtree is inspected to its bottom layer. At this point the display resolution and image resolution are matched and the display shows a 512×512 region of the quadtree image.

At the deeper levels the 512×512 window is restricted to lie on the boundaries of a 64×64 'chequer-board' on the image space of 4096×4096. This restriction corresponds to a selection of branches from the root of the modified tree being made; if a branch is selected then it is (completely) displayed. The selected branches are converted into a quad-list and displayed as described in §3.1.

4.2. On DisArray

DisArray has been programmed to do a straightforward depth-first walk over the tree. At each node a check is made: if the node represents an area which is outside the window ignore it otherwise display the leaf or recurse.

A pixel cannot lie on a plane boundary therefore it can be inserted into memory without any problem. The smallest leaf which can lie on a plane boundary depends on the position of the window. If the leaf lies on a plane boundary the two or four planes which are involved have to be written to in turn in order to write the leaf to memory.

Performance and possible modifications

The DisArray Quadtree Machine offers little in terms of efficiency for pixels - conventional frame stores are as good or better at pixel access - the DQM only wins on larger leaves.

Since the DQM does not need the (four) nearest neighbour connections which DisArray possesses the machine could easily be built with a larger array, say 32×32 or even 64×64. Such a machine could exploit the leaf size distribution rather better than the current 16×16 array machine. With quadtrees fully expanded to the depth which corresponds to the plane size they would be processed very rapidly. Also a considerable increase in efficiency would result from an increase in plane size for browsing since the least efficient part of the algorithm is where leaves which lie on a plane boundary are dealt with.

4.3. On Aura

It is a straightforward matter to microprogram Aura to walk over a very large quadtree in order to display an arbitrarily placed window. The data structure held in memory is a *one-to-four* quadtree so that it is easy to step over the unwanted branches.

5. Octtree display algorithms

5.1. Approaches to octtree display

A simple algorithm for the display of an octtree from an arbitrary point of view is the painter's algorithm: if the order of the children of parent octants is appropriately chosen (which is easily arranged) a simple traversal of the octtree is all that is required since the octtree structure orders the octants correctly, Meagher [3]. Doctor and Torborg [1] do much the same thing but create an image quadtree.

The octtree data structure is such that for certain projections the faces of the octants which lie behind a given octant have a particularly simple relationship to each other. This can be exploited to give much improved algorithms for these important special cases. There are three such classes of projection for an octtree and in addition there are two other simple techniques for the display of an octtree.

The five ways in which an octtree represented object can be viewed with the prospect of fast display are:

(i) Any slice orthogonal to a coordinate axis.

(ii) Arbitrary sections through the object.

(iii) Six orthographic projections parallel to any image space edge.

(iv) Eight isometric views: in the direction from one corner of the image space to the diametrically opposite corner.

(v) Twelve 'semi-isometric' views: in the direction from one corner of a face of the image space to the diametrically opposite corner of the face.

In all these cases it is assumed that rotations of 90 degrees (about any axis through the centre of the image space and parallel to the coordinate axes) can be used in order to orientate the octtree conveniently.

All the possibilities are examined in the next subsections, though not in the order just given. For these algorithms any octtree data structure can be used though, as with the quadtree algorithms, if the linear list is used then a new tree structure has to be generated to enable parts of the octtree to be stepped over. With octtrees the memory overhead of a fully pointered structure is large and there can be a considerable advantage in the use of a simpler structure such as the linear list or *one-to-eight*. Another aspect of this is the heavy administrative update overhead of a large pointer structure.

The octant order often plays an important role in the simplicity of the explication of the algorithms which are described below. Thus for reasons of clarity a different octant order is used in each of the algorithms.

The coordinate system which is used throughout is a left handed Cartesian coordinate system, as shown in figure 15, with its origin at the front upper left corner of the image space which is a cube of side 2^N. The z-axis runs into the paper. The unit of length is one pixel.

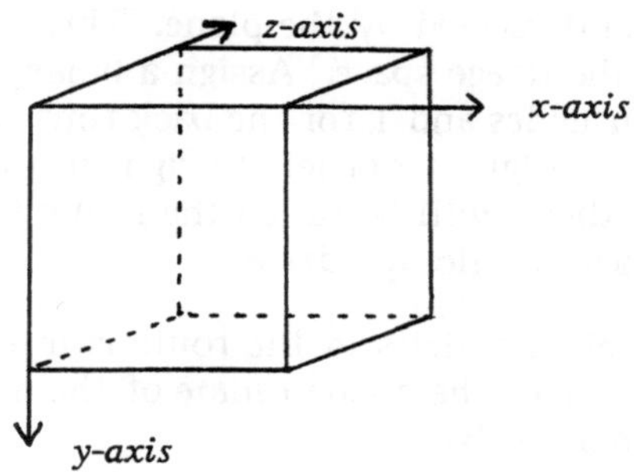

Figure 15. Coordinate system and image space

5.2. A plane section through an octtree image

General description of the algorithm

The problem here is to display a plane section of the image space one pixel thick; the plane section is to be parallel to the front face of the image space. The algorithm is similar to the quadtree scan conversion algorithm of §2.2 and is highly efficient. A full description of this algorithm together with code is given in [7]. This efficiency is important because in applications it offers the possibility of real time interaction with an octtree data structure. In order to see how the algorithm works consider how we can walk over just those nodes of an octtree which are intersected by a plane which is perpendicular to the z-axis.

First define an order on the children of a parent octant. For this algorithm the octants are ordered as follows. The front four octants (top left, top right, bottom left, bottom right) are numbered 0, 1, 2, 3 and the back four octants (top left, top right, bottom left, bottom right) are numbered 4, 5, 6, 7, as shown in figure 16.

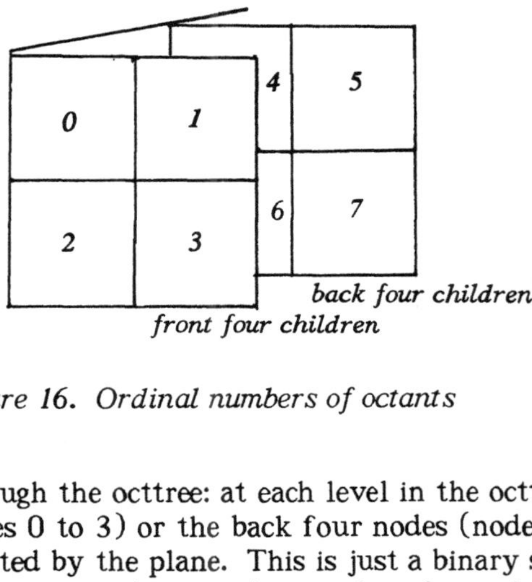

Figure 16. Ordinal numbers of octants

Now walk depth first through the octtree: at each level in the octtree choose either the front four nodes (nodes 0 to 3) or the back four nodes (nodes 4 to 7); choose the group which is intersected by the plane. This is just a binary search pattern on the z-axis within the image space. Assign a binary digit for each level in the tree: 0 for the front four nodes and 1 for the back four nodes. There are N levels in the tree so write these N digits from left to right in the order first level to Nth level. This list of binary digits will be called the route: they specify a route through the octtree which defines the slice quadtree.

If the sequence of binary digits in the route is interpreted as a binary number its value is just the value of the z-coordinate of the plane. The plane section through the image space is defined by

$$z = route, \qquad 0 \leqslant route < 2^N.$$

Assume an image space of 16×16 ($N = 4$) and take $route = 11$ (decimal) which is the eleventh section back out of sixteen. In binary 11 is 1011 so to pick out the required quadtree we go *right - left - right - right* down the octtree. In figure 17 the quadtree is depicted in heavy lines.

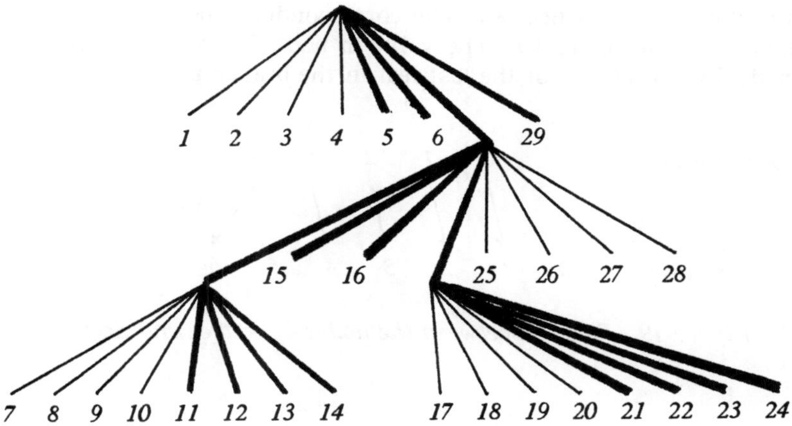

Figure 17. Plane section of image space: quadtree from octtree

The slice quadtree is shown in figure 18.

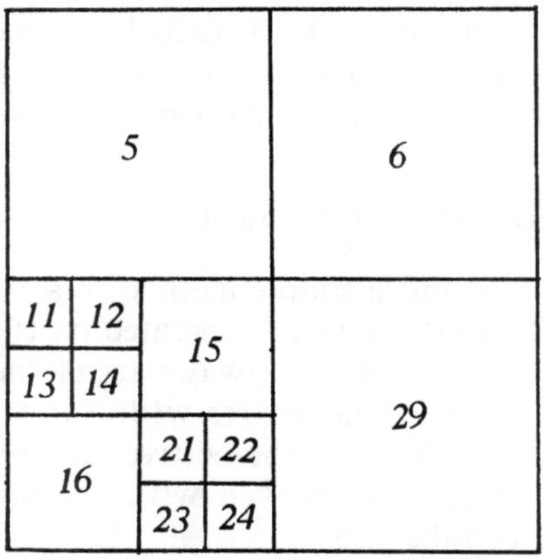

Figure 18. Section through z = 11 (image size of 16)

Notice that the section quadtree at $z = 11$ is identical to that at $z = 10$ because the octtree is only 3 layers deep and $N = 4$.

The dectree

The basic problem in the implementation of the algorithm is to see how to step over the unwanted branches of the octtree. If the octtree data structure has a suitable set of associated pointers these can be used. Another way is to make a dectree

(10-ary tree).

Each parent node in the octtree is given two extra children which contain offsets to enable the first or second group of four children to be stepped over, thus the octtree is converted into a dectree. The correspondence between the nodes in the two trees is shown in figure 19. The value in node 0 is the offset for node 5; the value in node 5 is the offset for the last leaf in the branch at node 9.

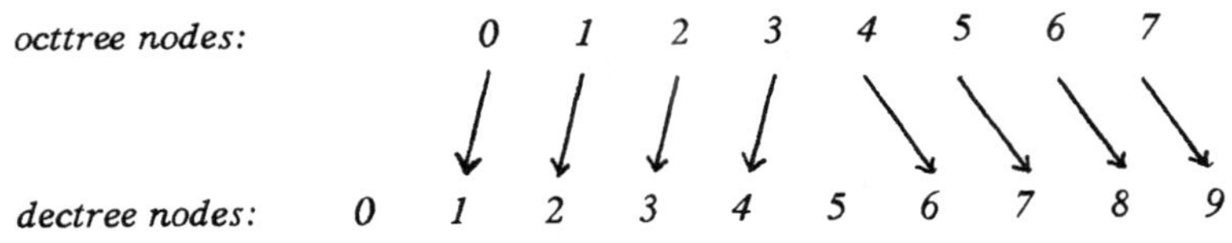

Figure 19. Relation between the nodes of octtree and dectree

Slice generation

Two procedures are needed: one to make the dectree and the other to walk over the quaternary subtree of the dectree. With the aid of the offsets stored in the first and sixth children together with a value for *route* the depth first walk over the dectree is modified into a depth first walk over a quadtree. The same dectree is used for all values of *route*.

In general the quadtree code which is generated will not be in its most compact form, i.e. there will be parents with four identical leaves for children. If it is to be transmitted, operated on, or stored then it needs to be compressed.

5.3. Arbitrary sections through the object

Michael Parsons has pointed out a simple method to section an octtree. The octtree which is to be sectioned and displayed is operated on (filtered) by a process which turns transparent all octants in the cut away part of the image space. Such a process requires a simple walk over the octtree with a test to check where the node is in relation to the section surface, i.e. the octtree is clipped to a three-dimensional window. The filtered octtree is displayed with one of the algorithms which are described in the next three subsections.

In many practical situations the much more efficient slice algorithm can be used.

5.4. Orthographic projection of an octtree

The problem

In order to simplify the description of the algorithm the octants are ordered as shown in figure 20, that is:

0 : top left front *1 : top left back*
2 : top right front *3 : top right back*
4 : bottom left front *5 : bottom left back*
6 : bottom right front *7 : bottom right back*

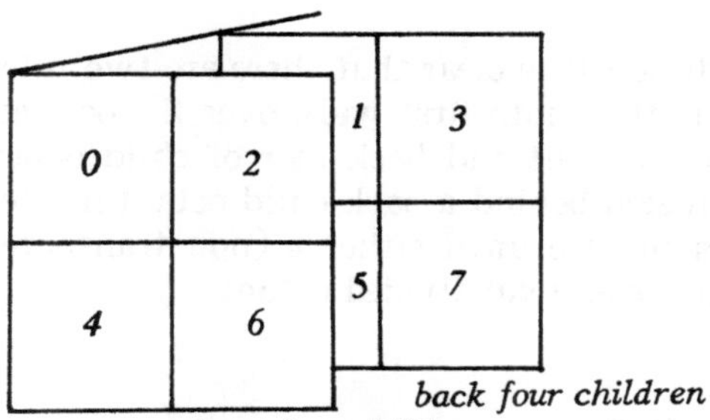

Figure 20. Ordinal numbers of octants

The fundamental problem is to identify those octants the front faces of which are visible, or partially visible, when orthographically projected onto the front face of the image space (the plane $z = 0$). These projected front faces form the leaves of a quadtree which will be called the ortho-quadtree.

The algorithm

A full description of this algorithm together with code is given in [7] (erratum: the first test in FindNode is incomplete). In the depth first walk over the octtree the four pairs of front and back child octants are visited in turn in the order just defined. A transparent octant has a colour value of zero. A procedure WalkOcttree has the structure:

(1) If a front octant is neither subdivided nor transparent then put out its colour and skip the back octant;

(2) If the front octant is subdivided then recurse, and skip the back octant;

(3) If the front octant is not subdivided and is transparent then the octant behind it, the back one of the pair, has to be examined:

  (i) If this back octant is subdivided then recurse;

  (ii) If it is neither subdivided nor transparent then put out its colour;

  (iii) If the back octant is not subdivided and is transparent then the region behind it (i.e. behind the *parent* octant) will have to be found and examined;

(a) If this region is an octant which is the same size or larger than the transparent one in front then if it is transparent the region behind it will have to be found and examined otherwise put out its colour;

(b) If the region is a subdivided octant of the same size then recurse from this octant.

From this description it is clear that there are two intertwined procedures. On the one hand there is the depth first walk over the octtree which is interrupted when both members of a front and back pair of child octants are transparent. On the other hand the region behind a back child octant has to be found and examined for its colour and structure until either a (non transparent) colour is found or it is necessary to walk over a subdivided octant.

The z-line binary tree

The basic difficulty is now reduced to that of being able to identify the leaf or branch on the octtree which corresponds to the region immediately behind the current back octant. The solution is simple.

Denote the north and south children by 0 and 1, respectively; the west and east children by 0 and 1, respectively; the front and back children by 0 and 1, respectively. List the three numbers in the order just given to denote a child octant, e.g. the south, east, front child is denoted by 110; interpret this as a binary number, six, and it corresponds to the scheme shown in figure 20.

Continuation of this numbering scheme with the recursive subdivision of the image space gives a method for the identification of any octant. The numbers are locational codes, see [9], [10]. Knowledge of the size of an octant and its locational code allows its neighbours to be found easily on the octtree; in particular the octant behind it.

Let the digits in the route be octal digits. With the octant order as defined in figure 20 each octal digit is made up from the y, x, and z binary digits in that order from left to right. An example should make this clear. Assume an image space of 32×32. The route 47060 (octal) in binary is 100 111 000 110 000. The first (left most) bit of each octal digit, expressed in binary, gives 11010; the middle bit of each octal digit gives 01010; the last bit (right most) of each octal digit gives 01000. As binary numbers these give the y, x, and z coordinates of the point; in decimal the values are 26, 10, 8, respectively.

Keep the bits in the binary representation of the route which correspond to the x and y coordinates fixed and allow the remaining bits (the z coordinate bits) to take all possible combinations of values. If there are n octal digits in the route this generates a set of $n!$ routes that define a binary tree on the octtree. The octants that correspond to these routes are all of the same size and have the same x and y coordinates: they lie one behind the other in the order that they appear in a depth first walk over the binary tree. If an octant on the octtree is not subdivided to this size there will be 'virtual octants' of this size: a larger octant could be subdivided to this level. This binary tree is called the z-line binary tree for the route.

An example

Consider the walk over the octtree in figure 21 which generates its ortho-quadtree. All ● nodes are coloured, perhaps differently, and o nodes are transparent.

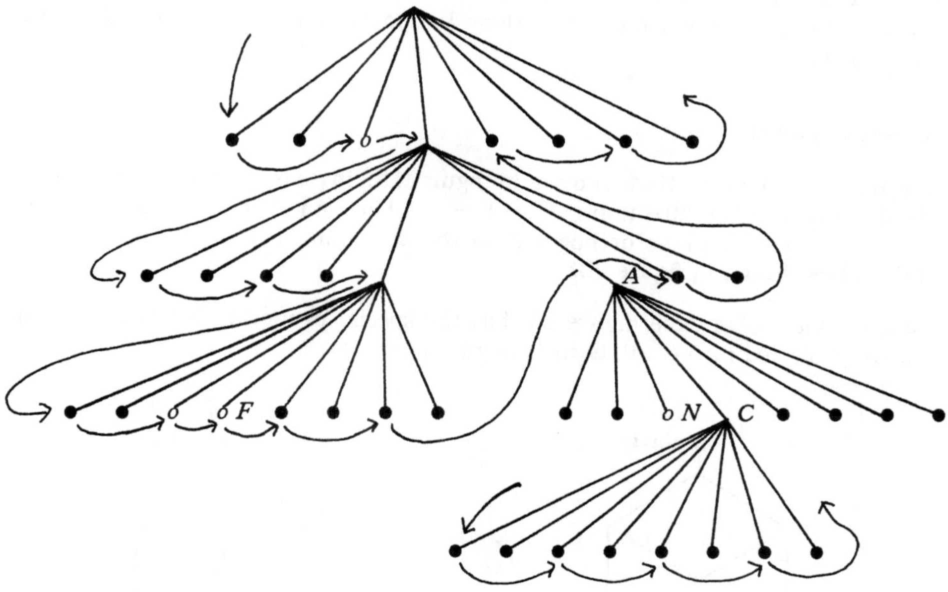

Figure 21. Octtree with walk to generate ortho-quadtree

Initially WalkOcttree is called: the (depth first) walk steps over any part of the octtree which is obscured from view by a coloured leaf in front of it, as shown by the arrowed path. At the node labelled F (the back node of a pair of transparent nodes) the walk is interrupted in order to find the octant behind F: it is N. The next node on the z-line binary tree (through F) is the node A. At node A a walk over the z-line binary tree starts: node N is transparent; node C behind it is subdivided and the same size as node F so call WalkOcttree. The walk over the branch at C completes the inspection of the region behind node F so we return and continue the original call of WalkOcttree.

In order to be able to move quickly over those nodes of the octtree which are not needed for the ortho-quadtree an auxiliary octtree is created. Appropriate offsets are inserted in the auxiliary octtree to allow us to step over branches of the object octtree very cheaply. This is analogous to the sextree except that the octtree and its offsets are kept separate, there is no necessity for this but is saves some copying.

Offsets are not needed at the bottom layer of the tree. The auxiliary octtree will be considerably smaller than the octtree, in terms of the number of nodes. In addition, the code for walking over the bottom layer can be optimised.

Remarks on the algorithm

No part of a leaf is visited more than once and leaves that are completely obscured are not visited at all: it is this which gives this algorithm its advantage over the painter's algorithm. In general the ortho-quadtree code that is generated needs to be compressed. Depth cues can be incorporated without any appreciable overhead. An implementation in C which runs on a Vax 780 processes an octtree of 30,000 nodes in one second; there are optimisations yet to be done which should reduce this significantly.

5.5. Isometric views

The coordinate system is that shown in figure 15; in this section it is viewed towards the origin in the direction $(-1, -1, -1)$. The isometric projection projects the octant faces onto a plane orthogonal to the direction $(1, 1, 1)$. Child octants are numbered as shown in figure 20.

The isometric view of a cube, figure 23, has the special property that the edges of the cube are projected into equilateral triangles, figure 24.

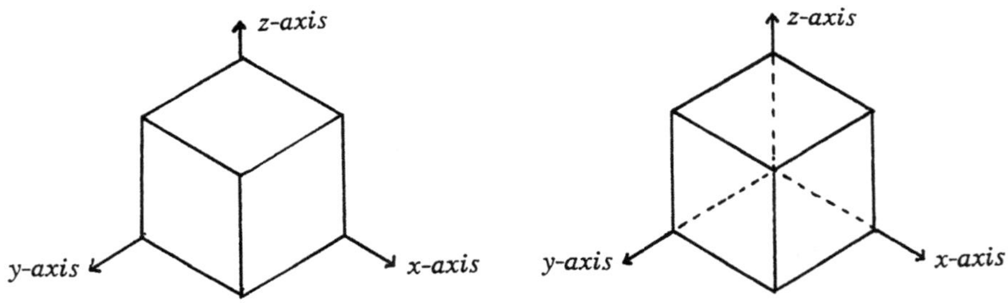

Figure 23. Isometric view of a cube: solid and 'wire frame'

Yamaguchi, Kunii and Fujimura [16] have pointed out that this property, together with the hierarchical order of the octtree, can be exploited to give an efficient algorithm to generate an isometric view of an object which is represented as an octtree.

In figure 25 an isometric view of a cube is shown, with its eight octants indicated by the dashed lines. The isometric projection of the edges of the octants produces the pattern of equilateral triangles shown in figure 26. In figure 26 seven minor hexagons can be drawn inside the major hexagon, the minor hexagons are just half the size of the major hexagon. The major hexagon contains 24 triangles and the minor hexagons are each made up from six triangles. Each of the seven minor hexagons corresponds to one or two (in the case of the centre hexagon) octants of the cube, c.f. figure 25. Each triangle corresponds to half of a face of one or more octants. In figure 27 the numbers in the triangles give the ordinal numbers (*vide* figure 20) of the octants which project onto the triangle in view order, i.e. the nearest octant first.

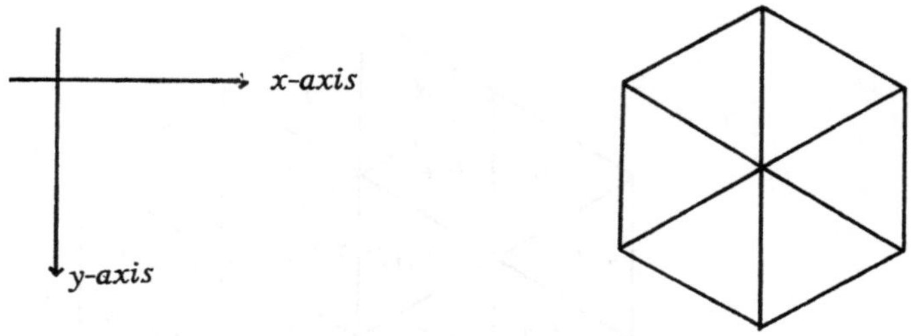

Figure 24. Isometric projection of cube faces onto plane

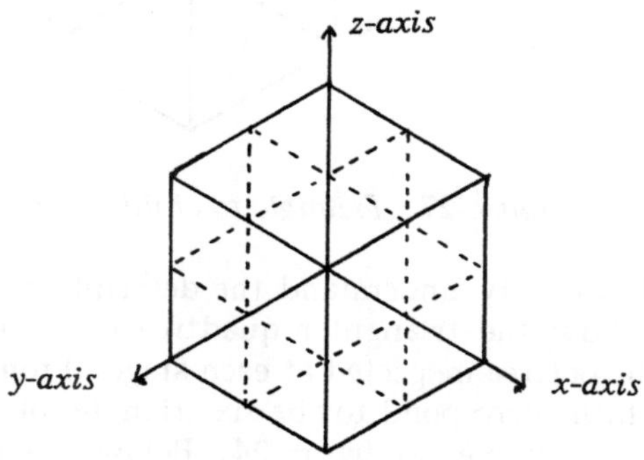

Figure 25. Isometric view of a cube with eight child octants

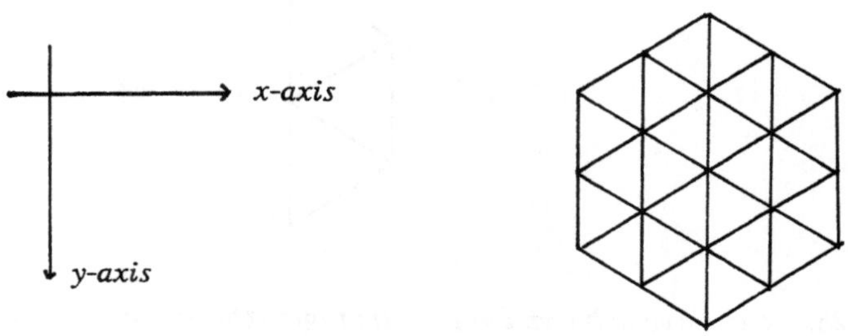

Figure 26. Projection of the front faces of the eight child octants onto a plane

When a child octant is subdivided the minor hexagon (in figure 26) which corresponds to this child octant is replaced by a subdivided hexagon of the same size. The number scheme shown in figure 27 can be extended to keep track of the octant-triangle mapping by the use of a locational code, e.g. [9], [16].

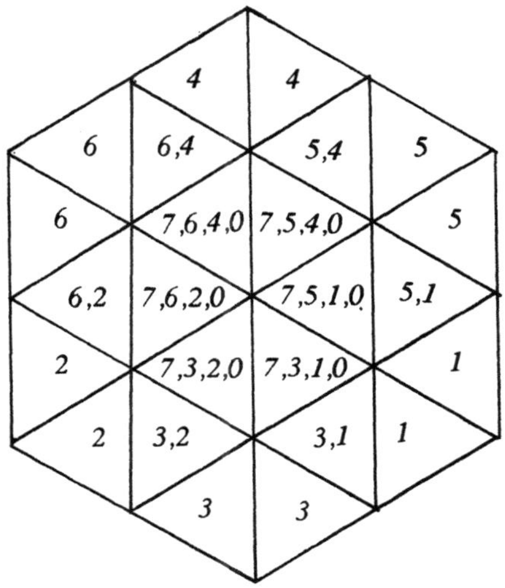

Figure 27. Triangle to child octant map

I have been unable to fully understand the description, by Yamaguchi, Kunii and Fujimura [16], of how the triangular quadtree is built up but it appears to be depth first with the octtree inspected at each stage. From the root of the tree there are six children which correspond to the six triangles of the isometric projection of the image space onto a plane, see figure 24. Below this all the branches are quadtrees: these correspond to the (recursive) subdivision of triangles into four equilateral triangles as shown in figure 28.

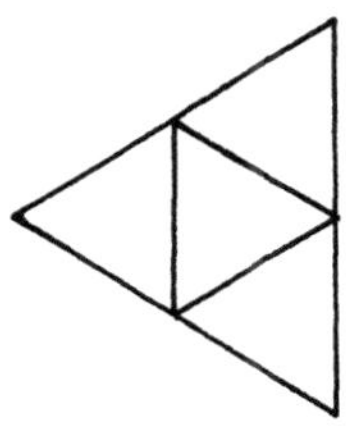

Figure 28. Recursive subdivision of a triangle (there are six possible orientations)

When complete, the triangular quadtree is ready for display.

5.6. Semi-isometric views

There are 12 other views of an octtree represented object which have a simple structure similar to that of the isometric view. These views are in the direction of one corner of a face of the image space to the diametrically opposite corner of the same face.

The octtree is projected onto a plane where the image is built up from rectangles (which correspond to the triangles of the isometric projection).

6. Hardware for octtree display

Meagher [4], [5] has built an octtree engine. The machine is high-tech and high cost. Unfortunately I have been unable to discover much about this machine and only rather ambiguous performance figures are given in the papers. However, there are some indications as to the approach which has been taken.

Meagher [5] states that the internal representation format which is used is an octtree and from the references which he gives we might guess that it is a variant of the fully linked list which is used. No description of any algorithms is given.

The structure of the machine is shown in figure 29.

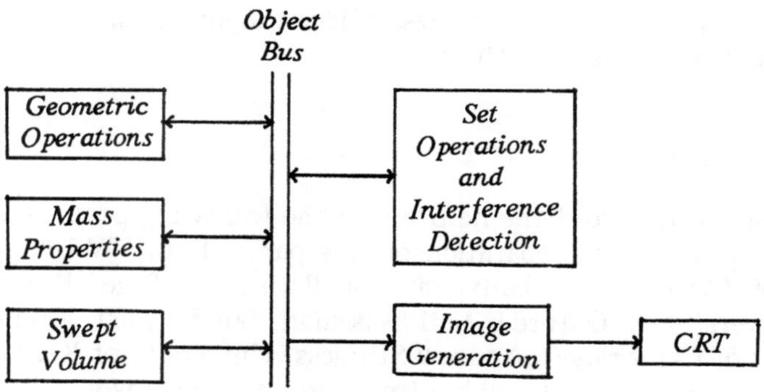

Figure 29. Meagher's octtree machine

The different hardware modules (only some are shown here) perform specific solid modelling tasks and they communicate over the object bus which can transfer up to 40 million nodes per second. This figure suggests that the eight children of any parent node in the octtree are transferred in parallel. It should be remarked that the linear list quadtree does not lend itself to the degree of parallel processing which is possible with the other data structures. In [4] Meagher states that the engine can generate images at approximately one million nodes per second but does not make clear just what this means. Images of 600,000 nodes can be displayed in about one second [4], though it is not clear whether there are any restrictions of any sort.

7. Final Remarks

The Quad-list Machine is a purpose built quadtree display terminal. The novel and important feature of the machine is that it refreshes the image from a quad-list rather than a frame buffer. In its present form its main drawback is its weak connection to its host, although there is no reason why this could not be changed.

DisArray was built as a RasterOp processor with some powerful general purpose processing capability which can be used for the display of quadtree data structures. A modification of the machine would form a reasonably simple (hardware) quad-tree terminal which could still be used for general purpose manipulations on quad-trees in microcode. The machine demonstrates one way in which parallel processing can be exploited in the context of quadtrees.

The Aura machine is a front-end to a high performance graphics workstation. It converts a *one-to-four* quadtree to run-length code very fast. Except for large quadtrees it is expected to run fast enough to refresh directly from the quadtree in the host.

For octtrees some efficient algorithms exist for special display viewpoints, of particular note for its efficiency is the 'slice' algorithm. Other viewpoints and perspective views have to be done with less efficient algorithms; however, with hardware these can give good response times.

Acknowledgements

It is a pleasure to record the help which the following people have given to me so generously during the preparation of this paper: Philip Willis and David Milford (School of Mathematics, University of Bath), Ian Page (Programming Research Unit, University of Oxford), Neil Wiseman, Ian Stewart (Computer Laboratory, University of Cambridge), Andrew Sturgess (University of Kent). All have contributed in major ways through discussions of their work, both published and unpublished. In addition I owe both Phillip Willis and Ian Page for their generous hospitality on extended visits to their respective institutions. I should like to thank Michael Parsons (University of Kent) for his comments on a draft of the paper. I am indebted to Kazunori Yamaguchi (University of Tokyo, Japan) for sending me copies of papers by his group, and also to Salah Habib (Consultant, London) for references to Donald Meagher's recent publications.

References

[1] Doctor, L.J. and Torborg, J.G., "Display Techniques for Octtree-Encoded Objects", *IEEE Computer Graphics and Applications* 1, pp. 29-38 (1981).

[2] Gargantini, I., "Linear Octtrees for Fast Processing of Three-Dimensional Objects", *Computer Graphics and Image Processing* 20, pp. 365-374 (1982).

[3] Meagher, D., "Geometric Modeling Using Octree Encoding", *Computer Graphics and Image Processing* 19, pp. 129-147 (1982).

[4] Meagher, D.J., "A New Mathematics for Solids Processing", *Computer Graphics World* November (1984).

[5] Meagher, D.J., "The Solids Engine: A Processor for Interactive Solid Modeling" *Nicograph '84* (Tokyo, 1984).

[6] Milford, D.J. and Willis, P.J., "Quad Encoded Display", *IEEE Proc. (Part E: Computers and Digital Techniques)* 131, pp. 70-75 (1984).

[7] Oliver, M.A., "Two Display Algorithms for Octtrees", in Bo, K. and Tucker, H. A. (editors), *Eurographics '84* (North-Holland, 1985).

[8] Oliver, M.A. and Wiseman, N.E., "Operations on Quadtree Encoded Images", *The Computer Journal* 26, pp. 83-91 (1983).

[9] Oliver, M.A. and Wiseman, N.E., "Operations on Quadtree Leaves and Related Image Areas", *The Computer Journal* 26, pp. 375-380 (1983).

[10] Oliver, M.A., King, T.R. and Wiseman, N.E., "Quadtree Scan Conversion", in Bo, K. and Tucker, H. A. (editors), *Eurographics '84* (North-Holland, 1985).

[11] Page, I., "DisArray: A 16 × 16 RasterOp Processor", in Ten Hagen, P. J. W. (editor), *Eurographics '83* (North-Holland, 1984).

[12] Samet, H, "Algorithms for the Conversion of Quadtrees to Rasters", *Computer Vision, Graphics, and Image Processing* 26, pp. 1-16 (1984).

[13] Stewart, I. P., "Quadtrees: Storage and Scan Conversion", to appear in *The Computer Journal,* November (1985).

[14] Sturgess, A. C., "Algorithms to Represent Solid Objects", unpublished dissertation, University of Kent, U.K. (1985).

[15] Willis, P.J. and Milford, D.J., "Browsing High Definition Colour Pictures", to appear in *Computer Graphics FORUM* 4, Number 3 (1985).

[16] Yamaguchi, K., Kunii, T. L., and Fujimura, K., "Octtree-Related Data Structures and Algorithms", *IEEE Computer Graphics and Applications* 1, pp. 53-59 (1984).

Intermediate data structures for display * algorithms

Marloes L.P. van Lierop

Dept. of Mathematics and Computing Science
Eindhoven University of Technology
P.O. Box 513
5600 MB Eindhoven
The Netherlands

ABSTRACT

This paper describes two algorithms and implicit data structures to display 3D scenes composed of polygons on a raster device. Both algorithms are based on the so-called painter's technique; the first one uses a depthsort algorithm for the visible surface calculation à la Newell, Newell, and Sancha ([1]), the other one uses a priority tree as proposed by Fuchs, Kedem, and Naylor ([2]).

Both algorithms were designed to be used in interactive applications. In order to update an image on the screen as fast as possible and to prevent the recomputation of the whole image after a change in the scene has occurred, an intermediate representation of the scene is needed. This intermediate representation might also be of use in detecting which polygon is meant when a pixel on the screen is pointed at.

For both display algorithms some intermediate representations will be considered, as well as the implications of alterations in the scene upon both these representations and their display.

1. Introduction

With the decreasing prices and increasing performance of raster graphic displays in the last few years, high quality computer generated images came into reach of all kinds of applications. Various algorithms were developed for generating images, given a scene and a viewing specification. An important part of such an algorithm is the visible surface calculation. Some well-known techniques are ray casting, z-buffering, depthsort, the scan-line algorithm, and the Warnock algorithm,

* These investigations were supported by the Netherlands Technology Foundation (STW).

The algorithms described in this paper are based on the painter's algorithm. This algorithm paints polygons on the screen one after another, the ones close to the viewpoint overwriting the ones far away. Hence the overwriting property of raster displays is exploited; an important property in which raster displays differ from vector displays.

In section 2 the programming language CG (C extended with some graphical elements) is described, as far as it is of interest for the subject of this paper. Section 3 deals with data structures for a depthsort like algorithm, and section 4 with a display algorithm that uses a Binary Space Partitioning Tree. Finally, section 5 contains hardware considerations, including parallel processing, and some concluding remarks.

2. CG

For the investigation and comparison of the algorithms and their associated data structures, we needed a programming language to write graphical application programs. For this purpose we extended the language C with some graphical elements, and called this extension CG. The most important aspects of CG are the hierarchical structure of the objects and the way interaction is handled. A preprocessor has been developed that translates CG programs into plain C. For a complete description of CG we refer to [3]; in this section only those aspects will be dealt with that are of interest for the intermediate data structures.

Besides the basic types char (and its derivative string), int, float, and double of C, CG is provided with the types **point, polygon, link,** and **linklist.** Values of type point represent geometrical points in three-dimensional space. From points, polygons may be formed. Values of type polygon represent coloured two-dimensional surfaces in three-dimensional space. They are used to form 3D scenes, which may be displayed on a raster graphic screen. Scenes may be composed of subscenes, which are on their turn scenes, maybe composed of subscenes, etc. To describe this hierarchy, the type link is introduced. Each scene, which is labeled with a unique name, consists of a bag of polygons, and a bag of links which represent the references to subscenes. These references are joined with a transformation matrix and a list of attributes.

Formally, a value of type link is a 3-tuple consisting of the name of a scene, a real (4 x 4) matrix, and an attribute list. If scene S contains a reference to scene T with matrix M and attribute list A, that is to say, if the 3-tuple $<T,M,A>$ occurs in the link bag of S, then the polygons of T, transformed by premultiplying their coordinates with M, form part of S, and the attributes in A are associated with all those polygons. In the directed graph, obtained by conceiving each reference as a directed edge from the scene containing the reference to the scene referenced, no cycles are allowed. In the sequel, this graph will be referred to as the **CG graph.** Note that the polygons that form part of a scene S are the polygons in the polygon bag of S plus the polygons that form part of the scenes referred to by S, transformed by the matrix that occurs in the associated link.

Though we have included attribute lists in the links, we will not work them out in this paper. How attributes are associated with scenes, how they are combined, and all other questions on attributes, is subject of a joint research project in Leiden and Amsterdam, and can be found in [4] and [5].

As an example, suppose that the scenes S_1, S_2, and S_3 have the following polygon and link bags.

scene	*polygon bag*	*link bag*
S_1	p_1, p_2	$< S_2, M_1, A >, < S_2, M_2, A >, < S_3, M_3, A >$
S_2	p_3	$< S_3, M_4, A >$
S_3	p_4	$\emptyset$

The associated CG graph is shown in figure 1.

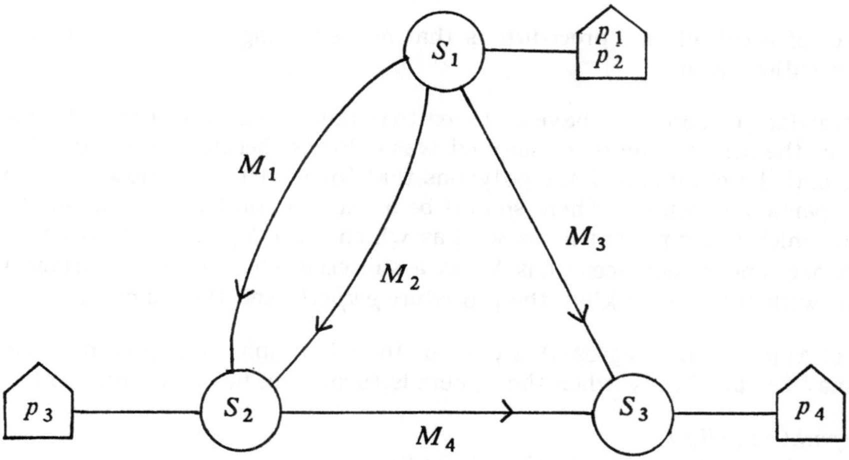

Figure 1. An example of a CG graph.

S_1 consists of the polygons

p_1
p_2
$M_1\ (\times)\ p_3$
$M_2\ (\times)\ p_3$
$M_3\ (\times)\ p_4$
$(M_1 \times M_4)\ (\times)\ p_4$
$(M_2 \times M_4)\ (\times)\ p_4$

where $(\times)$ and $\times$ denote the transformation of a polygon by a matrix and matrix multiplication respectively.

One of the most important operations on scenes is displaying them on the screen. For this purpose CG knows the procedure

display(nm,vs)
string nm; viewspec vs;

The effect of a call to this procedure is that the scene with name *nm* is displayed on the screen. To transform the 3D coordinates in which the scene is defined into the two-dimensional coordinates of the screen, the viewing transformation as specified by *vs* is applied. As a matter of fact, the hidden surfaces are not shown. The display of a scene *S* results in the display of all polygons that form part of *S*.

After the call *display(nm,vs)*, every change in scene *nm* will result in an update of the image on the screen. In other words, *display* turns on a camera which records every change in the scene that was displayed by the latest call of display. To turn off the camera, CG knows the procedure

enddisplay().

The effect of a call of this procedure is that no new image will be displayed until *display* is called again.

For interaction purposes, we have assumed that there is an input device that selects a pixel on the screen. The pixel selected was coloured because of the display of a scene *S*, and therefore one of the polygons that form part of *S* caused the pixel to get that particular colour. There should be a way to point out to the application program which polygon that is, as well as which scene S_1 has that polygon in its polygon bag, and which scene has S_1 as a subscene, etc. For this purpose CG is provided with the type linklist, the procedure *getpath*, and the function *getlink*.

Values of type linklist represent a path in the CG graph. The procedure *getpath*, which may be called only when the camera is turned on, has four arguments:

getpath(nm,p,ll,n)
*string *nm; polygon *p; linklist *ll; int *n;*

where, due to a call, the variables will get the following values, depending upon the screen contents and the pixel pointed at,

**nm*: the name of the scene passed as an argument to the most recent call of display;

**p*: the polygon in the CG graph due to which the pixel pointed at has got its value;

**ll*: the list of links representing the path in the CG graph from **nm* to the scene whose polygon bag contains **p* ;

**n*: the length of **ll* .
Note that **n* == 0 iff **p* belongs to the polygon bag of **nm* .

In order to process the information obtained by a call to *getpath*, CG is provided with the function

link getlink(lol,i)
linklist lol; int i;

that returns the $i-$th link of the linklist *lol*.

For example, if the scenes S_1, S_2, and S_3 have the same polygon and link bags as in the previous example, and *display* is called for scene S_1, and the pixel pointed at has got its colour due to the polygon $(M_1 \times M_4)$ $(\times)$ p_4, then, after the call *getpath(nm,p,ll,n)*, *nm* refers to S_1, *p* to p_4, *ll* to $(<S_2,M_1,A>, <S_3,M_4,A>)$, and n to 2. Afterwards, *getlink(ll,1)* and *getlink(ll,2)* yield $<S_2,M_1,A>$ and $<S_3,M_4,A>$ respectively.

As said already in the introduction, the intermediate data structure we aim at should serve two purposes: to prevent the recomputation of the entire image after a scene has been altered, and to be useful in detecting the polygon due to which a selected pixel has got its colour. With respect to CG, the second purpose should be embodied in the implementation of *getpath*. It implies that the intermediate data structure should contain information about the paths in the CG graph. The first purpose implies that alterations in the scene displayed should be efficiently worked out in the intermediate data structure, and that the display process should operate on this intermediate data structure instead of the CG graph of the scene.

The only operations provided in CG to change existing scenes are

addpol(nm,pol)
string nm; polygon pol;

addlink(nm,lk)
string nm; link lk;

to add polygon *pol* and link *lk* respectively to the polygon bag and link bag of the scene with the name *nm*, and

delpol(nm,pol)
string nm; polygon pol;

dellink(nm,lk)
string nm; link lk;

to remove the polygon *pol* and link *lk* respectively from the polygon bag and link bag of the scene with name *nm*. These operations may result in changes of the CG graph, of the intermediate data structure and of the screen. Updating the CG graph, the intermediate data structure, and the screen, due to a call of one of the above operations, will be dealt with in the next two sections.

Irrespective of the way the display procedure is implemented, the CG graph must be traversed to get all the polygons that form part of the scene to be displayed. For this traversal a recursive procedure may be used. Along with each polygon, its corresponding path in the CG graph (i.e. a list of links) should be generated and stored because of the procedure *getpath*. For this purpose, a list is created while traversing the CG graph, containing the names of all scenes that are subscenes of the scene currently displayed. With each entry in the list, the appropriate linklist is associated, and, for sake of convenience, a transformation matrix that is the result of multiplying the matrices of the links in the linklist. Because a scene may appear more than once as a subscene of another scene, the list may contain various entries for one name. From now on we will refer to this list as the Path List. The Path List may be seen as an intermediate data structure which is independent of the implementation of *display*. Other useful information, like bounding boxes and plane equations, may be computed and generated during the traversal.

The procedure, given in listing 1, traverses the CG graph to generate all polygons (and associated data) that form part of the scene with name *nm*, where each polygon is transformed by matrix *mt*. Furthermore, during that traversal, the Path List is updated by creating a new element each time a subscene is encountered, where the associated path from *nm* to that subscene is concatenated with *ll*. We assume that the Path List is a global object, whose elements are of type PATH-LISTELMT. The function *updlist(nm,ll,mt)* creates a new element with value *{nm,ll,mt}* in the Path List, and returns a pointer to this element.

```
traverse (nm, ll, mt)
string nm; linklist ll; matrix mt;
{
        PATHLISTELMT *lp, *updlist( );

        lp = updlist (nm, ll, mt);
        for ( "each polygon p in the polygon bag of the scene with name nm" ) {
                "tp = polygon resulting from applying matrix mt to p";
                "pl = plane equation of tp";
                "bb = bounding box of tp";
                ...
                "output (tp, pl, bb, *p, lp, ...) ";
        }
        for ( "each link <S,M,A> in the link bag of the scene with name nm" ) {
                "m = matrix resulting from the premultiplication of M with mt";
                "l = linklist resulting from the concatenation of ll and <S,M,A>";
                traverse (S, l, m);
        }
}
```

Listing 1.

As a result of the call *display(nm,vs)*, the procedure *traverse(nm,l,m)* will be called, where *l* is the empty linklist, and *m* is the view transformation matrix or the identity matrix, depending on the wish to generate the polygons in viewing coordinates or in world coordinates.

3. Depthsort

The basic idea of the *depthsort* algorithm, as introduced in [1], is to perform the visible surface calculation by sorting the polygons by their distance from the viewpoint, and use the painter's algorithm by displaying the ones at far distance before the ones that are close.

Sorting is done in viewing space, hence the polygons that form part of the scene that is to be displayed, first have to be transformed by the viewing transformation that was specified in the call to *display*. This transformation, as well as clipping against the view volume and, if necessary, the perspective transformation, may all be embedded in the traversal of the CG graph, by which the polygons generated by the CG traversal algorithm are the polygons in view space on which the depthsort algorithm may operate directly. These polygons are initially sorted in a list on maximal distance from the viewpoint. From this list the depthsort algorithm extracts the polygons in order of display, wherever necessary splitting up polygons to resolve ambiguities, for example when cyclically obscuring polygons occur.

Because of *getpath*, the polygons generated by depthsort need to be stored, such that their associated CG path and a pointer to the original polygon in the CG graph are available. In the sequel, the list of polygons and additional data, as generated by depthsort, and sorted in display order, is called the Display List. In this list, a pointer to a Path List element is associated with each polygon, containing the corresponding path. Furthermore, each polygon is associated with a pointer to the original CG polygon, and some additional information, like plane equation, bounding box, etc. An element of the Display List will therefore have the following structure:

3D polygon in viewing coordinates
pointer to Path List element
pointer to polygon in CG graph
bounding box
pointer to plane equation
...

To display a polygon from the Display List, a projection operation is needed, maybe a window-viewport transformation, and a polygon scan conversion.

With the Display List, we have come to the second intermediate representation, this one being implied by the *display* algorithm. We will first discuss how it might be of use in the procedure *getpath*. If a pixel is selected on the screen, *getpath* should be able to detect the polygon in the CG graph due to which this pixel got its colour. This may be achieved by going through the polygons in the Display List, in REVERSE display order, until a polygon is detected whose image on the screen encloses the selected pixel. The order in which the polygons are accessed, guarantees that the correct polygon is detected. For this detection, a point-in-polygon test is needed. If the polygon is detected, the necessary information, like its original in the CG graph, and its associated path, is available in the Display List and the Path List.

We will now discuss the implications of alterations in the scene lastly displayed, on both the Display List and Path List and on the screen contents. We assume that the camera is on at the moment an alteration occurs. In the previous section, we mentioned the CG procedures that may change scenes: *delpol*, *dellink*, *addpol*, *addlink*.

The first one, *delpol(nm,pol)*, removes polygon *pol* from the polygon bag of scene *nm*. If scene *nm* is a subscene of the scene currently displayed, then there are polygons in the Display List that refer to *pol*, and these polygons should be deleted from the Display List. They are easily detected by testing each element of the Display List for having a polygon pointer that points to *pol*. The Path List does not change at all. There is no need to perform the *depthsort* algorithm again in order to update the screen, because the display order of the remaining polygons in the Display List has not changed. Therefore displaying the polygons of the updated Display List is sufficient.

The *CG* procedure *dellink(nm,lk)* removes link *lk* from the link bag of scene *nm*. As a consequence, if *nm* is a subscene of the scene currently displayed, each element in the Path List whose *CG* path contains *lk* should be deleted, as well as each element in the Display List referring to one of these Path List elements. Again, this is achieved by testing the elements of the Display List, now for having a pointer to a Path List element whose path contains *lk*. Afterwards, the Path List is updated. The screen is updated by displaying the remaining polygons of the Display List in the same order.

The *CG* procedure *addpol(nm,pol)* adds polygon *pol* to the polygon bag of scene *nm*. If *nm* is a subscene of the scene currently displayed, say scene *S*, the number of polygons that form part of *S* might increase with more than one polygon, because various paths in the *CG* graph may lead from the node associated with *S* to the node associated with *nm*. For each occurrence of *nm* in the Path List, the associated matrix is applied to *pol*, and the resulting polygon is to be inserted in the Display List. With this insertion, a problem arises: we would like to keep the order of the elements in the Display List unchanged, except for the insertion of the new polygons. However, in general this is not possible, because the insertion of a new polygon may disturb the display order of those polygons already present, as is shown by the following example. In figure 2 some polygons in viewing space are shown; the projection plane is the xy-plane, and the viewer is supposed to be at location $z = -\infty$. The display order of the polygons in figure 2a is P_1, P_2, because the polygons do not hide each other, and in this case the one with the greatest z-value is displayed first. However, if polygon P_3 is added, like in figure 2b, the display order becomes P_2, P_3, P_1. Therefore, the *depthsort* algorithm must be applied again in order to determine the display order of the extended set of polygons. Naturally, only the polygons to be inserted need to go through the viewing transformation and clipping process; the other ones are available already in viewing coordinates. The screen is updated by displaying the polygons in the order as generated by *depthsort*.

The same holds for *addlink(nm,lk)*, if *nm* is a subscene of the scene currently displayed: the *depthsort* algorithm must be applied again on the polygons occurring in the Display List plus the polygons that are to be inserted due to the addition of link *lk* to the link bag of scene *nm*. These additional polygons are generated in the following way: for each occurrence of *nm* in Path List the call *traverse(T,LL,MM)* is performed, where *lk* is supposed to be the triple <*T*,*M*,*A*>, and *LL* is the linklist resulting from concatenating the linklist associated with *nm* in the Path List with *lk*, and *MM* is the matrix resulting from premultiplying *M* with the matrix associated with *nm* in the Path List. The Path List is updated during the traversals of the *CG* graph. The screen is updated by

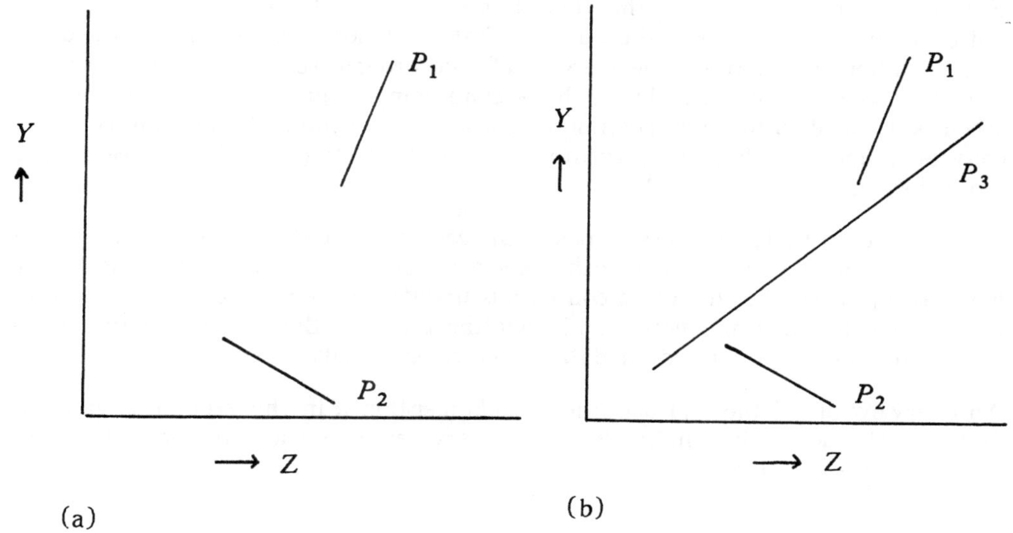

Figure 2. The display order of the polygons is P_1, P_2 in (a) and P_2, P_3, P_1 in (b).

displaying the polygons in the order as generated by *depthsort*.

If the same scene is to be displayed with another view specification, the existing Display List is of no use at all, and all computations must be performed again. This is a serious drawback of the algorithm. The next section deals with a display algorithm where the intermediate data structure is independent of the viewing specification.

As said before, the *getpath* procedure, in this setup, needs a point-in-polygon test in order to detect the polygon due to which a selected pixel on the screen got its colour. Quite another solution for this detection problem is to add another intermediate data structure to the number of representation levels, one especially suited for fast polygon detection. If a polygon is displayed, a set of pixels is selected by scan conversing the polygon, and this set of pixels is assigned a value in the bit planes of the raster device, representing the colour of the polygon in question. If one has a set of pseudo bit planes at one's disposal, it would be possible to store not only the colour of a polygon, but also a pointer to the corresponding element in the Display List, by which means each pixel is associated with an indirect reference to the polygon due to which that pixel got its colour. This solution requires a lot of extra memory, so compression is desirable. One could think of the linear quadtree representation called *leafcode*, as re-introduced by Gargantini in [6], or *run length* encoding. We will refer to this new representation as the Item Buffer. The creation of the Item Buffer should happen simultaneously with the polygon display, and be based on the same scan conversion algorithm.

For both representations of the Item Buffer mentioned above, overwriting the buffer with a new polygon should be a fast operation. For the linear quadtree representation, this implies the merging of two ordered sequences, where one has priority above the other, followed by a condensing step; for run-length encoded schemes, it requires the superposition of runs. Which combination of polygon scan conversion and Item Buffer representation is most effective, should be investigated more closely.

Having an Item Buffer at one's disposal, the *getpath* procedure is trivial. Since the Item Buffer must be consistent with the screen contents, updating the Item Buffer is necessary whenever the screen contents is updated. It depends on the application and on the efficiency of creating and updating the Item Buffer whether the introduction of this new intermediate data structure brings advantage.

An overview of all the representation levels mentioned in this section, is given in figure 3. The dotted box indicates an auxiliary representation, the dashed one an optional representation.

4. Binary Space Partitioning tree

The Display List as described above, has the disadvantage that an overall recomputation is needed if another view of the same scene is required. In order to prevent this, the polygons in world coordinates have to be rearranged, such that given a particular view, the actual display order of the polygons is easily derived. The Binary Space Partitioning (BSP) tree, introduced by Fuchs, Kedem, and Naylor in [2], yields such an arrangement.

In a BSP tree, each node is associated with a polygon, such that all polygons in the left subtree of a node N lie entirely on the negative side of the polygon associated with N, and all polygons in the right subtree on its positive side. For a polygon with plane equation

$$\mathrm{a}x + \mathrm{b}y + \mathrm{c}z + d = 0$$

the positive side consists of those points (x,y,z), where

$$\mathrm{a}x + \mathrm{b}y + \mathrm{c}z + d \geqslant 0$$

and for the negative side

$$\mathrm{a}x + \mathrm{b}y + \mathrm{c}z + d < 0$$

holds.

For a particular view, the display order of the polygons is determined by an in-order traversal of the BSP tree, depending on the position of the viewpoint with regard to the node's polygon. This is based on the property that if the viewpoint is on the positive side of a polygon p, p can not be obscured by any polygon on the negative side of p. Furthermore, the polygons on the negative side of p can not obscure any of the polygons on the positive side. The reverse holds if the viewpoint is on the negative side of p. Hence, the display order of the polygons is easily determined by a recursive procedure that operates on a BSP tree and which, depending on the position of the viewpoint with regard to the root polygon, calls

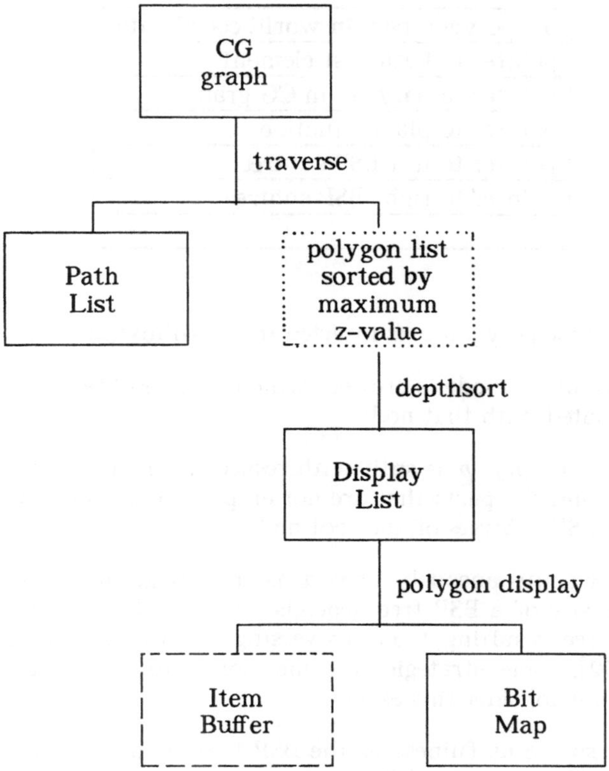

Figure 3.

Representation levels in the depthsort like display algorithm.
· · · indicates an auxiliary representation,
- - - indicates an optional representation.

itself for the left subtree, displays the polygon in the root, and calls itself again for the right subtree, or just the other way around. The viewing transformation, clipping, and projection, are now part of the polygon display.

If a BSP tree is to be constructed for the polygons of a particular scene, the CG graph must be traversed first in order to generate all the polygons that make up that scene. Similar to the Display List, each node in the BSP tree should also contain pointers to the CG polygon of which it is a part and to the element in the Path List that contains the associated path. Because the plane equation plays an important part in various calculations, it is also included in the node. Hence, a typical BSP node will contain the following fields.

3D polygon part in world coordinates
pointer to Path List element
pointer to polygon in CG graph
pointer to plane equation
pointer to left BSP subtree
pointer to right BSP subtree
...

Given a BSP tree, a new polygon *p* is inserted in the following way:

- if the tree is empty, a node is created, which becomes the root of the BSP tree, and *p* is associated with that node;
- if the tree is not empty, *p* is split with respect to the polygon associated with the root node, and the parts that are not empty are recursively inserted in the corresponding BSP subtrees of the root node.

We have chosen for simultaneously traversing the CG graph and constructing the BSP tree. Since the size of a BSP tree depends on the order in which the polygons are inserted, the tree resulting from traversing the CG graph may not be the optimal one. In [2], some strategies are mentioned to minimise the number of nodes; here we do not consider this aspect.

We will now discuss the usefulness of the BSP tree in the procedure *getpath*. If a pixel is selected on the screen, the BSP tree must be traversed again to detect the polygon due to which the pixel in question got its colour. This traversal should be such that the order in which the nodes are entered is the reverse of the order in which the nodes are entered by the display algorithm. Again, this traversal might be performed recursively, for instance by the function *detect* (see Listing 2), that operates on a BSP tree and returns the node associated with the polygon in request, or NULL if the polygon is not contained in the tree.

However, to detect whether a polygon gives a particular pixel a colour, either that polygon again needs to be transformed, clipped, etc, because it is stored in world coordinates, or the equation in world coordinates of the ray that connects the viewpoint with the pixel in question should be computed. One way to prevent these computations, is to use an Item Buffer as described in the previous section, where the pointers now refer to a node in the BSP tree. The function *detect* is not needed then at all.

Another solution is to store the 2D polygons that are the result of transforming, clipping, and projecting the polygons of the BSP tree. If they are stored in the BSP tree itself, a recomputation of the viewpoint's position with regard to the node's polygon is still needed in the function *detect*. This might be resolved by associating a three-valued mark with each node, standing for being neutral, having the current viewpoint on its positive side, or on its negative side respectively. These marks should be set during the first traversal of the tree for the current view. This way the BSP tree becomes a mixture of view-dependent and view-independent

```
NODE *detect (node)
NODE *node;
{
      NODE *nd;

      if ( "the viewpoint is on the positive side of the polygon
            associated with *node" )
            if ( ( nd = detect (node → rightsubtree) ) != NULL )
                  return (nd);
            else if ( "the polygon associated with *node gives the
                        selected pixel a colour" )
                        return (node);
                  else return ( detect (node → leftsubtree) );
      else
            if ( ( nd = detect (node → leftsubtree) ) != NULL )
                  return (nd);
            else if ( "the polygon associated with *node gives the
                        selected pixel a colour" )
                        return (node);
                  else return ( detect (node → rightsubtree) );
}
```

Listing 2.

data, where the structure of the tree is view-independent. The view-independent data contained in the nodes consists of a polygon p in world coordinates, a reference to the CG polygon of which p is a part, a reference to a Path List element, and a plane equation. The view-dependent data consists of the polygon in device coordinates that is the result of transforming, clipping, etc., polygon p, and a mark denoting the position of the current viewpoint with regards to p. We will refer to this tree as the Extended BSP tree. The structure of a node of the Extended BSP tree is as follows.

3D polygon part in world coordinates
pointer to Path List element
pointer to polygon in CG graph
pointer to plane equation
pointer to left BSP subtree
pointer to right BSP subtree
2D polygon in device coordinates
three-valued mark
...

If one does not want the BSP tree to contain view-dependent data, one might choose to store the 2D polygons in a separate list, arranged in display order. For this solution, instead of the procedure *detect*, only a point-in-polygon test is needed. This list will be referred to as the 2D Display List. Each element consists of a 2D polygon (in device coordinates) and a reference to the BSP node whose associated polygon is the original of the polygon in the list.

We now come to the aspect of updating the (Extended) BSP tree, the 2D Display List or Item Buffer, if present, and the screen, assuming that the camera is on. The same strategy as described in the previous section may be used to generate all the polygons that become part of the scene currently displayed because of a call to the CG procedures *addpol* or *addlink*. Adding these polygons to the (Extended) BSP tree is no problem since the creation of the tree is based on adding polygons to an existing tree.

One might choose to handle the update of the (Extended) BSP tree and the screen as two separate steps, by first adding a polygon to the tree and then traversing it again for its display. It is more attractive, however, to traverse the tree only once, simultaneously adding the polygon parts and computing the updated image. Because of the last task, the tree should then be traversed in display order. For the Extended BSP tree this is very easy because of the marks in the nodes that determine the display order traversal for the current view. For the plain BSP tree, the position of the viewpoint with regards to each node's polygon must be recomputed in order to determine the display order traversal.

When traversing the tree in display order, adding parts of the polygon that is to be inserted at the appropriate places, the polygons whose nodes are traversed before any new polygon part is inserted, do not need to be displayed again. All the other polygons do, together with the inserted parts. If a plain BSP tree is used without a 2D Display List, all polygons that are to be displayed need to be transformed, clipped, etc., which implies a lot of recomputations. For the Extended BSP tree, recomputations are reduced to a minimum; only the parts of the newly inserted polygon need to go through the transforming, clipping, etc., process, while the 2D polygons already present in the nodes only need a scan conversion.

The same holds if a plain BSP tree is used in combination with the 2D Display List. Updating the BSP tree, the 2D Display List, and the screen may be done simultaneously. The tree traversal starts at the root, the list traversal at the bottom, i.e. at the firstly displayed polygon. Each time a polygon is encountered in the tree, the list traversal proceeds one element. For the synchronisation it is required that each node in the tree has a corresponding element in the list, so polygons that fall outside the view volume after transformation, still need to have an (empty) element in the 2D Display List. If, during traversal of the tree, a polygon part is added, this part is subsequently transformed, clipped, etc., and the result is inserted in the 2D Display List. Display of the polygons in the 2D Display List starts as soon as a new element is inserted.

The Item Buffer, if present, is updated in the same way as the screen.

As a result of the CG procedure *delpol*, a polygon is removed from the polygon bag of a scene. In the (Extended) BSP tree, all nodes that refer to that polygon must be deleted. However, if a node is deleted, the left- and right-subtree should be united in order to form one (Extended) BSP subtree, and this is definitely not a simple operation. To keep things as simple as possible, we choose for the possibility to have "empty" nodes in the (Extended) BSP tree: no valid polygon is associated with such nodes anymore, only a plane equation. This plane equation is needed for future traversals of the tree. Of course, if a tree contains a lot of "empty" nodes, one might consider the creation of a new (Extended) BSP tree.

To detect all nodes that refer to the polygon that is to be deleted, the tree must be traversed. Since the deletion of a polygon from the (Extended) BSP tree implies the display of all remaining polygons, a display order traversal is obvious; for each node, the polygon is either deleted or displayed. If an Item Buffer is used, it is updated simultaneously with the screen. If a 2D Display List is in use, it might be traversed and updated simultaneously with the tree traversal.

As a result of the procedure *dellink*, a link is removed from the link bag of a scene. In the (Extended) BSP tree, all nodes that have this link in its associated path, must be removed. Again, the removal of these nodes and the display of the remaining nodes may be performed in one display order traversal of the tree.

Updating the Path List, necessary whenever *addlink* or *dellink* is called, is done in the same way as described in the previous section.

Although the plain BSP tree is independent of the view, the Extended BSP tree, the 2D Display List and the screen are not, of course, and need to be updated every time the view changes. In this case the (Extended) BSP tree must be traversed again in order to generate the new list of polygons.

In figure 4, two configurations of representation levels are shown, the first one with a plain BSP tree, the other one with the Extended BSP tree. Again, dashed boxes indicate optional representations.

5. Concluding remarks

The display algorithms, in combination with the intermediate data structures as described in the previous sections, are thought to be useful in interactive raster graphics applications. Most of the algorithms are not implemented by us yet, so conclusions about performances are not available yet. The CG preprocessor, which translates CG programs into plain C, has been implemented except for the procedure getpath, which is, however, about to be finished. The first display algorithm, based on depthsort and the Display List as intermediate data structure, has also been implemented, but the scenes on which it was tested were too simple to reveal any useful information about its performance.

Most ideas expressed in this paper are not new at all: the depthsort algorithm dates from 1972, the BSP tree idea from 1969. We believe, however, that the idea to use the algorithms in combination with appropriate intermediate data structures in an interactive environment is worth investigating.

Finally, we would like to discuss the possible use of special hardware and/or parallel processors in order to speed up things. The traversal of the CG graph, where polygons are generated that are to be consumed by either depthsort or the BSP tree algorithm, might be done by numerous processors, since the order in which the polygons are generated is not important at all and the traversals of the subtrees of a node are fully independent.

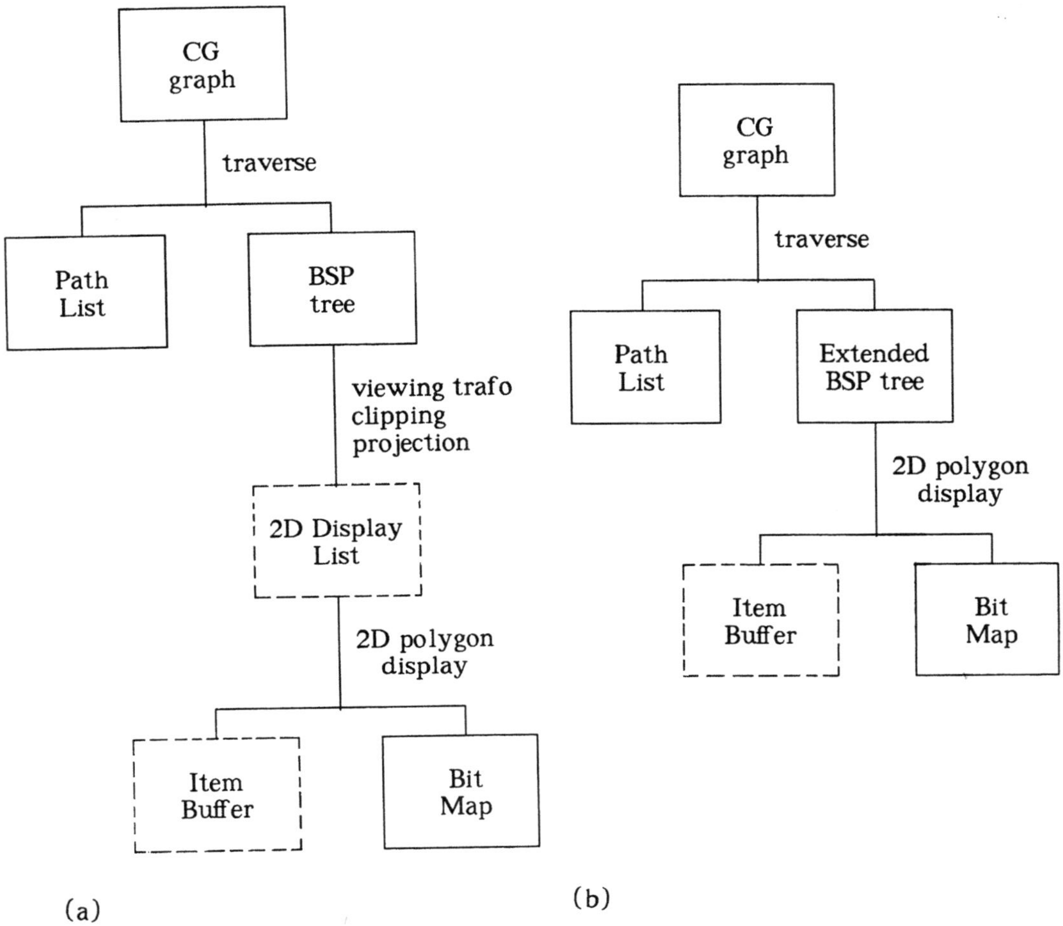

Figure 4.

Representation levels of the BSP tree display algorithm; in (a) a plain BSP tree is used, in (b) an Extended BSP tree. - - - indicates an optional representation.

In the environment of the depthsort algorithm, these processors generate the polygons from its assigned part of the CG graph, update the Path List as well as the auxiliary list (where the polygons are sorted by maximum z value), from which depthsort will extract the (split) polygons in display order, creating the Display List. Parallellising the depthsort algorithm is not a trivial problem, and it remains to be seen if it can be done at all.

Displaying the polygons of the Display List is done in sequential order, so parallel processing is not possible here either. However, since the depthsort algorithm creates the Display List sequentially from top to bottom, i.e. the polygons that are to be displayed firstly are generated firstly, a processor that performs depthsort and a processor that performs the display of the polygons from the Display List, might be linked in a pipeline, which is also a kind of parallel processing.

If the Display List and the screen have to be updated by removing elements from the List and displaying the remaining ones, again a sequential pass is required.

The creation of the (Extended) BSP tree might be done by parallel processors, since the extensions of the left and right subtree of a node are fully independent. Traversing the (Extended) BSP tree to generate the polygons in display order, however, cannot be done in parallel, unless the traversal is done in order to create the 2D Display List. This List, on its turn, must be traversed sequentially when displaying its elements.

The traversal of the CG graph and the creation of the (Extended) BSP tree may be "pipelined", as well as the traversal of the (Extended) BSP tree and the display of the polygons.

Some important operations that have to be performed are the point-in-polygon test, the polygon splitting operation, and the polygon scan conversion. As for the first one, we know that people at the Philips Research Laboratories in Eindhoven have implemented this test in hardware for 2D cases, where it takes them 1.5 μsec to test whether a point is inside a quadruple. The polygon scan conversion has been implemented in hardware already. As for the splitting operation, which might be seen as a special form of clipping, there is also hardware available.

References

[1] Newell, M.E., R.G Newell, and T.L. Sancha, *A Solution to the Hidden Surface Problem*, Proc. ACM National Conference (1972), pp. 443-448.

[2] Fuchs, Henry, Zvi M. Kedem, and Bruce F. Naylor, *On Visible Surface Generation by à priori Tree Structures*, Proc. Siggraph 80, in: ACM Comp. Graphics, **14,** 3 (July 1980), pp.124-133.

[3] Peters, F.J., L.R.A. Kessener, and M.L.P. van Lierop, *Language extensions to study data structures for raster graphics*, Dept. of Mathematics and Computing Science, Eindhoven University of Technology, internal report.

[4] Teunissen, W.J.M, and J. v.d. Bos, *A Model for Raster Graphics Language Primitives*, Data Structures for Raster Graphics; Proceedings of a Workshop, EurographicSeminar Series, Springer Verlag, 1985.

[5] ten Hagen, P.J.W., and C.G. Trienekens, *Pattern Representation*, Data Structures for Raster Graphics; Proceedings of a Workshop, EurographicSeminar Series, Springer Verlag, 1985.

[6] Gargantini, I., *An effective way to represent quadtrees*, CACM, **25,** 12, (1982) pp. 905-910.

Data structures for ray tracing

Frederik W. Jansen

Dept. of Industrial Design
Delft University of Technology
Oude Delft 39A
2611 BB Delft
The Netherlands

ABSTRACT

Methods to improve the efficiency of the ray tracing process are reviewed. Special attention is given to algorithms for tracing a ray through box and cell structures of hierarchical box and spatial subdivision methods.

1. Introduction

Ray tracing [1] is a very elegant hidden surface algorithm that has provided some of the finest examples of image synthesis in raster graphics. Ray tracing effectively models optical effects, such as mirroring reflections, cast shadows and transparency with refraction. The price for this sophistication is the long processing time for the picture generation process, and hence the interest in methods and data structures to improve the efficiency of the ray tracing process. The ray tracing algorithm in its simplest form can almost do without any auxiliary data structure. It can be characterized as a brute force method and it is therefore most natural to consider a multiprocessor or a VLSI implementation for the most time consuming components. Although a hardware implementation will undoubtedly be the ultimate answer, efficient software methods will provide sufficient and flexible solutions for the moment, and lead to a better understanding so that the entire process can be optimized.

In section 2 the principles of ray tracing are summarized and in section 3 methods and data structures that have been proposed for improving the efficiency of ray tracing, are described.

The main components in the ray tracing process are the geometric search for surfaces to be intersected and the intersection calculation itself. In this paper we will concentrate on the geometric search problem. In general, the cost of searching algorithms depends on the structure of the set of items being searched. If the set of items is already sorted, the search can be performed more efficiently. Most methods that are reviewed in section 3 are based on this principle. The item buffer method uses preprocessing based on a depth sort to find the first intersected surface element for each pixel; the hierarchical box methods exploit a binary search strategy; the spatial subdivision methods sort the surface elements by location. When the overhead introduced by the methods grows, it may be worthwhile to study the efficiency of the algorithms that work on the data structures. In section 4, algorithms for tracing a ray through a box or cell structure are discussed.

2. Ray tracing

2.1. Ray tracing

The 'point-by-point' approach of ray tracing was first described by Appel [2]. For every 'pixel' of the image plane that is located between the eye and the scene, a ray is cast from the eye point into the scene and a search is made for intersections with objects (fig.1).

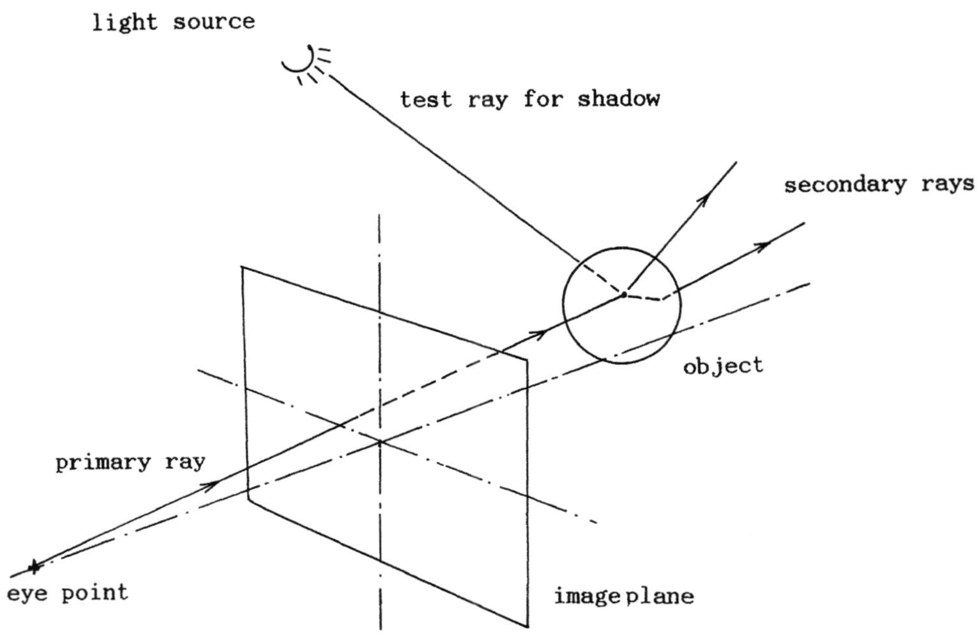

Figure 1.

Ray tracing: for every pixel of the image plane a ray is cast in search for object intersections. If the ray does not intersect an object the pixel is set to the background colour.

If an intersection is found, new rays can be cast to calculate shadows (e.g. is there another object between the light source and the intersected surface) or to simulate mirroring reflections and transparency with refraction [1]. We will call the ray from the eye point into the scene the 'primary' ray and the additional rays the 'secondary' rays. Secondary rays can themselves be offsprings of other secondary rays. A further improvement is obtained with the concept of distributed ray tracing [3], for modeling motion blur, depth of field, and anti-aliasing.

Ray tracing is a non-projective method. Most other standard hidden surface algorithms are projective methods: the surface elements of the objects are projected onto the image plane and a visibility calculation is performed, based on a depth sort prior to projection for all surface elements of the object (list priority algorithms), a depth sort for every pixel (z-buffer algorithms), or a depth sort for each scan-line segment (scan-line algorithms). The projective methods are restricted to solve the hidden surface problem in one direction, and can strongly benefit from coherence and efficient sorting techniques [4]. In the multi-directional case of ray tracing the use of coherence and sorting is not so straightforward.

2.2. Object representations

With respect to the search for ray surface intersections, it is important to distinguish two methods of object representation:

- The object is defined as a polygon model or approximated with a net of polygons (faceted model). If the approximation is accurate, the number of polygons is large. Faceted models typically consist of 10-50k polygons.

- The geometric model is not approximated but defined analytically as a procedural representation or as a surface model with quadratic and cubic surface representations.

Both model representations can be derived from the same primitive instancing, sweep or procedural input representation scheme. While for the faceted modeling the input representation is converted into a consistent boundary model, for the analytical approach the input representation is converted into parameters for a ray intersection procedure. For a hybrid approach see Potmesil [5]. For the faceted models, the ray intersection calculation is simple and the same for all primitives. For the analytical approach, the intersection calculation is different for every primitive and often benefits from special shape features. Algorithms have been published for ray tracing sweep defined objects [7],[8],[9], bicubic patches [6], fractals and other procedurally defined objects [7].

For the two representation schemes, the ray intersection problem can be stated differently:

- For the faceted models we search for the high chance candidates among a very large set of polygons; the ray intersection problem itself is trivial. The problem is to select the relevant subset without testing all the elements of the total set.

- For the other approaches, since the ray intersection calculations are, except for the basic primitives, rather expensive, we try to avoid any unnecessary intersection calculation. The problem is to select, with a simple test from a small set, all objects that are intersected.

2.3 Ray tracing CSG models

CSG models are objects defined by applying transformations and boolean operations to primitive solids. The CSG model is internally represented as a binary tree. Each leaf node is a primitive object; each intermediate node is the composite object formed by applying the operator at the node to the sub-objects defined by the left and right branches of the node; the root node corresponds to the complete object. Remarkably, ray tracing was the first hidden surface algorithm for viewing CSG models that did not need an explicit boundary evaluation of the CSG representation. The CSG ray tracing algorithm originates from Goldstein and Nagel [10]. Roth [11] discusses several techniques to improve the efficiency of this algorithm. Only recently other CSG versions of standard hidden surface algorithms have been published [12],[13],[14]. In the CSG ray tracing algorithm, the search for visible surfaces is combined with the determination of valid surfaces. Valid surfaces are surfaces of primitives that contribute to the boundary of the resulting composite object. The determination of valid surfaces is based on a ray classification method [15]. Descending the CSG tree down to the leaves, the ray is classified with respect to the primitive solids, and returning upwards the tree, the classifications of left and right subtrees are combined (see fig.2).

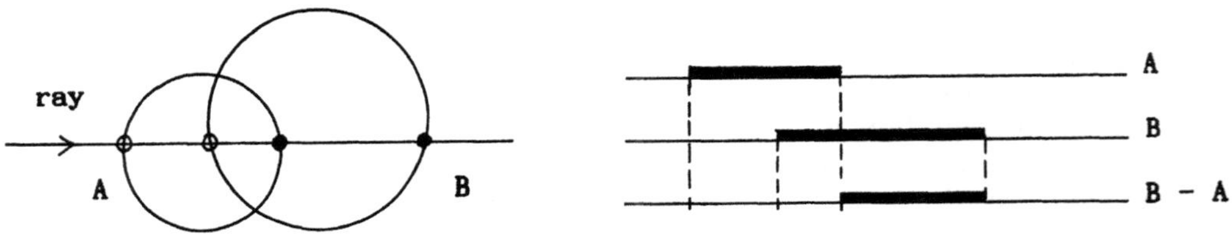

object: B - A

o intersection point with primitive
• valid point

Figure 2.

The ray intersections with the primitives are calculated and the first valid point is the intersection of the ray with the object.

Only in the extra CSG evaluation do CSG ray tracing algorithms differ from standard ray tracing methods. In the following we only give special attention to CSG models if the data structure influences the CSG evaluation. The term 'objects' is used for standard surface models; in case of a CSG model, one should read 'primitive solid' for 'object'.

3. Methods to improve the efficiency of the ray tracing process

3.1. Image coherence

We already referred to the brute force character of the method. A method to reduce the number of rays is to exploit image coherence: neighbouring pixels will often have the same intensity. After sampling the picture at a low resolution, new rays are cast only at those places where intensity gradients occur [1],[11]. This technique is effective and especially suitable in a previewing context [17],[18]. For complex pictures, however, the image coherence drops to a low level and the gain of this method is small.

In the following we concentrate on the activities within one ray tracing operation.

3.2. The item buffer

The idea behind the item buffer is surprisingly simple, but only recently brought forward by Weghorst, Hooper and Greenberg [19]. The basic notion is that casting a primary ray is the inverse of the projection of an intersected surface element on the image plane. We can therefore use a projective hidden surface method to determine which surface element covers a pixel. For each pixel a pointer to a surface element or item is stored. For faceted models the method is very effective because only one intersection calculation has to be carried out to find the exact intersection point. For the other representations it may be advantageous to store additional information in the item buffer to avoid the intersection calculation completely.

For CSG models more information is needed. If additional rays are to be cast, it is necessary to know which primitives are active on an intersection point. A method to provide this information is given in [14] (see fig. 3).

3.3. Bounding volumes

A naive implementation of the ray tracing algorithm tests every object for intersection with the ray. In most cases the intersection calculation is expensive. It is therefore preferable to enclose the objects in a bounding volume with a simple ray intersection test. Only if the ray intersects the bounding volume, a ray intersection with the object is calculated (fig. 4).

A simple implementation uses rectangular boxes oriented towards the viewing direction. More elaborated implementations incorporate arbitrarily oriented boxes and multiple types of bounding volumes. A first alternative for the rectangular box is the sphere. Spheres are less effective for some objects than boxes but are direction independent and are thus more easy to test for intersection with secondary rays [1],[11] chosen according to an intersection complexity-versus-volume trade-off function. For complicated objects, such as sweep objects, special or

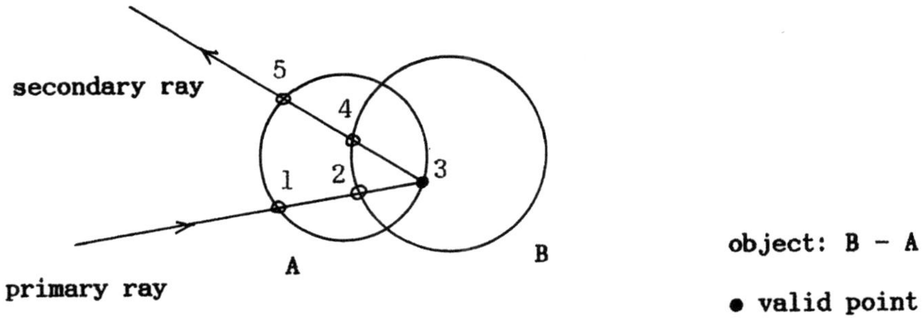

Figure 3.

For a correct interpretation of the intersection points 4 and 5 we need to know that the start point of the secondary ray is contained in primitive A and B.

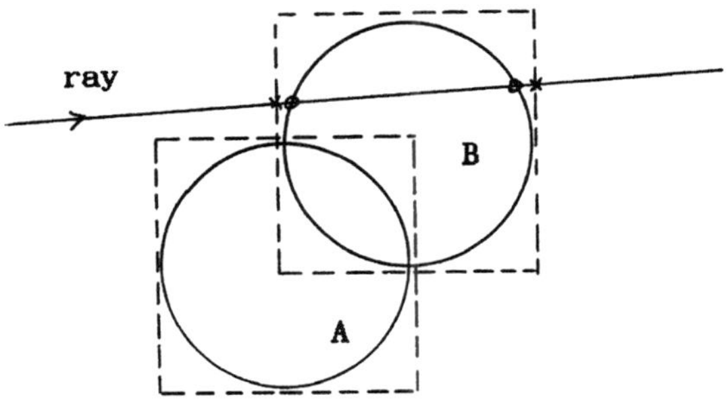

Figure 4.

If the ray intersects the enclosing box of an object, the object is tested for intersection.

multiple bounding volumes are used [7],[8].

3.4. Hierarchical box methods

A natural extension of the previous method is a hierarchy of bounding volumes. Given the bounding volumes of the objects a tree of enclosing volumes is created with the bounding volumes of the objects at the leaves and at every intermediate node a bounding box that encloses the boxes of the subtrees. The notion of enhancing hidden surface algorithms with a hierarchical data structure originates from

Clark [20]. The hierarchy of enclosing volumes guides the search for object intersections with the ray. If the ray does not intersect the enclosing volume at the root, it does not intersect any object. If the ray intersects the root, the tree is recursively descended to test for ray intersections with the bounding volumes of the subtrees (fig. 5).

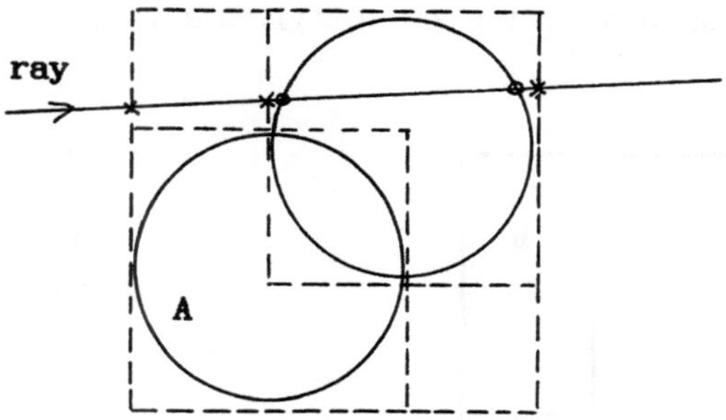

Figure 5.

If the ray intersects the box of the composite node, the boxes of the subnodes are tested.
When the ray misses a box, that node or subtree is discarded.

A simple implementation uses rectangular boxes oriented towards the view direction. More elaborated implementations incorporate:

- Arbitrarily oriented bounding volumes.
  Rubin and Whitted [21] refer to Brooks et al. [22] who utilize arbitrarily oriented rectangular parallellepipeds. The ray is transformed for every level of the box-hierarchy.

- Geometric ordering.
  The optimal conditions for the tree organization are:

  - overlap of object enclosures in space is minimal,
  - the tree is balanced and organized in such a way that it reflects the geometric distribution in space.

  An efficient tree organization corresponds with a logical hierarchical decomposition of the scene [11],[19]. Savings from tree optimalization algorithms are therefore not expected.

- Dynamic z-bounding.
  If an intersection point is found we can discard all subtrees with bounding volumes behind the intersection point in the ray direction. Descending the tree the subtree with the nearest enclosing volume is tested first. For CSG models the z-bounding is only valid for primitives that are not involved in difference and intersection operations [11].

- Tree pruning.
  For the primary rays we can take advantage of object coherence. For a given part of the screen only a subset of the total number of objects has to be tested for intersection. Objects outside this area can be temporarily pruned from the tree. This reduces the number of box tests at the cost of some preprocessing. A suitable partitioning of image space is given by the projections of the enclosing boxes, (see fig. 6). The box test now reduces to a point in interval test. In [18] an indication is given of the efficiency gain for a scanline approach. A similar approach based on areas on the screen is given in [23].

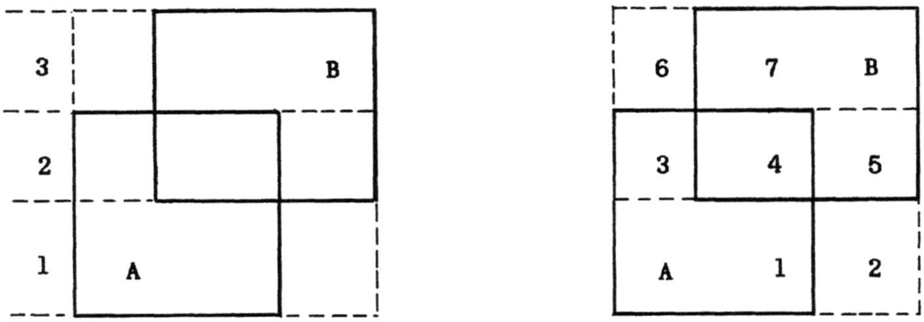

Figure 6.

The projections of the enclosing boxes divide the image plane in partitions. Left (for scanline processing) in three areas, 1: A, 2: A+B, and 3: B. Right (for optimal area coherence), 2 and 6: empty, 1 and 3: A, 4: A+B, and 5 and 7: B.

For very large polygon models, the hierarchical enclosing box method tends to become inefficient: if an object contains more than a few hundred polygons the ray intersection with that object becomes quite laborious. Rubin and Whitted [21] therefore extended the enclosing box hierarchy down to the polygon level. Because of the great amount of data involved in a complete expanded tree, the composition tree is dynamically expanded when needed for the ray intersection. Up to the object level, the tree is static and kept in memory. The 500 boxes last generated are also kept to benefit from object coherence. Another approach mentioned by Rubin and Whitted [21] is a recursive binary subdivision of the object box. This is a hybrid version of the hierarchical box method and a spatial subdivision method to be discussed in the following paragraph.

For ray tracing CSG models the hierarchical box structure can be combined with the CSG tree. Pruning of the box tree includes also pruning of the CSG tree [24],[18],[23].

3.5. Spatial subdivision methods

For faceted models it is preferable to choose a data structure that is independent of the hierarchical object structure. Instead of using bounding volumes, we divide object space in cells and classify the objects or polygons according to their position in these cells. A simple implementation divides the object space in a rectangular grid or cell structure, and stores the objects or polygons that are contained in a cell, in a bucket related to that cell. Prior to the ray-object intersection calculation, the ray is intersected with the cell structure to find the cell first intersected. If no ray-object intersection is found in this cell, we search for the cell next intersected by the ray and test the objects or polygons contained in that partition of object space. We proceed until the first intersection point, if any, is found. A number of methods have been developed that differ in the use of:

- Fixed or adaptive cell structures.
  In the adaptive variant, the cell structure accommodates the spatial distribution of the items. A useful scheme is to allow up to a maximum number of items in a cell. When the number of items exceeds this maximum, the cell is divided and the contents of the cell are redistributed over the new cells.

- Regular or arbitrarily sized cells.
  Both versions are mentioned by Rubin and Whitted [21]. The arbitrarily sized cells are created by dividing parent cells according to a load balancing strategy.

- Access to data by tree traversal or by index in a directory.
  With the tree traversal method, the object space is recursively subdivided and the hierarchy is represented by a tree. The object data is accessed via the leaves of the tree. With the directory index method, an address computation is done on basis of the position of a point (coordinates), followed by a lookup in a directory table (spatial index).

The EXCELL method of Tamminen [25],[26] provides a spatial index to an adaptive cell structure created by recursive binary subdivision (fig. 7). A ray tracing algorithm for this structure is given in [27]. An octree like structure is used by Glassner [28]. Access to the data is by tree traversal. Dippe and Swensen [29] use a cell structure with a fixed number of arbitrarily shaped tetrahedra. Cells are adapted in size to contain an equal distribution of data over the cells. The structure is used to distribute the ray tracing load over a fixed number of parallel processors.

For ray tracing CSG models with a spatial subdivision method, it is not preferable to use the standard ray classification method, but the classification on ordered points [15]. It is not necessary to calculate all the intersection points of the ray with the object. We only need to calculate the intersection points until a valid point is found [12]. For every intersection point found, we perform a CSG evaluation with the CSG tree after pruning the absent primitives from the tree. A primitive is absent when an even number of intersection points for that primitive are encountered. In [14] a method is given to exploit CSG coherence for ray tracing CSG models.

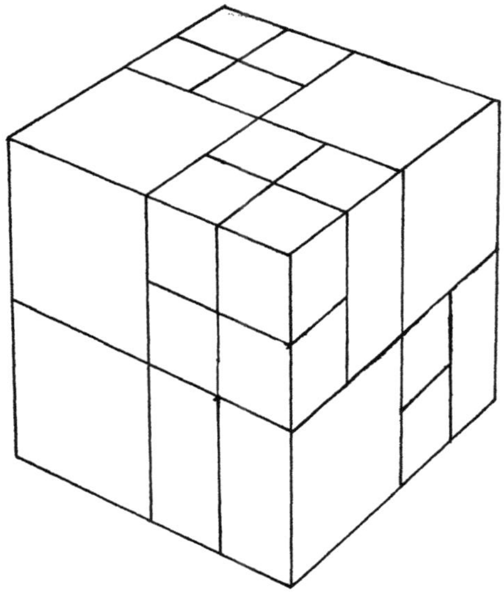

Figure 7. Adaptive cell structure

4. Ray tracing algorithms for cell and box structures

4.1. Ray traversal methods

If we compare the hierarchical box method with the spatial subdivision method we can distinguish two main differences in approach:

- the box structure is object oriented and the cell structure is space oriented,
- with the hierarchical methods the ray intersection proceeds top-down instead of bottom-up for the spatial subdivision methods.

The natural ray tracing algorithm for the hierarchical box method descends the hierarchical tree and tests the ray for intersection with the boxes of the subnodes. All subtrees that fail to pass the box and z bounding tests are discarded and pruned from the tree. At the leaf level the ray is intersected with the objects and while returning upwards the intersection intervals of the left and right subtree are combined. The ray classification of the root gives the final ray-object intersection intervals.

The natural ray tracing algorithm for the cell structure takes a bottom-up approach and proceeds by local access. First the intersection of the ray with the total structure is calculated and the cells are stepwise traversed by calculating the intersection of the ray with the cell planes and determining which cell is traversed next.

We can imagine two other methods using similar data structures but instead of the pure tree traversal or the pure local access method, we take a hybrid approach of traversing the binary tree, meanwhile looking for the first partition, intersected by the ray. We will call this approach the recursive ray traversal method.

4.2. Algorithms

The combination of ray traversal methods and box and cell structures leads to the following algorithms:

A. Standard hierarchical box method.
See fig. 8a and listing 1.

B. Recursive ray traversal for an enclosing box hierarchy.
A cell structure is build using the enclosing boxes of the objects. The procedure is as follows:

- for every composite node the ray is clipped recursively at the side planes of the subtree boxes. In case of overlapping boxes the node is dynamically expanded to a subtree with at most twelve leaf nodes. In most cases the number is less than twelve because the ray does not traverse all partitions.

- while descending, we search for the node that is first intersected by the ray.

- for every leaf node the object is intersected and a flag is set to prevent multiple intersection computations of the ray with the same object. A leave node can contain zero, one or several objects.

In fig. 8b an example is given of the box partitioning. For the algorithm see listing 2.

C. Recursive ray traversal for space subdivision structure.
We now apply the same tree descending technique on the cell structure. When the ray intersects the cell structure, we recursively subdivide the ray and proceed with the cell first intersected by the ray. If the ray intersects only one cell, the polygons in that cell are tested for intersection. This approach can be taken if the cell structure is created by a recursive binary subdivision or can be recursively halved. The algorithm is the same as B except for the simpler splitray procedure.
See fig. 8c and listing 3.

D. Standard spatial subdivision method.
A spatial index (directory) is used in the example for accessing the polygons that are contained in the cell.
See fig. 8d and listing 4.

```
procedure raytrace(node);

begin
  if boxintersect(box(node)) then
    if kind(node) = composite then
      begin
        raytrace(left(node));
        raytrace(right(node));
        combineintervals
          {merge left and right ray classifications}
      end
    else {ray/object classification}
      rayintersection(objectnr(node))
end;
```

Listing 1. Standard ray intersection of hierarchical box structure.

```
procedure raytrace(node,alpha1,alpha2); {alpha is ray parameter}

begin
  if boxintersect(box(node)) then
    if kind(node) = composite then
      begin
        splitray(first,second,alpha3); {clip ray to one of the box planes}
        raytrace(first,alpha1,alpha3); {first intersected box partition}
        raytrace(second,alpha3,alpha2) {second intersected box partition}
      end
    else {ray/object classification}
      rayintersection(objectlist(node))
end;
```

Listing 2. Recursive traversal of hierarchical box structure.

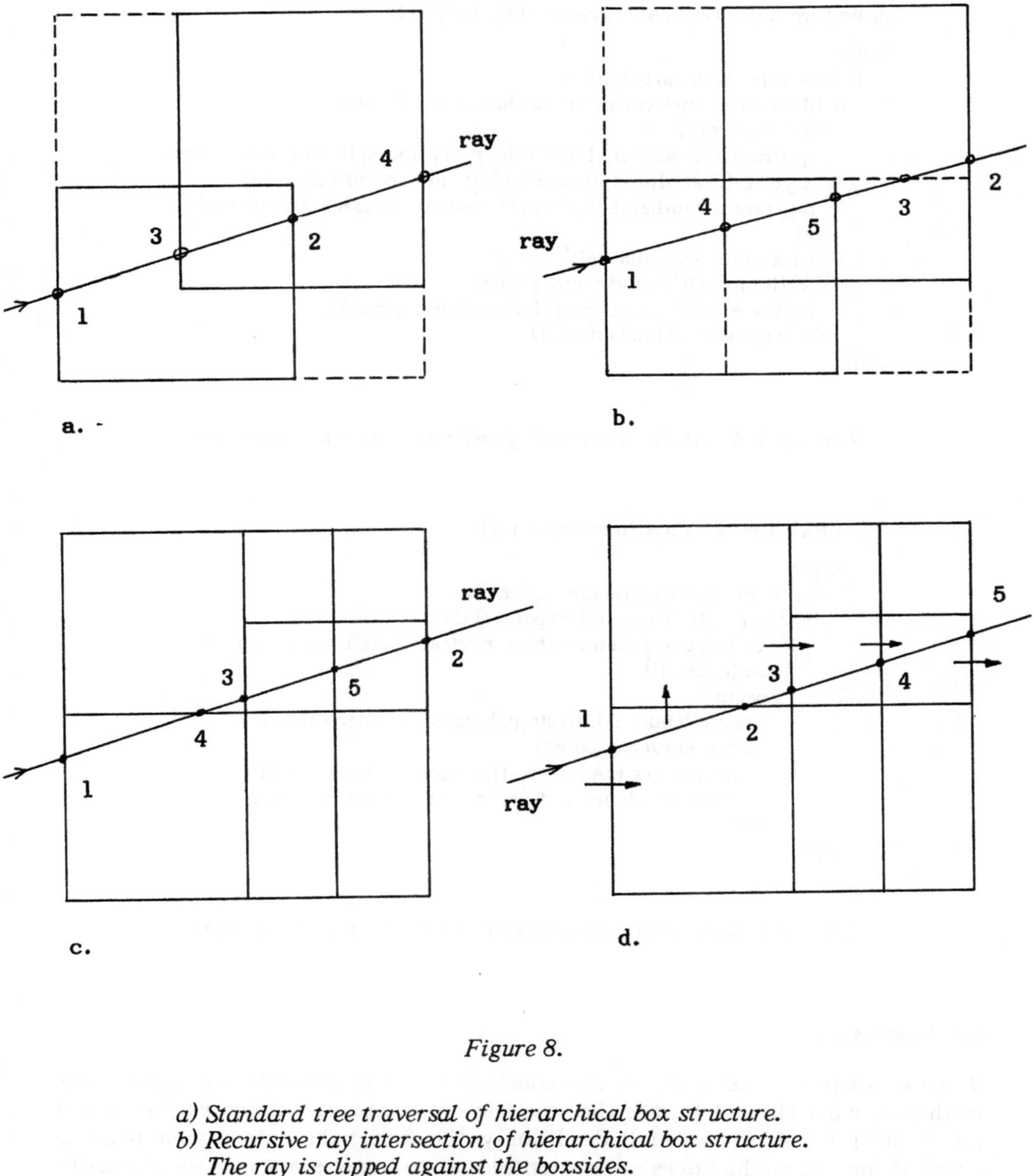

Figure 8.

a) Standard tree traversal of hierarchical box structure.
b) Recursive ray intersection of hierarchical box structure. The ray is clipped against the boxsides.
c) Recursive ray intersection of cell structure. The ray is subsequently halved, similar to the creation of the cell structure.
d) Sequential ray intersection of cell structure.

```
procedure raytrace(directoryrange,alpha1,alpha2);

begin
  if {ray intersects partition} then
    if {directory range covers more than one cell} then
      begin {clip ray}
        splitray(first,second,alpha3); {clip ray and split directory range}
        raytrace(first,alpha1,alpha3); {first intersected partition}
        raytrace(second,alpha3,alpha2) {second intersected partition}
      end
    else {ray intersects one cell}
      if cellkind(cell)=subdirectory then
        raytrace(subdirectoryrange(cell),alpha1,alpha2);
      else raydatacell(bucket(cell))
end;
```

Listing 3. Recursive traversal of cell structure with directory.

```
procedure raytrace(directory,point);

begin
  while inbox(box(directory),point) do
    with cell(directory,index(point)) do
      if (celltype = directory) then raytrace(subdirectory,point)
        else {datacell}
          begin
            raycell(bucket); {tests polygons for intersection}
            updateray(box,point)
              {calculates the intersection point of the ray with
                the cell planes and find new testpoint in next cell}
          end
end;
```

Listing 4. Sequential traversal of cell structure with directory.

4.3. Discussion

If we compare the methods, we can conclude that the standard hierarchical box method is most efficient in case the object intersections are not too expensive and the number of objects is limited. If only the first valid intersection point is searched for, the method does not guarantee that no unnecessary intersection calculations are performed. Method B clips the ray at the box sides and reduces the ray classification to limited intervals that are processed stepwise. The method guarantees, at the cost of extra overhead, that no unnecessary intersection calculations are done. The method is a generalization of the z-bounding technique. For faceted modeling, method C seems preferable when all intersection points are searched for and method D seems more suitable when only the first (valid) intersection point is needed and the average number of traversed cells is small compared to the total number of cells that is traversed by a ray that is traced completely through the structure. Experimental results are required for a more quantitative comparison of these methods.

5. Conclusions

An overview was given of published methods for improving the efficiency of ray tracing. Experimental results and efficiency gains of these methods are given in [18],[19],[23] and [28]. Two new ray tracing algorithms for recursive box and cell structures are given based on a combination of the hierarchical access method of the box structure and the local access of the cell structure methods.

Acknowledgements

I would like to thank Jack van Wijk and Wim Bronsvoort for their comments on an earlier version of this paper and for the discussions on this subject through the years, the results of which are embedded in the contents of this paper.

References

[1] Whitted, T., An improved illumination model for shaded display, Communications of the ACM 23(1980)6, 343-349.

[2] Appel,A.A., Some techniques for shading machine renderings of solids, SJCC 1968, AFIPS Conf. Proc. Vol. 32(1968), 37-45.

[3] Cook,R.L., Porter,T., Carpenter,L., Distributed ray tracing, Computer Graphics 18(1984)3, 137-145. Siggraph84.

[4] Sutherland,I.E., Sproull,R.F., Schumacker,R.A., A characterization of ten hidden-surface algorithms, ACM Computing Surveys 6(1974)1, 1-55.

[5] Potmesil,M. Generating three-dimensional surface models of solid objects from multiple projections. IPL-TR-033, Image Processing Lab. Rensselaer Polytechnic Institute, New York, Oct 1982.

[6] Kajiya,J.T., Ray tracing parametric patches, Computer Graphics 16(1982)3, 245-254, Siggraph82.

[7] Kajiya,J.T., New techniques for ray tracing procedurally defined objects, Computer Graphics 17(1983)3, 91-102, Siggraph83.

[8] van Wijk,J.J., Ray tracing objects defined by sweeping cubic splines, to appear in ACM Transactions on Graphics.

[9] van Wijk,J.J., Ray tracing objects defined by sweeping a sphere. in: K.Bo and H.A. Tucker (eds), proc. Eurographics84, 73-82.

[10] Goldstein,E., Nagel,R., 3D visual simulation, Simulation 16(1971)1, 25-31.

[11] Roth,S.D., Ray casting for modeling solids, Computer Graphics and Image Processing 18(1982)2, 109-144.

[12] Atherton,P.R., A scan-line hidden surface removal procedure for constructive solid geometry, Computer Graphics 17(1983)3, 73-82, Siggraph83.

[13] Okino,N., Kakazu,Y., Morimoto,M., Extended depth-buffer algorithms for hidden surface visualization, IEEE Computer Graphics and Applications 4(1984)5, 79-88.

[14] Jansen,F.W., A CSG list priority hidden surface algorithm, to appear in proc. Eurographics85.

[15] Lee,Y.T., Requicha,A.A.G.,"Algorithms for computing the volume and other integral properties of solids. II. A family of algorithms based on representation conversion and cellular approximation. Comm. of the ACM 25(1982)9, 642-650.

[16] Whitted,T., Weimer, D.M., A software test-bed for the development of 3-D raster graphics systems, Computer Graphics 15(1981)3, 271-277, Siggraph81.

[17] Jansen,F.W., Wijk,J.J. van, Previewing techniques in raster graphics, Computers and Graphics 8(1984)2, 149-161.

[18] Bronsvoort,W.F., Wijk,J.J. van, Jansen,F.W., Two methods for improving the efficiency of ray casting in solid modelling, CAD 16(1984)1, 51-55.

[19] Weghorst,H., Hooper,G., Greenberg,D.P., Improved computational methods for ray tracing, ACM Transactions on Graphics 3(1984)1, 52-69.

[20] Clark,J.H., Hierarchical geometric models for visible surface algorithms, Communications of the ACM 19(1976)10, 547-554.

[21] Rubin,S.M., Whitted,T., A 3-dimensional representation for fast rendering of complex scenes, Computer Graphics 14(1980)3, 110-116. Siggraph80.

[22] Brooks,J. et al., An extension of the combinatorial geometry techniques for modeling vegetation and terrain features. MAGI Inc. NTIS AD-782-883. June 1974.

[23] Sears,K.H., Middletich,A.E., Set-theoretic volume model evaluation and picture-plane coherence. IEEE Computer graphics and Applications 4(1984)3, 41-46.

[24] Woodwark,J.R., Quinlan,K.M., Reducing the effect of complexity on volume model evaluation, CAD 14(1982)2, 89-95.

[25] Tamminen,M., The EXCELL method for efficient geometric access to data, Thesis, Acta Polytechnica Scandinavica, Mathematics and Computer Science Series no.34, Helsinki, 1981.

[26] Mantyla,M., Tamminen,M., Localized set operations for solid modeling, Computer Graphics 17(1983)3, 279-288, Siggraph83.

[27] Tamminen,M., Karonen,O., Mantyla,M., Ray-casting and block model conversion using a spatial index, CAD 16(1984)4, 203-208.

[28] Glassner,A.S., Space subdivision for fast ray tracing, IEEE Computer Graphics and Applications 4(1984)10, 15-22.

[29] Dippe,M., Swensen,J., An adaptive subdivision algorithm and parallel architecture for realistic image synthesis, Computer Graphics 18(1984)3, 149-158, Siggraph84.

An approach for a PHIGS machine

Salim S. Abi-Ezzi
Michael A. Milicia

Center For Interactive Computer Graphics
Rensselaer Polytechnic Institute
Troy, N.Y. USA

ABSTRACT

The Programmer's Hierarchical Interactive Graphics System (PHIGS) proposal specifies a powerful interface for the development of interactive graphics applications. Throughout the development of PHIGS, emphasis has been placed on providing a high level of functionality along with the ability to provide rapid, dynamic display modifications. Any implementation of PHIGS should strive toward the ultimate goal of providing real-time support for the full functionality. This goal will be impossible to achieve using current, readily available graphics hardware. This is due to the inherent complexity introduced by the desired level of functionality and not to any of the specific approaches that PHIGS has taken to providing that functionality. One possible solution to this problem is the development of a "PHIGS machine." Such a machine will play the role of a PHIGS logical workstation. This machine must include customized hardware to perform many of the functions required to meet the PHIGS specifications. Some of the more important PHIGS features which one must consider when approaching the architecture of such a machine include structure manipulation, structure traversal and the viewing pipeline.

1. Introduction

The Programmer's Hierarchical Interactive Graphics System (PHIGS) is a proposed 2/3-D graphics programming standard under development by the American National Standards Institute (ANSI) committee X3H3. The Graphical Kernel System (GKS) is an already existing, well-accepted international standard for 2-D graphics [Ende84] and is currently being extended to 3-D *. An important question that must be asked is whether or not the PHIGS proposal offers significant

---

* We assume that the reader is familiar with GKS, as well as the basic graphics concepts covered in [Fole82]. All subsequent references in this paper to GKS will refer to the 3-D version.

enough improvements over GKS to justify the existence of a second standard. The answer to this question is that it depends on what type of application programs we are considering.

PHIGS is specifically intended to satisfy the needs of application programs whose requirements include the following:

1. Definition, display and manipulation of *geometrically related* (i.e. hierarchically defined) objects.

2. A high degree of interactivity which necessitates frequent dynamic modification of graphical entities.

Since the design of PHIGS is customized for support of these types of applications, the programmers of such applications should see significant improvements over GKS. However, if these features are not required, there may be no strong motivation for the use of PHIGS over GKS.

Thus, PHIGS is not intended to be a competing standard with GKS. It is simply intended to provide better support for the particular constituency mentioned above. In fact, compatibility with GKS is a highly desired goal of PHIGS. The GKS specification is being used as the primary reference point for PHIGS development. Differences will only be introduced when they are necessary to better satisfy the requirements of the PHIGS constituency. Most of the basic features of PHIGS are identical or very similar to those of GKS. These include sophisticated, flexible 3-D graphics output primitives, all of which are subject to a complex viewing process.

In the next section, we will give a high level overview of the key features of PHIGS. This will be followed by a discussion of the major differences between PHIGS and GKS and a comparison of their relative complexities from an implementation point of view. We then go on to discuss the idea of developing a PHIGS machine. The ultimate goal of this machine is to provide real-time support for the full functionality of PHIGS.

Many of the issues presented here arose out of work being done at the Rensselaer Polytechnic Institute Center for Interactive Computer Graphics on an experimental implementation of PHIGS [Abi-85]. The results of this work are discussed with the ANSI PHIGS committee on a regular basis.

2. A brief overview of PHIGS

This section is intended to give the reader a general understanding of the major features of the PHIGS model. It is by no means intended to be a complete treatment of the features covered and many features are omitted entirely.

2.1. The basic PHIGS model

The data grouping mechanism used by PHIGS for the definition and manipulation of graphical data is called a *structure*. A PHIGS structure can be viewed as a sequential list of heterogeneous *structure elements*. A structure element may be one of the following:

1. An output primitive - This may be a polyline, polymarker, text, cell array, fill area, fill area set, and generalized drawing primitive.

2. A modeling transformation - This specifies a change in the modeling coordinate system in which the application is defining its data.

3. A view selection - This specifies changes in the camera position and parameters with respect to the world coordinate system.

4. An attribute selection - This specifies a change in a primitive's attribute setting from within the structure.

5. An invocation to another structure - This permits arranging structures into acyclic networks.

6. A symbolic label - This type of element is useful for specifying a target for subsequent structure edit operations.

7. Application data - This type of element provides a limited capability for integrating application data into the graphics model. It has no graphical significance.

8. A name set constructor - This specifies an update to the current name set attribute (defined later).

Once a PHIGS structure has been defined, it can be edited at the structure element level. PHIGS provides functions to (re)open a structure at any time and modify it by inserting or deleting individual elements. This is done in a manner similar to that of a standard line editor. Functions are provided to position the *element pointer* to any location within the structure. The effect of subsequent edit operations is dependent upon the position of this pointer.

2.2. Structure processing for output

PHIGS structures are created and stored in a centralized data storage facility. They can exist and can be manipulated independently of any particular workstation. In order to associate a given structure with a particular workstation for display, the structure must be *posted* to the workstation. This association is maintained until the structure is explicitly *unposted*. All structures in the centralized data storage facility are available for posting to all workstations at all times.

A workstation processes a posted structure for display by sequentially processing each of its elements. This is referred to as structure *traversal*. During traversal, an attribute selection element is processed by setting the current value of the given attribute in a workstation-maintained state list to the requested value. The processing of a transformation element causes a requested change to be made to the current modeling transformation which will then affect subsequent output primitives. A view selection element causes a change in the current viewing specification. This will also affect subsequent output primitives. An output primitive element is processed according to the current attribute, transformation, and view settings and then displayed. Label and application data elements are ignored when processing a structure for display. Perhaps the most important type of structure element in PHIGS is the one which allows the invocation of other structures. This is what provides PHIGS with its powerful hierarchical modeling capability. The processing of these elements is rather involved but deserves a fairly detailed treatment.

A "structure call" is similar to a parameterless procedure call in a programming language. Upon encountering a "call structure" element during traversal, the following actions occur:

1. The processing of the calling structure (the parent) is suspended.

2. The current "environment" in effect at the time of the call (e.g. transformation and attribute settings) is saved on a system stack.

3. Control is passed to the called structure (the child) which then executes to completion. The initial environment for the child structure is that which it inherits from its parent. This may subsequently be changed from within the child structure.

4. On return from the child structure, the parent's environment is restored from the system stack to its original state prior to the call. Thus, a child structure cannot affect its parent's environment.

5. Processing of the parent structure is resumed with the element immediately following the call.

One important consequence that should be noted about the traversal process described above is that attributes and transformations are "bound" to individual output primitives dynamically during traversal. Thus, the exact appearance of a primitive is dependent upon the environment in effect at the time it is encountered.

Conceptually, once a structure is posted to a workstation, its associated network is traversed continually for display. Ideally, the continual nature of traversal implies that any change resulting from a structure edit should be immediately reflected on the displays of all workstations to which the structure, or one of its ancestor structures in the hierarchy is posted.

2.3. PHIGS input model

The PHIGS input model is basically the same as GKS. The only major difference between the two is in the pick mechanism. Since the PHIGS model is hierarchical, it requires that a pick device return a *pick path* which represents the path through the structure which leads to the picked primitive. This is necessary to distinguish between the possibly many instances of the same primitive within a structure network. The detectability of an object in PHIGS is handled through the name set mechanism which is described in the next section.

2.4. Name set mechanism

At each point during structure traversal, PHIGS has the concept of a *current name set*. This set is modified dynamically during traversal in response to the Add To Name Set and Remove From Name Set structure elements. Each time a change is made, the new current name set is associated with all subsequent output primitives in a structure until it is again changed or the end of the structure is reached. Name sets are similar to attributes in that they are saved and restored on structure calls, and are inherited by child structures.

Intuitively, the name set associated with a primitive is intended to represent the set of logical classes to which that primitive belongs. Name sets are used in conjunction with workstation-associated sets which are called *filters*. These filters specify which primitives should currently be highlighted, invisible, and/or pickable on that workstation. Associated with each of these three characteristics at each workstation, is an *inclusion filter* which specifies what classes of primitives are to have the corresponding characteristic, and an *exclusion filter* which specifies which classes are to be specifically excluded from having the characteristic. As an example, a primitive whose associated name set is NS, is pickable on a workstation whose pick inclusion filter is PI and whose pick exclusion filter is PE, if and only if *BOTH* of the following conditions hold:

$$NS \cap PI \neq \emptyset$$
$$NS \cap PE = \emptyset$$

Invisibility and highlighting are handled in an analogous manner.

2.5. PHIGS viewing pipeline

All output primitives in PHIGS are specified by the application programmer in *modeling coordinates* (MC). However, in order to ultimately display an output primitive, it must be mapped to *device coordinates* (DC). In this paper, we refer to the sequence of operations which must be applied to a primitive to convert it from MC to DC, as the *viewing pipeline*. See left side of Figure 1. These operations may include scaling, rotation, translation, projection (perspective or parallel), and clipping. The entire pipeline is three-dimensional and all transformations are expressed as 4x4 homogeneous matrices. Each primitive passes through three intermediate coordinate systems on its way from MC to DC for a total of five distinct coordinate systems.

An application program begins by specifying each logical graphics object in its own MC system. A *modeling transformation* is used to map an object defined in MC to a particular *instance* of the object in *world coordinates* (WC). This is the way in which objects are composed to form a specific configuration in a single WC system. The remainder of the pipeline is devoted to creating a particular view of the configuration that we have constructed in WC. The next step is the application of a *viewing transform* which changes from WC to *viewing coordinates* (VC). The VC system (UVN space) is one which is oriented so that the desired *view plane* is parallel to the UV plane. A view volume, projection reference point, and projection type are then specified relative to the VC system. A *projection* is then applied which maps the view volume to a viewport in the next coordinate system called

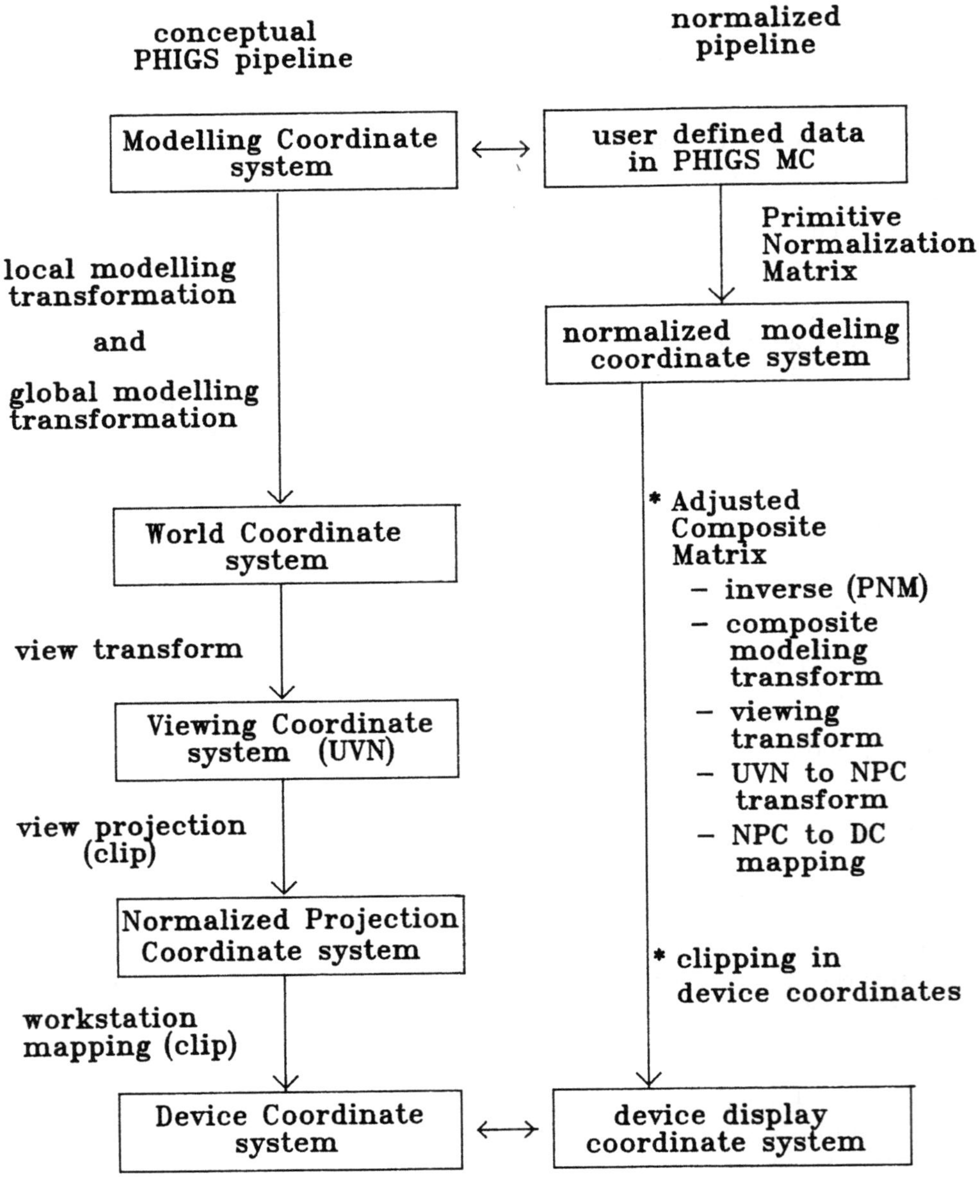

Fig 1– The normalization of the PHIGS viewing pipeline

normalized projection coordinates (NPC). NPC space is simply a unit cube. Finally, a *workstation transformation* is applied which performs an isotropic mapping from a window in NPC to a viewport in *device coordinates* (DC).

As mentioned previously, the entire pipeline is three-dimensional, so it is up to the device to determine the method by which the 3-D image in DC is to be displayed on the 2-D physical view surface of the workstation. The techniques which can be used include simply dropping the z-coordinates, or creating a hidden surface image.

3. Overview of relative complexities of PHIGS and GKS

It should be clear from the preceding section that the only differences between PHIGS and GKS stem from the desire to provide integrated support for the modeling and dynamic modification of hierarchically related graphics entities. This is reflected in PHIGS by the specification of an n-level, hierarchical graphics model in which attributes are dynamically bound to primitives. In this model, there is only one master copy of each structure. However, this single copy may be referenced several times to create the effect of multiple instances. PHIGS hierarchies also impose a dynamic, downward inheritance of attributes and transformations. The PHIGS model may be contrasted to the GKS segment model which only provides a one-level hierarchy with static attributes. In the GKS model, there must be a separate copy of a segment for each of its "instances".

The desire for dynamic modifications to the graphics display is supported in PHIGS by providing the ability to perform editing of previously defined structures at the structure element level. The editing of a structure automatically affects all instances of that structure in all structure networks. To achieve the same effect in GKS would require the deletion and recreation of an entire segment for each "instance" of the segment being changed.

One of the major concerns that has been raised regarding the PHIGS proposal is the inherent complexity of its implementation relative to that of a more traditional approach like GKS. We would like to address this question by looking at the problem in two separate parts. First, there is the complexity introduced by the provision of high-level graphics primitives and a sophisticated viewing process. We agree that real-time support for these features presents a significant challenge. In fact, this is a problem which can probably *only* be adequately addressed through the development of more sophisticated graphics hardware. However, these particular concerns are equally applicable to GKS since the differences between the two standards in this respect are minimal.

Second, we must consider the implications of the PHIGS hierarchical model and dynamic editing capabilities. The argument usually made in this regard is that the dynamic traversal of PHIGS structure networks with traversal time binding of attributes and transformations is a very expensive process. The claim is also made that the situation is aggravated by the fact that edits typically require a complete retraversal of the affected hierarchies. These are very valid concerns but they are not caused by the specifics of the PHIGS model. They are simply complexities which are inherent in the support of the truly hierarchical graphics environment which is desired by the PHIGS constituency. The same complexities would be present if we attempted to do hierarchical modeling with GKS. The only difference would be that the management of the hierarchies and the required traversal process would be embedded within the application program rather than be explicitly represented in the graphics model.

Similarly, the additional requirement of the PHIGS constituency for dynamic modifications would also require frequent "retraversals" by an application program using GKS. In fact, for this type of application, GKS would probably be less efficient since even simple edits would, in general, require deletion and recreation of several copies of entire segments to achieve the effects desired by the application. This would require much more data transfer between the application and the workstations than the PHIGS approach, which would allow us to directly update the single copy of the structure being edited. With GKS, it would also be the responsibility of the application to determine which segment copies on what workstations are affected by the change. This would require that the application "understand" the implicit hierarchy which is being modeled.

Our conclusion here is that for applications which do *not* require dynamic modification and/or hierarchical modeling capabilities, the use of PHIGS may indeed lead to unjustified performance degradation. In these cases, GKS would probably be the standard of choice. However, for those applications which *do* require these capabilities, PHIGS should be the standard of choice. For these types of applications, the use of PHIGS will not introduce any unnecessary performance penalties. However, it *will* provide a much more natural model for the application programmer as well as a large portion of the required graphics and modeling support that would otherwise have to be handled by the application program. These two characteristics together will lead to significant improvements in application programmer productivity.

However, there are indeed valid concerns about the potential performance problems associated with *any* graphics system which attempts to provide support for highly interactive, 3-D graphics applications which require a truly hierarchical modeling capability. Although these problems may be justified by the amount of function being provided, they must still be addressed. In this paper, we propose to deal with these problems by introducing customized hardware to perform many of the crucial functions required for the graphics support in such an application. Based on the above discussion, it is clear that many of the basic components required for such a machine (e.g. those which process output primitives through the viewing pipeline) would be equally necessary in supporting either a GKS or a PHIGS environment. However, we will concentrate specifically on the idea of a *PHIGS machine* which will include functions above and beyond those needed for GKS.

4. Inherent Complexities of PHIGS Implementations

As previously stated, one of the major goals of PHIGS is the ability to provide rapid, dynamic articulation of geometrically related graphical entities. Achieving this goal will depend in a large part on the efficiency of the structure traversal (display) process and how often complete traversals must be performed. It is fairly obvious that the PHIGS traversal process in its full generality is likely to be an extremely computation-intensive task. One of the biggest bottlenecks in this process will be the processing of primitives through the viewing pipeline. This is due to the fact that in general, with the full functionality of PHIGS, the viewing process may include the following types of operations :

1. Transforming a cell array (pixel array) by a general 4 × 4 homogeneous matrix and then clipping it.

2. Pattern fill - This includes projecting a parallellogram to an arbitrary plane, mapping an N × M pattern to the parallellogram, replicating the pattern to fill the interior of a fill area or fill area set primitive, and finally applying transformation and clipping to the filled primitive.

3. Generating stroke precision text given a string, text plane and position, text up vector, text path, text alignment, character height, character expansion factor, and character spacing.

In addition, PHIGS structure network traversal will include the following functions due to its hierarchical nature :

1. Each time the current name set is changed, we must perform set operations to determine the highlighting, invisibility and pickability attributes for subsequent output primitives.

2. Return a complete pick path for a picked primitive.

In addition to the above, future modifications to PHIGS are likely to call for support for hidden line/hidden surface removal (HL/HSR) during traversal and the introduction of a modeling clip in the modeling coordinate system of the viewing pipeline. Both of these features are very desirable to the application programmer and add considerably to the modeling value of a PHIGS structure. However, they will also lead to significant increases in the complexity of the already expensive traversal process.

Since complete traversal of a structure network is potentially such a costly proposition, we may next ask ourselves how often complete traversals must be done. Obviously, it must be done for the initial display of an image. But what about the effect of subsequent structure edits? Can we identify certain types of structure edit operations for which we can define shortcut methods to make the necessary changes on the display without a *complete* retraversal of all structures in the networks affected by the edit? Unfortunately, in general, the answer to this last question is no. It can easily be shown that the vast majority of edit operations, no matter how simple they may seem (e.g. insert or delete a single element), will require a complete retraversal of all affected structure networks to update the display appropriately. There are only a few types of edit operations which, if applied in very specific contexts, could be handled without a complete retraversal. However, the cost of detecting these highly specialized cases will outweigh any benefits to be gained by treating them in a special efficient manner.

A last point worth mentioning here is that floating point processing is needed by the traversal process. This is the case since PHIGS places no limits on the MC system in which the user defines his data. In addition, the modeling coordinate system, as well as the view of the WC system, may get changed from within a structure. This situation eliminates any scheme that could be used to normalize coordinates to integer values prior to traversal.

5. A PHIGS machine

We have seen that the traversal of a PHIGS structure to generate a graphics image is a very complex operation which requires floating point support. Since traversal is so complex, and must be done frequently, it is not feasible to do it in many of the current generation graphics devices. Even those devices that provide the functionality needed for traversal will have a problem in doing it fast enough. A PHIGS machine would be an attempt to deal with this situation. Therefore, one critical requirement of a PHIGS machine is to be able to perform the traversal process fast enough to allow rapid display modification. This points toward doing traversal in hardware and utilizing parallel processing techniques. We will give a high-level overview of a possible architecture for such a system.

The machine basically takes the place of the PHIGS logical workstation. It is organized as a display processing system which controls a high resolution color raster display with double buffers. The basic components of the machine are a floating point *general purpose processor* (GPP), a *graphics system controller* (GSC), and several *special purpose VLSI processors* (SPP). For the sake of exposition, we will assume that these processors communicate with one another over a single bus. See Figure 2. This would not be practical in a final design due to the large amount of communications that will be required.

5.1. The general purpose processor

The GPP controls the overall operation of the PHIGS machine. It is organized into two independent processors, P1 and P2, which share a common memory. Processor P1 has two basic tasks. The first is to handle the interface with the *workstation independent section* (WSIS) of PHIGS. The second is to manage the memory which it shares with processor P2. P2 is responsible for managing the continual traversal of the posted structure networks.

5.1.1. Processor P1 - Handling the WSIS interface

There is a two-way communication between P1 and the WSIS. On the one hand, P1 receives structure content, structure edits, and state table updates from the WSIS and records them in the shared memory. On the other hand, P1 sends inquiry results and graphical input data to the WSIS. P1 is also responsible for performing the functions necessary to support deferral mode. This guarantees that P2 is always traversing the correct data. For example, upon receiving structure or attribute changes from the WSIS, P1 must either perform the required updates immediately (if deferral mode is set to As Soon As Possible), or queue these changes (if deferral mode is set to Wait). Queued changes are applied either when the deferral mode is changed or when an explicit update is requested.

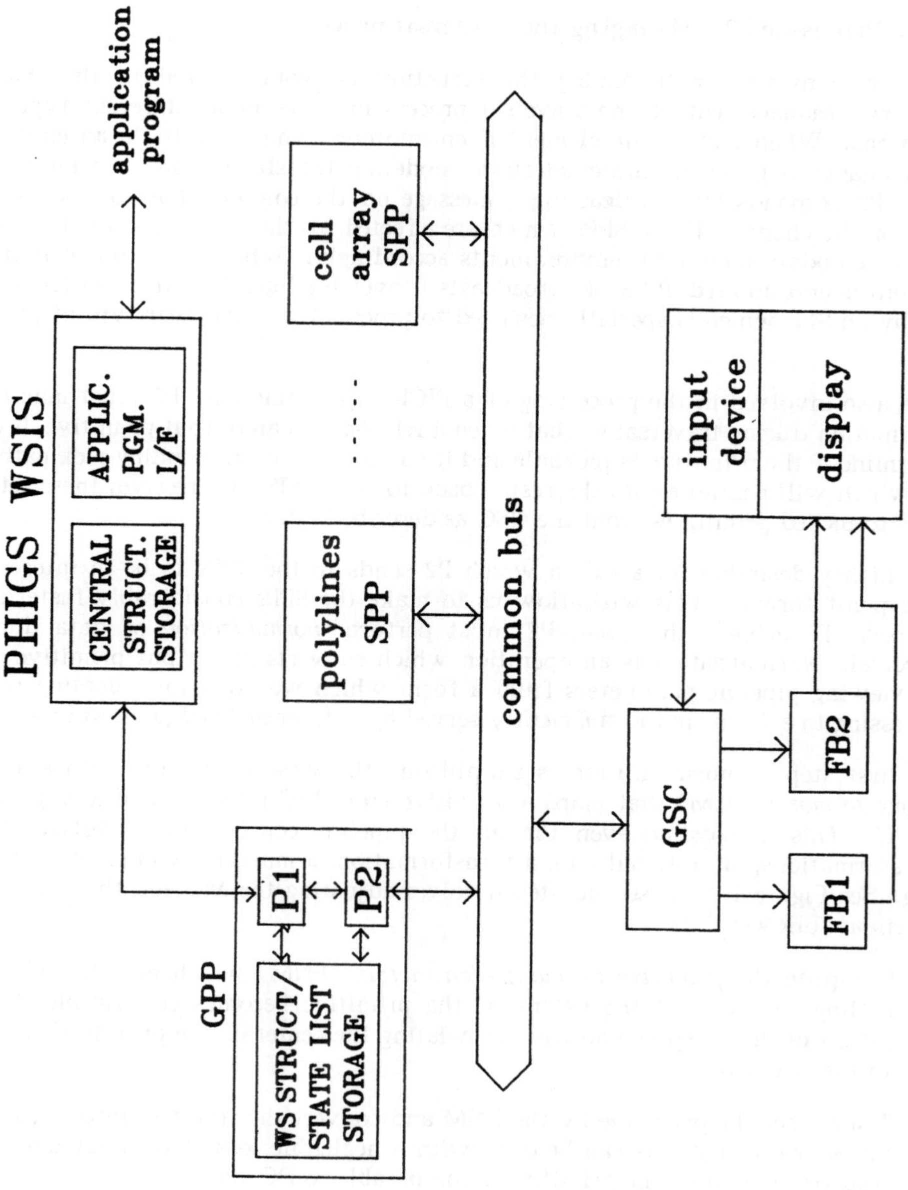

Fig 2- Architecture of a PHIGS machine

5.1.2. Processor P2 - Managing the traversal process

P2 is responsible for traversing the structure networks stored in the shared memory. Management of the traversal process involves many different types of functions. When a structure element is encountered which results in an environment change (e.g. an attribute selection, modeling transformation, or view selection), P2 responds by broadcasting a message on the common bus to inform the SPPs of the change. Those SPPs which are affected by the change receive the message and update their local environments accordingly. When an output primitive element is encountered, P2 again broadcasts it over the bus. It is received from the bus by an SPP which is specially designed to process that particular type of primitive.

P2 is also involved in the processing of a PICK input function. P2 must maintain information during traversal so that given a reference to an output primitive, it can determine if the primitive is pickable and if so, send the corresponding pick path to P1, which will communicate the result back to the WSIS. P2 receives these references to picked primitives from the GSC as described later.

It is highly desirable for all data which P2 sends to the SPPs to be in integer or fixed point format. This will allow us to make the SPPs considerably faster and cheaper. To achieve this goal, P2 must perform *normalization* of data during traversal. Normalization is an operation which converts an output primitive and the viewing pipeline parameters from a form which would require floating point processing to a form that is sufficiently served by integer or fixed point support.

The first step of normalization is simplifying the viewing pipeline into a single *composite matrix* (CM) that maps a primitive from MC into DC, and a single clip in DC. This is possible even though the pipeline conceptually involves three transformations, an optional clip, a transformation, a mandatory clip, and a mapping. See Figure 1. The second step involves adjusting the MC and the composite matrix as follows:

1. Compute the *primitive normalization matrix* (PNM) which has the effect of scaling MC so that the extent of the primitive becomes comparable to the extent of device space and then translating the center of the primitive's extent to the center of MC.

2. Transform the primitive by the PNM and convert the result to integer coordinates. Note that this can be done with a negligible loss of accuracy since the resulting extent of the primitive is comparable to DC space.

3. Adjust the CM to compensate for the effect of the PNM. This is done by multiplying the inverse of the PNM by the CM to produce the *adjusted composite matrix* (ACM).

4. Convert the ACM to a fixed point format. Note that this may be done with a negligible loss in accuracy since the ACM is mapping between two comparable coordinate systems. This ACM will be used in place of the original CM in the viewing pipeline.

Notice that P2 must perform normalization dynamically during traversal. Upon reaching a primitive, P2 computes an estimate of the extent of this primitive. P2 recomputes the ACM and the effective clipping window in DC whenever the viewing pipeline is changed or when a primitive's extent differs considerably from the extent of the previous primitive.

5.2. The special purpose processors

An SPP is a VLSI chip designed specifically to handle one type of PHIGS output primitive. Note, however, that an SPP for one type of primitive (e.g. text) may call on an SPP for a simpler type of primitive (e.g. polyline) to complete its task. An SPP maintains a local list of the attribute settings for the type of primitive which it supports. It also keeps a local copy of the ACM and the clipping window. When P2 broadcasts environment updates which affect a particular SPP's settings, the SPP accepts such updates and adjusts its local settings accordingly.

An SPP applies the ACM transformation, clipping, and the appropriate attributes to each output primitive that it receives. This processing of the primitive results in the broadcasting of a series of *pixel update messages* over the bus. Each such message is a 3-tuple consisting of a pixel's location, color, and priority. The priority is used to resolve conflicts during traversal which arise from multiple writes to the same frame buffer location.

The fact that data is normalized before it reaches the SPPs greatly simplifies their design and adds to their speed. This is especially true if we want to design the SPPs as systolic systems [Mead80], since such systems are known to deal best with the homogeneity of the integer format as opposed to the floating point format. Furthermore, there are many cases where normalizing only a few values will allow us to avoid floating point processing for a much larger number of values. For example, in the case of a cell array, we normalize the 3 points that constitute the parallellogram, and reap the benefit for every point in the cell array grid. The same situation exists in handling stroke precision text. Only the text extent is considered for normalization while the benefit is extended to all the points that constitute the strokes. Hence, normalization is a desirable feature since its costs are vastly outweighed by its benefits.

5.3. The graphics system controller

The system uses a double-buffering approach which allows us to create a new frame buffer image in one buffer while the other buffer is being used to refresh the display. The GSC manages both of these buffers as well as the hardware input devices. It receives two types of messages over the bus. First, there are the pixel update messages sent by the SPPs. Second, there are control commands sent by the GPP. It also receives data from the input devices.

The GSC associates a *priority* with each pixel in the frame buffer being constructed. Whenever a pixel update message is received, the priority of the update is checked against the priority currently associated with the pixel. The pixel is updated only if the update priority is higher than the current priority. The priority of an update is set by the SPP which generates the update. These priorities are organized on a multi-level scheme. Equal priorities at level i are resolved by examining the priorities at level $i+1$. If priorities are equal at all levels, an arbitrary choice is made. At least one level of priority must correspond to the traversal order of the primitive which resulted in the pixel update. Thus, primitives are uniquely identifiable by this level of priority. This "order-based" priority will insure that primitives can be processed in parallel while still guaranteeing the same results that would occur if they were processed sequentially. It is also convenient for the implementation of PICK input as described below. Additional levels of priority can lead to many useful effects. For example, we can do Z-buffering for HL/HSR at no extra cost by having the first level priority of a pixel correspond to the depth of the primitive at that pixel, while the second level is based on the traversal order as described above. Such an image space technique for HL/HSR allows us to avoid the complexities of the PHIGS viewing pipeline and traversal process.

In order to process a PICK input function, the PICK device would transmit a pixel location to the GSC. The GSC would then monitor that location during traversal and determine the priority of each pixel written there. These priorities would then be sent to processor P2 by way of the bus. Since each priority uniquely identifies a primitive, P2 can use this information to complete pick processing.

Each time a complete traversal of all posted structure networks is completed, the GPP broadcasts a message over the bus. This is received by the GSC and used as a signal to swap frame buffers.

5.4. The use of parallelism

There are many places in which parallelism is utilized in the PHIGS machine. At one level, there is parallelism within the processing performed by the SPPs. For example, transforming, clipping and painting a polyline will be handled by a systolic system such as that described in [Fuch82]. At the next higher level, we process several primitives in parallel using several SPPs. It is possible to use several SPPs of the same type for frequently used primitives such as the polyline. This second level of parallelism requires the use of pixel priorities as described above to guarantee correct results.

Also, since the execution of a "substructure" cannot have any effect on the results of its caller, we have yet another level of parallelism which allows the processing of called structures to proceed in parallel with their callers. This requires the use of several P2 (traversal) processors. This last level of parallelism would require a more sophisticated form of pixel priorities. In essence, it would require that each instance of a primitive be identified to the SPPs by the unique *path* through the structure network which leads to the generation of that instance.

6. Conclusion

We have seen that the viewing pipeline of any graphics system which supports high level 3-D output primitives with a large number of attributes is a very complex process. In order to achieve real-time dynamics in such a system, we will require specialized hardware support. In fact, specialized hardware has been identified as a crucial element for real-time support even in simpler systems such as 2-D GKS [Enca84].

Adding the PHIGS concept of dynamic traversal of structure networks complicates the problem even further. We will have to depend on a custom VLSI approach which utilizes as much parallelism as possible. Fortunately, the type of processing required is very amenable to a parallel design. We have identified what we feel is a possible approach to the high-level architecture of such a machine. Future work will involve refining the architecture and examining the requirements of the individual components more closely. In particular, we plan to address the design of a more elaborate communications scheme between the various processors, and to explore the idea of using systolic algorithms to solve some of the basic problems which are involved.

Acknowledgements

The work described in this paper has been supported by the CICG Industrial Associates Program and National Science Foundation grant ISP79-20240. The opinions expressed in this paper are those of the authors, and do not necessarily reflect the views of the sponsoring organizations.

References

[Abi-85]
Abi-Ezzi, S. S., A. J. Bunshaft, "An Implementer's View of PHIGS", *RPI CICG Technical Report*.

[GKS]
American National Standards Institute, Graphical Kernel System, December 26, 1984.

[Enca84]
Encarnacao, J. L., R. Lindner, M. Mehl, G. Pfaff, W. Strasser, "A VLSI Implementation of the Graphics Standard GKS", *Computer Graphics Forum*, Vol. 2, No. 2/3, Aug. 1983, pp.115-121.

[Ende84]
Enderle, G., K. Kansy, G. Pfaff, *Computer Graphics Programming, GKS- the Graphics Standard*, Springer-Verlag, New York, 1984.

[Fole82]
Foley, J.D., A. van Dam, *Fundamentals of Interactive Computer Graphics*, Addison-Wesley, Reading, Massachusetts, 1982.

[Fuch82]
Fuchs, H., J. Poulton, A. Paeth, A. Bell, "Developing Pixel-Planes, A Smart Memory-Based Raster Graphics System", *Proceedings of the 1982 Conference on Advanced Research in VLSI*, M.I.T., pp.137-146.

[GKS-3D]
Draft Functional Description - Graphical Kernel System for Three Dimensions, ISO/TC97/SC5/WG2-N277.

[Mead80]
Mead, C. A., L. A. Conway, *Introduction To VLSI Systems*, Addison-Wesley, Reading, Massachusetts, 1980.

[PHIGS]
Draft American National Standard for the Functional Specification of the Programmer's Hierarchical Interactive Graphics System (PHIGS), X3H3/85-21, February 18, 1985.

Using linear quadtrees to store vector data *

Hanan Samet
Clifford A. Shaffer

Computer Science Department and
Center for Automation Research
University of Maryland
College Park, Maryland 20742

Robert E. Webber

Computer Science Department
Rutgers University, Busch Campus
New Brunswick, New Jersey 08903

ABSTRACT

The linear quadtree is adapted to store vector data by defining a new data structure called a *segment quadtree.* It uses a constant or bounded, amount of storage per node, represents straight lines exactly (i.e., it is not a digitized representation), and enables updates in a consistent manner (i.e., when a vector feature is deleted, the database can be restored to the state it would have been in had the deleted feature never been inserted). The segment quadtree is shown to meet these requirements whereas existing quadtree-like methods (e.g., the edge quadtree, strip tree, etc.) fail to satisfy them. In order to illustrate the usefulness of the segment quadtree, sample algorithms are discussed to insert and delete line segments as well as perform boundary following. The space requirements of segment quadtrees are also investigated.

1. Introduction

The region quadtree representation [Klin71, Same84a] has gained extensive use as a data structure for region representation in image processing, computer graphics, automated cartography, and other fields. It is a hierarchical data structure that is based on the principle of regular decomposition. Due to the large amounts of data involved in such applications, it is useful to use a representation for the quadtree

* This work was supported in part by the National Science Foundation under Grant DCR-83-02118 and in part by the U.S. Army Engineer Topographic Laboratory under contract 70-81-C-0059.

that does not involve pointers. The linear quadtree [Garg82] is one such representation that stores the image as a collection of leaf nodes each of which is encoded by a number corresponding to a sequence of directional codes that locate the leaf along a path from the root of the quadtree.

We are interested in using the linear quadtree as a uniform representation for data corresponding to regions, points, and vector features. The uniformity facilitates the performance of set operations such as intersecting a vector feature with an area, etc. Use of a linear quadtree for point and region data is well understood; however, this is not the case for vector features. While there are several hierarchical data structures for vector features, they are either not based on regular decomposition (e.g., the strip tree [Ball81]), do not handle more than one vector feature (e.g., the strip tree), or do not cope with the intersection of vector features (e.g., the edge quadtree [Shne81]). For vector features, a good linear quadtree representation must also have the following three properties. First, it must use a constant, or bounded, amount of storage per node. This rules out the PM quadtree [Same85b]. Second, straight line segments should be represented exactly (not a digitized representation). Third, updates must be consistent, i.e., when a vector feature is deleted, the data base must be capable of being restored to a state identical (not an approximation) to that which would have resulted if the deleted vector feature had never been added. The line quadtree [Same84b] is eliminated because it only handles rectilinear vector features. Hunter and Steiglitz's [Hunt79] adaptation of the quadtree for polygons is likewise of no use since it only approximates the lines. The edge quadtree [Shne81] was designed primarily for representing curves and thus does not handle connected edges in a manner that permits consistent updates.

In order to meet the above requirements, we present a new data structure, termed a *segment quadtree*. We show how it can be used in conjunction with linear quadtrees to represent collections of vector features consisting of sets of connected straight line segments termed *polygonal maps*. The remainder of this paper is organized as follows. Section 2 reviews the region quadtree and other attempts to use quadtree-like data structures for storing vector feature data. Section 3 describes the segment quadtree while Sections 4, 5, and 6 show, respectively, how line segments are inserted into segment quadtrees, how they are deleted, and how a boundary represented by a segment quadtree is followed. Section 7 contains a worst-case analysis of the size and storage requirements of segment quadtrees as well as some empirical data. Section 8 summarizes the current state of, and future plans for, the investigation of the segment quadtree.

2. The quadtree and previous line representations

The region quadtree represents region data by successive subdivision of the image array into four isomorphic quadrants. Given an image and its binary array, if the array is not composed entirely of 1's or entirely of 0's, then we subdivide it into quadrants, subquadrants, ..., until we obtain square blocks (possibly single pixels) that consist entirely of 1's or entirely of 0's. As an example, the region in Figure 1a is represented by the 2^3 by 2^3 binary array in Figure 1b. The resulting blocks for the array of Figure 1b are shown in Figure 1c and the quadtree in Figure 1d.

Below we consider quadtree representations for line and point data. One of the first issues we must face is the location of a point specified with d bits of precision in a node of depth d. In order to simplify the theoretical analysis of Section 7, we treat the point as being located in the center of the node at level d in the quadtree. However, results analogous to that of Section 7 hold for other treatments. Thus this is not a restriction on the implementation.

The PR quadtree [Oren82, Same84a] is an adaptation of the region quadtree to handle point data. Given an image representing a set of points, the image is subdivided into quadrants, subquadrants, etc., until each quadrant contains at most one point. The collection of points in Figure 2a is represented by the PR quadtree of Figure 2b.

As mentioned in Section 1 our goal is a unified approach to the treatment of points, regions, and vector features. Thus we must find a similar decomposition criterion for vector features. Unfortunately, the strip tree [Ball81] does not meet our requirements as it is not based on a regular decomposition. Other candidates are reviewed below.

In the *edge quadtree* of Shneier [Shne81] a region containing a vector feature, or part thereof, is repeatedly subdivided into subquadrants until each quadrant contains at most one curve that can be approximated by a single straight line segment. Each leaf node contains the following information about the edge passing through it: magnitude (i.e., 1 in the case of a binary image or the intensity in case it is a grey-scale image), direction, intercept, and a directional error term (i.e., the error resulting from the approximation of the curve by a straight line using a measure such as least squares). If a line segment terminates within a node, then a special flag is set and the intercept denotes the point at which the segment terminates.

Applying this process leads to quadtrees in which long straight edges can be stored in a few large leaves. However, small leaves are required in the vicinity of corners, intersecting edges, close approaches between curves, or areas of high curvature. Of course, many leaves will contain no edge information at all, since they are not intersected by a curve. As an example of the decomposition that is imposed by the edge quadtree, consider Figure 4 which is the edge quadtree corresponding to the polygonal map of Figure 3 when represented on a 2^4 by 2^4 grid.

A serious drawback of the edge quadtree is its inability to handle the meeting of two or more edges at a single point (i.e., a vertex) except as a pixel corresponding to an edge of minimal length. In other words, we don't know the nature of the vertex - e.g., the number of edges intersecting it. This means that boundary following as well as deletion of line segments cannot be properly handled in the vicinity of a vertex at which more than one edge meets. Another quadtree variant which is closely related to the edge quadtree is the formulation of Hunter and Steiglitz [Hunt79], termed an *MX quadtree* in [Same84a]. It considers the border of a region as separate from either the inside or the outside of that region. Figure 5 shows the MX quadtree corresponding to the polygonal map of Figure 3. The MX quadtree has problems similar to those of the edge quadtree in handling vertices. Again, a vertex is represented by a single pixel. Thus boundary following and deletion of line segments cannot be properly handled. Worse is the fact that an MX quadtree only yields an approximation of a straight line rather than an exact representation as done by the edge quadtree. Furthermore, note that the edge quadtree in Figure 4 contains considerably fewer nodes than the MX quadtree in Figure 5.

The *linear edge quadtree* is a variant of the edge quadtree that has been adapted for incorporation in a geographic information system [Same84c]. In this scheme, the leaf nodes of the quadtree are stored in a list (maintained in a B-tree) in the order in which they would have been visited by a preorder traversal of the tree. Each node contains three fields; an address, a type, and a value field. The address field describes the size of the node and the coordinates of one of the corners of its corresponding block. The type field indicates whether the node is empty (i.e., WHITE), contains a single point, or contains a line segment. Unlike Shneier's [Shne81] formulation, a line segment may not end within a node since in the existing implementation the value field is not large enough to contain the location of an interior point as well as a slope. Thus endpoints and intersection points are represented by single pixel-sized point nodes. The value field of a line segment indicates the coordinates of its intercepts with the borders of its containing node. Vertices are represented by pixel-sized nodes with the degree of the vertex stored in the value field. Figure 6 illustrates the linear edge quadtree representation. Note the difference in the decomposition of the region containing the vertex H in Figures 4 and 6.

The linear edge quadtree has a number of deficiencies. All vertices and endpoints are stored at the lowest level of digitization, i.e., in nodes deep in the tree. There is no mechanism for following a line segment, as each node describes only that portion of a line segment which is contained within the borders of the node. In particular, given a node that contains a single point, there is no indication as to which of the neighbouring nodes are connected to the point by a line segment.

An important criterion for evaluating whether or not astorage representation handles line segments properly is if the successive insertion and removal of the same line segment leaves the map unchanged. Since the edge quadtree nodes store only local information, it is extremely difficult to restore nodes, by merging, which had been split apart by the original insertion. For example, it is not easy to determine the endpoints of the edges emanating from a given vertex. Thus over time, the representation's compactness could deteriorate until it becomes equivalent to the MX quadtree (i.e., line segments are represented by pixel-sized nodes).

An alternative approach to storing vector feature data is the PM quadtree [Same85b]. The PM quadtree evolved from a desire to adapt the PR quadtree to store a polygonal map in a manner which preserves the relationship between edges and vertices. In essence, whenever a group of line segments meet at a common point, those segments can be organized by the linear ordering derived from their orientation. Three variations of the PM quadtree, termed PM_1, PM_2, and PM_3, have been developed.

The PM_1 quadtree is based on a decomposition rule that permits more than one line segment to be stored at a node only if they meet at a vertex that lies within the borders of that node. Figure 7 shows the PM_1 quadtree corresponding to the polygonal map of Figure 3. From the decomposition of the line segments CD and CE, we observe that the representation of line segments which meet at narrow angles may require a large number of nodes.

The PM_2 quadtree permits more than one line segment to be stored at a node even when the vertex they share is not within the borders of that node. Figure 8 shows the PM_2 quadtree that corresponds to Figure 3. Note that the PM_2 quadtree requires fewer nodes than the PM_1 quadtree for the same map. However, we observe that when a line segment passes near a vertex that is not incident on it (e.g., segment DF passing near point E in Figure 8), it is possible that many nodes may be required to separate them.

The PM_3 quadtree is based on the same decomposition rule as the PR quadtree. All line segments that pass through the node are broken into a fixed number of separate groups. There is one group for all the lines that radiate from the vertex in the node. The remaining line segments are ordered according to the pair of sides of the node's containing block that they intersect. The group of line segments radiating from a vertex is organized by angular orientation and the remaining groups of line segments are organized by their intercepts with the side of the region represented by the node. Figure 9 is the PM_3 quadtree that corresponds to Figure 3. Note that the block containing vertex E has two line segments intersecting the vertex (i.e., EA and EC), and one line segment (i.e., DF) for the line segment intersecting the South and West boundaries of the block.

Although useful for storing polygonal maps in core, it is not easy to incorporate the PM_2 or PM_3 quadtrees into the fixed-width fields of the linear quadtree disk-based representation. The problem is that the amount of information stored at a single quadtree node varies widely. For example, in the PM_3 quadtree, a node can contain both a vertex and a set of line segments that do not pass through the vertex. The PM_2 quadtree represents an improvement in the sense that a node either corresponds to a vertex or a set of line segments but not both. The PM_1 quadtree limits a node further to correspond either to a vertex or to a single line segment. This is more compatible with the node size limitation posed by the linear quadtree. Indeed, the segment quadtree, presented in the next section, can be viewed as a linear quadtree adaptation of the PM_1 quadtree.

3. The segment quadtree

The segment quadtree has three types of nodes: 1)empty or WHITE, 2)vertex, and 3)line (i.e., a node containing a line segment whose endpoints are boundaries of the block corresponding to the node). A linear quadtree representation stores each node type in the same (fixed) amount of space. This space should be minimized since WHITE nodes will also be of the same size as line and vertex nodes, even though for them we need only to store information distinguishing them from line and vertex nodes.

A line node in the segment quadtree is defined to contain precisely one line segment which enters from one side and exits through another side. With each line node we store the coordinates of the vertices of the line of which it is a component. This enables us to determine easily whether or not two neighbouring line nodes are part of a larger line segment. Without this information, we cannot properly merge nodes after deletion of a nearby line segment. Note that recording the coordinates, although requiring more space, is preferable to recording the slope and intercept values for the line because it avoids precision errors as well as keeps all information in integer format.

We next consider the problem of storing vertex nodes. A vertex node in the segment quadtree is defined to contain precisely one vertex and no line segments which do not intersect the vertex. This is identical to the definition of the PM_1 quadtree. With each vertex node we store the x and y coordinates of the vertex that it represents.

In order to be able to perform boundary following, we must be able to follow line segments which extend from a vertex. This requires us to investigate the neighbouring nodes of the vertex node. There are three cases. First, if a neighbour is empty, then there are no line segments extending from the vertex in that direction. Second, if a neighbour contains a single line segment, then we can check the slope of that line segment to determine whether or not it intersects the vertex. Finally, if the neighbour is a vertex, then we must be able to detect whether or not there exists an edge joining the two vertices. The solution is to store an eight bit descriptor with each vertex node that indicates which of the sides and corners are exited by one or more line segments. Using this scheme, whenever two vertices are contained in adjacent nodes, one of three situations can arise:

(1) The corresponding sides (or corners) are not exited through;

(2) the corresponding sides (or corners) are exited through; and

(3) the side for one node is marked as exited through, and the corresponding side of the other node is not exited through.

(1) indicates that no line segment joins the two vertices (e.g., the boundary between vertices B and C in Figure 10), while (2) indicates that a line segment does join the vertices (e.g., the boundary between vertices A and B in Figure 10). (3) signifies that no line segment passes between the two vertices and that the vertex node with the exited side is larger than the vertex node with the unexited side (since there must be another node on that side into which a line segment exited). For example, consider vertices B and D in Figure 10. Note that all the nodes neighbouring a given node on an exited side must be inspected since more than one line segment may exit from that side (e.g., the East side of the node containing vertex D in Figure 10).

In summary, segment quadtree nodes may contain either a vertex in which case each line segment in the node intersects the vertex, or at most a single line segment which enters and exits the node. The resulting decomposition is identical to that of the PM_1 quadtree; however, the information stored is different. Figure 11 shows the segment quadtree corresponding to the polygonal map of Figure 3. Compare this with the PM_1 quadtree of Figure 7.

An important aspect of the above decomposition rule is that it does not allow any case where there might be an unbounded decomposition of the tree. This would result if we would have taken as our decomposition rule one that did not permit a quadrant to contain more than one line segment. In the segment quadtree all vertices must be specified at some level of resolution, which will correspond to some depth in the tree. This resolution, say d , is a function of the minimum separation between any two vertices. The maximum depth of the segment quadtree depends on two further factors: the minimum separation between a vertex and a line and the minimum separation between two lines. These factors are analyzed further in Section 7.

In the case of geographic data, images are constructed from sequences of line segments that intersect only at their endpoints. Note that if a user wishes to specify two intersecting line segments, then four line segments must be specified. In the following, we assume that this minor preprocessing of the data has already been done.

4. Insertion into the segment quadtree

The data model used by the above analysis assumes that line segments do not intersect (except at their endpoints). This model is appropriate for cartographic data; however, the data structure is not restricted to such data. Below we show how to handle intersecting line segments by creating vertex points at the intersection of a collection of line segments. We shall also use this extended model in the discussion of deletion of line segments from the segment quadtree.

Insertion of a line segment into a segment quadtree proceeds as follows. If the line segment is to be inserted into a region represented by an internal node of the quadtree, then it is clipped against each of the quadrants of that region and the appropriate component of the line segment is inserted into the corresponding subquadrants. Once a line segment has been clipped, it is important to remember whether its end points were vertices of the original line segment or artifacts of the clipping operation.

Upon encountering a leaf node there are three possible courses of action depending on its type - i.e., empty, line, or vertex. If the leaf is empty and the component of the line segment contains two vertices (i.e., it is the unclipped line segment), then the region is further subdivided. If the leaf is empty and the component of the line segment contains one vertex, then the node becomes a vertex node and is marked exited in the direction of the intercept of the line segment with the border of the node. If the component of the line segment contains no vertices, then the node becomes a line node.

If the leaf is a line node, and the line segment to be inserted contains any vertices, then the node must be decomposed. Otherwise, we must determine if the components of the line segment and the line represented by the line node intersect within the region bounded by the node. If they intersect, then a new vertex is formed at the intersection point with the borders of the node being marked as exited as appropriate for the four line segments radiating from that vertex. Otherwise, the nodes are decomposed further until the two line segments are not contained within the same node.

If the leaf is a vertex node, and the component of the line segment either contains another vertex or does not intersect the vertex, then the leaf node must be further decomposed and the line segment insertion procedure continues. If the component of the line segment intersects the vertex and contains no new vertex, then we need only mark the edges of the node that intersect the line segment as exited.

5. Deletion from the segment quadtree

Deletion of a line segment from a segment quadtree is achieved by applying a two-step process to each quadtree node through which the line segment passes. First, we must remove the information corresponding to the presence of the line segment. Second, we must merge empty nodes as well as nodes that correspond to a line segment once the nodes containing the removed vertex have been replaced by empty nodes.

The first step of removing the information corresponding to the presence of a line segment is quite easy. We simply repeat the decomposition of the line segment as though it were to be inserted, locating those segment quadtree leaf nodes which contain the segment. Line nodes are marked WHITE. Vertex nodes require more work since the sides of the containing leaf through which the segment exits may also be exited by another (undeleted) line segment. Therefore, the neighbours along these sides must be examined to see if they contain another line segment. If not, then the vertex segment bit marking that side as exited is turned off. If, after this process, no side of the node's block remains marked as exited, then the line segment being deleted is the only one intersecting that vertex, and the node is marked WHITE.

Merging eligible nodes is somewhat more complicated; but since it is possible to determine which neighbours of a node are connected by a line segment, it is feasible. Each node which contained a portion of the line segment being deleted must be considered as a potential candidate for merger with its three siblings. The following algorithm should be applied to each such node.

A node and its three siblings may be merged if they are either 1) all WHITE, 2) all line nodes representing portions of the same line, or 3) a single vertex with line segments all of which intersect the vertex. The first two cases are easily determined by comparing the values of the node and its siblings - the siblings in this case will all be at the same depth in the tree. The third case might be difficult to determine, since two line segments may intersect at a vertex which either is not contained within the region covered by the node and its siblings, or is stored at a lower level in one of its sibling's subtrees.

In order to handle this last case, it is necessary to check the subtrees of each sibling of the node to determine if all line segments stored intersect at the same vertex. If the vertex is not contained in these siblings, then we must check the siblings of the node's ancestors until either 1) the vertex is located, or 2) additional line segments or vertices are encountered which would not allow the nodes to merge. Note that a special situation arises when exactly two line segments meet at a vertex and they are collinear. In such a situation, the appropriate nodes are merged to form a line node instead of being merged to form a vertex node as would have otherwise happened in the third case.

For example, consider the deletion of line segment AE from Figure 3, the result of which is shown in Figure 12a. The leaf node marked I is the result of merging since it now contains only portions of line segment AG. The node containing vertex E is no longer marked as exited on the North. Figure 12b shows the result of deleting segment CE from Figure 12a. In the course of deleting the line segment all leaf nodes in the SE quadrant will be merged to form the node marked II.

6. Traversing the border of a polygon

In order to traverse the border of a polygon we must first locate it. This can be accomplished, for example, by visiting successive western neighbours of a node (having started with some leaf representing a region that is internal to the polygon in question) until either a line or a vertex node is reached. This can be achieved using the neighbour finding techniques described in [Same82, Same85a].

If a line node is reached, then proceed down the line segment represented by the line node such that the interior of the polygon is on the right. If a vertex node was found (instead of a line node), then examine all the line segments radiating from that vertex in the counterclockwise direction looking for the segment that forms the minimum interior angle with it. We are now positioned to perform a clockwise traversal of the perimeter of the polygon.

At each step of the traversal, we are either entering a line segment node or a vertex node. If we are entering a line segment node, then all we must do is calculate the new neighbour. The information in the line node should be checked for consistency with the information used to calculate the entry into the line node. However, since directions only change at vertex nodes, nothing new is learned from a line segment node except that the border hasn't changed direction yet.

If we are entering a vertex node, then the neighbours of the vertex node are visited in a counter-clockwise manner (from the node we enter from) until the next line segment radiating from the vertex is located. This insures that the line segment found is the next line segment met in the clockwise traversal of the perimeter of the polygon (in case the vertex is intersected by many line segments). For example, suppose we are following the border of the polygon ABCEA in Figure 11 and we are moving along line segment BC in the direction of C. Upon reaching vertex C, we must search in a counter-clockwise direction in order to locate segment CE, rather than segment CD which is part of an adjacent polygon.

7. Space requirements

Earlier work [Same85b] on PM quadtrees analyzed the storage requirements in terms of the distances between vertices in the map and the angles formed by line segments in the map. Although such an analysis is technically correct, it is seldom the case that we categorize a map in such terms. A more common way of describing a map is in terms of the precision with which the locations of the vertices of the map are measured. We shall use this technique in the following analysis of the PM_1 quadtree (which is equivalent to the analysis of the segment quadtree).

As has been observed elsewhere [Same85b], the key factor in the analysis of the storage requirements of the PM_1 quadtree is the maximum depth of the quadtree. Given the maximum depth, say d, it is clear that the number of quadtree nodes representing a polygon will be proportional to 2^d (except in certain degenerate cases). This follows from the analysis of the MX quadtree performed by Hunter [Hunt79] and is definitely superior to using a 2-dimensional array to store the same information with a corresponding storage requirement of 4^d. Of course, PM quadtrees are usually considerably more compact than MX quadtrees (as will be demonstrated in the empirical results at the end of this section). However, this is not revealed by our approach to the worst-case analysis of these structures.

Analyzing the worst-case storage requirements in terms of the maximum depth is particularly useful when contemplating a linear quadtree implementation because efficiency considerations require that the linear quadtree address be stored in an array whose elements have a fixed and bounded size. Each element of this array will have a width, in bits, equal to twice the maximum depth of the quadtree being stored. Hence the following analysis will yield a safe size for the linear quadtree address as a function of the number of bits used to store the coordinates of the map.

The situation that leads to a maximum depth for vertices stored with d bits of precision can be derived in the following manner. Observe that all the points that can be specified with d bits of precision form a 2^d by 2^d grid. Recall that the PM_1 (and segment) quadtree require that no node can contain two line segments unless they meet at a common vertex in the region of that node (here we can view an isolated vertex as a degenerate line segment). Thus the problem reduces to how small (or deep) a node can be and still fail to satisfy this requirement. First, we determine the closest approach (without touching) between a point, say C, on that grid and a line segment, say AF, connecting two other points (A and F) on that grid. Assuming that our grid of points corresponds to centers of pixels, we can see that this has placed the vertex C at the maximum depth for a map of one line segment and an isolated vertex. Now we find two other points, say W and Y, such that the angle formed by WCY is a minimum. Let W' be the intercept of the border of the node containing C with the line segment CW and let Y' be the intercept of the border of the node containing C with the line segment CY. We claim that on a map where all line segment intersections are represented by vertices with precision d, that the maximum depth of the corresponding PM_1 (or segment) quadtree is the depth necessary to separate W' from Y'. Figures 13 and 14 show the worst case positioning of A, C, F, W, and Y. In the following discussion we demonstrate that this is indeed the worst-case situation and calculate the corresponding worst-case depth.

First, let us consider how close C can approach AF. If we drop straight down from C onto the segment AF, we find a point G on AF. Although the distance between C and AF is not exactly the length of CG, AF is no closer to C than $1/\sqrt{2}$ times the length of CG. To find the length of CG, we argue from the similar triangles ACG and AHF that the ratio of the length of CG to the length of HF is the same as the ratio of the length of AC to the length of AH. If we assume that AC (and hence HF) is of unit length, then the length of AH is 2^d-1 and the length of CG is approximately 2^{-d}.

To see that this is the worst-case situation for a map of one line segment and an isolated vertex, we consider all the other possible combinations of points and observe that when we form the analogous similar triangles, either AC or HF (or both) is greater than 1 and hence the length of CG would be greater than that calculated above. If this was as far as the analysis went, then we would see that a node of width 2^{-d}, occurring at depth $2d$, would be sufficient. This would mean that to store vertices with d bits of precision in each coordinate, the linear quadtree address field must have room for $4d$ bits.

First, observe that the point G is not a vertex of our map (and would require more than d bits of precision to represent). Therefore, line segments that contain G as an endpoint are irrelevant to our analysis since we are looking at maps formed from vertices of the grid. Similarly, if a point below A (say B) were connected with H resulting in an intersection point, say D, with the line AF, this would also be irrelevant. This is because D would be a vertex of the map, but would not be representable in d bits of precision. However, by the above analysis we now know what level of decomposition is necessary to separate vertex C from its nearest non-intersecting line segment. Therefore, the only way we can cause nodes to be deeper is to realize that any line segments connected to C have to be in separate nodes once they leave the node containing C. The closest approach between two line segments connected to C, say CY and CW, occurs at their intersection, say Y' and W', with the border of the node containing C. Thus, we must find the smallest possible angle YCW and then calculate the length of Y'W'.

In order to calculate the length of Y'W' as shown in Figure 14, it is convenient to introduce a point Q such that WQC is a right angle (and hence WQ is of unit length). We shall also extend the line segment CY to CY'' where Y'', W, and Q lie on a straight line. Since triangles Y''WY and Y''QC are similar, the ratio of the lengths of Y''W and Y''Q is the same as the ratio of the lengths of WY and QC. Observe that the length of WY is 1 and the length of QC is 2^d-2. The length of Y''Q is the length of Y''W plus the length of WQ (which is 1). Therefore the length of Y''W is $1/(2^d-3)$ (which is roughly 2^{-d}). Next, we observe that the triangles Y''CW and Y'CW' are similar which means that the ratio of Y''W to Y'W' is the same as the ratio of WC to W'C. Similarly, by observing that the triangles WCQ and W'CQ' are similar, we find that the ratio of WC to W'C' is the same as the ratio of QC to Q'C. Therefore, the ratio of Y''W to Y'W' is the same as the ratio of QC to Q'C. Recall that the length of Y''W is $1/(2^d-3)$, and the length of QC is 2^d-2. Since the depth of the node containing vertex C is $2d$, the width of that node must be 2^{-d} and the length of Q'C must be 2^{-d-1}. By solving the equations, we find that the length of Y'W' is roughly $2^{-(3d+1)}$.

We can now complete our analysis by noting that the depth of a node of width $2^{-(3d+1)}$ would be $4d+1$. However, the above analysis assumes that we are trying to separate Y' from W', whereas in reality we want to separate Y'Y from its closest approach W'W. This can be handled by using $4d+2$ as an upper bound on the depth of the quadtree. Thus the linear quadtree address field should allow for

$8d + 4$ bits. Since d is usually the wordsize, in bits, on the computer, using 9 words to store the linear quadtree address might seem a bit extravagant. However, it should be noted that our worst-case example was rather eccentric and that typical data behaves much better. Below, we cite some typical maximum depths and node counts for four maps from a cartographic database with which we have been working [Same84c]. The various strategies for handling maps that require greater depth than a user is willing to allocate are beyond the scope of this paper.

The above results are of interest when establishing the correctness of an implementation, i.e., they indicate the worst-case depth for which we must allow. However, this is one situation when the worst case is truly rare. As an example, let us consider four maps (Figures 15 through 18) chosen from our geographic database. The Railline Map (Figure 15) shows the path of a railroad through a section of the Russian River area in California. The Powerline Map (Figure 16) presents analogous information about the local main powerline. The Cityline Map (Figure 17) indicates the border of the local municipality. The Roadline Map (Figure 18) is our most complicated map, since it details the local roadway network. Table 1 contains the number of vertices and edges in each of these maps. All of these maps consist of line segments whose vertices rest on a 512 by 512 grid. Thus each vertex would require 18 bits of information (2 9-bit coordinates) to represent. The above analysis would indicate that we would have to be prepared for the possibility of the quadtree having a depth of 40. However, such a depth is not even approached by our sample data, and in general is extremely unlikely.

Table 1. Size of the maps.

Map	No. of Vertices	No. of Edges
Powerline	15	14
Railline	17	16
Cityline	65	64
Roadline	685	764

Tables 2-4 summarize the storage requirements of the MX, linear edge (recall Figure 6), and segment quadtrees (equivalent to the PM_1 quadtree) for the four maps of Figures 15-18. In all cases the MX quadtree is larger than the segment quadtree by at least a factor of 7. More generally, we would expect the size of the MX quadtree to be roughly as large as the product of the average line length and the number of nodes in the corresponding segment quadtree. In the case of trivial (but often typical) maps, like the Powerline, Railline, and Cityline, we see that the linear edge quadtree is almost three times as large as the segment quadtree. This is because the average depth of a vertex node in the segment quadtrees for these two maps was observed to lie between 6 and 7 whereas the linear edge quadtree had to represent all of the vertex nodes at depth 9.

Table 2: Size of the MX quadtrees.

Map	Depth	Leaves	BLACK nodes	WHITE nodes
Powerline	9	1627	526	1101
Railline	9	2074	680	1394
Cityline	9	2770	1187	1583
Roadline	9	20566	8955	11611

Table 3: Size of the linear edge quadtrees.

Map	Depth	Leaves	Vertex nodes	Line nodes	White nodes
Powerline	9	178	28	27	123
Railline	9	229	31	25	173
Cityline	9	542	133	71	388
Roadline	9	7723	1590	1354	4779

Table 4: Size of the segment quadtrees.

Map	Depth	Leaves	Vertex nodes	Line nodes	White nodes
Powerline	7	64	20	11	33
Railline	8	70	22	12	36
Cityline	8	220	90	31	99
Roadline	12	2701	1067	509	1125

In a map of moderate complexity, such as the Roadline Map (the most complex we have gathered to date) we see that the linear edge quadtree is a bit smaller than three times the size of the segment quadtree. For the first time, we observe the occurrence of a segment quadtree deeper than the depth required by the digitization grid. In this case the digitization grid required a depth of 9 and the segment quadtree actually had a depth of 12. Observe that this depth of 12 is still a long way from the worst-case value of 40 calculated in the previous analysis. Although for this map, the maximum depth of the segment quadtree is greater (i.e., 12) than that of the linear edge quadtree (i.e., 9), we must look to the distribution of nodes by depth (see Table 5) to explain the difference in the number of nodes between the two trees. In essence, the average depth of the vertex nodes is smaller for the segment quadtree than for the linear edge quadtree thereby accounting for the smaller number of nodes in the segment quadtree. The importance of the reduction in the average depth of the vertex nodes in the segment quadtree is a consequence of the the observation that the decomposition of a line segment is identical in the linear edge and segment quadtrees once the line segment has exited the region of the vertex nodes representing its endpoints.

Table 5

Distribution of node types by depth for the segment quadtree of the Roadline map.

Depth	Vertex nodes	Line nodes	White nodes
0	0	0	0
1	0	0	0
2	0	0	4
3	2	0	8
4	10	3	39
5	73	33	110
6	184	106	226
7	286	152	272
8	242	123	208
9	165	46	159
10	104	25	98
11	1	17	1
12	0	4	0

8. Conclusions

The segment quadtree has been presented and shown to be a suitable data structure for representing vector feature data in conjunction with image databases using linear quadtrees. Methods for insertion and deletion of line segments in it, as well as its use in border following have been described. In the segment quadtree, deletion of line segments and border following can be accomplished using information local to the nodes representing a line segment. In contrast, such operations in the linear edge quadtree are much more difficult. Furthermore, the segment quadtree requires fewer nodes than the edge quadtree to store a collection of vector features since the vertices need not be stored at the lowest level of resolution as in the edge quadtree. This means that fewer nodes will be required to represent corners and intersections. Future work includes its implementation and integration into the geographical information system described in [Same84c], where it will replace the linear edge quadtree.

References

[Aho74] - A.V. Aho, J.E. Hopcroft, and J.D. Ullman, *The Design and Analysis of Computer Algorithms*, Addison-Wesley, Reading, MA, 1974.

[Ball81] - D.H. Ballard, Strip trees: A hierarchical representation for curves, *Communications of the ACM 24*, 5(May 1981), 310-321 (see also corrigendum, *Communications of the ACM 25*, 3(March 1982), 213).

[Garg82] - I. Gargantini, An effective way to represent quadtrees, *Communications of the ACM 25*, 12(December 1982), 905-910.

[Hunt79] - G.M. Hunter and K. Steiglitz, Operations on images using quad trees, *IEEE Transactions on Pattern Analysis and Machine Intelligence 1*, 2(April 1979), 145-153.

[Klin71] - A. Klinger, Patterns and search statistics, in *Optimizing Methods in Statistics*, J.S. Rustagi, ED., Academic Press, New York, 1971, 303-337.

[Oren82] - J.A. Orenstein, Multidimensional tries used for associative searching, *Information Processing Letters 14*, 4(June 1982), 150-157.

[Same82] - H. Samet, Neighbor finding techniques for images represented by quadtrees, *Computer Graphics and Image Processing 18*, 1(January 1982), 37-57.

[Same84a] - H. Samet, The quadtree and related hierarchical data structures, *ACM Computing Surveys 16*, 2(June 1984), 187-260.

[Same84b] - H. Samet and R.E. Webber, On encoding boundaries with quadtrees, *IEEE Transactions on Pattern Analyg)c and Machine Intelligence 6*, 3(May 1984), 365-369.

[Same84c] - H. Samet, A. Rosenfeld, C.A. Shaffer, and R.E. Webber, A geographic information system using quadtrees, *Pattern Recognition 17*, 6 (November/December 1984), 647-656.

[Same85a] - H. Samet and C.A. Shaffer, A model for the analysis of neighbor finding in pointer-based quadtrees, to appear in *IEEE Transactions on Pattern Analysis and Machine Intelligence*, 1985 (see also University of Maryland Computer Science TR-1432).

[Same85b] - H. Samet and R. E. Webber, Storing a collection of polygons using quadtrees, to appear in *ACM Transactions on Graphics*, 1985 (see also *Proceedings of Computer Vision and Pattern Recognition 83*, Washington, DC, June 1983, 127-132 and University of Maryland Computer Science TR-1372).

[Shne81] - M. Shneier, Two hierarchical linear feature representations: edge pyramids and edge quadtrees, *Computer Graphics and Image Processing 17*, 3(November 1981), 211-224.

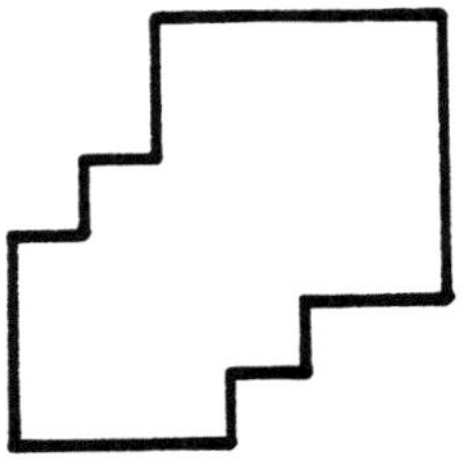

(a) Region.

0	0	0	0	0	0	0	0
0	0	0	0	0	0	0	0
0	0	0	0	1	1	1	1
0	0	0	0	1	1	1	1
0	0	0	1	1	1	1	1
0	0	1	1	1	1	1	1
0	0	1	1	1	1	0	0
0	0	1	1	1	0	0	0

(b) Binary array.

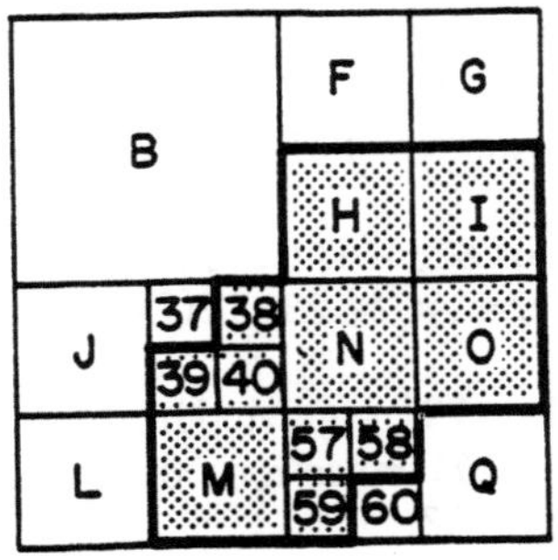

(c) Block decomposition of the region in (a). Blocks in the region are shaded.

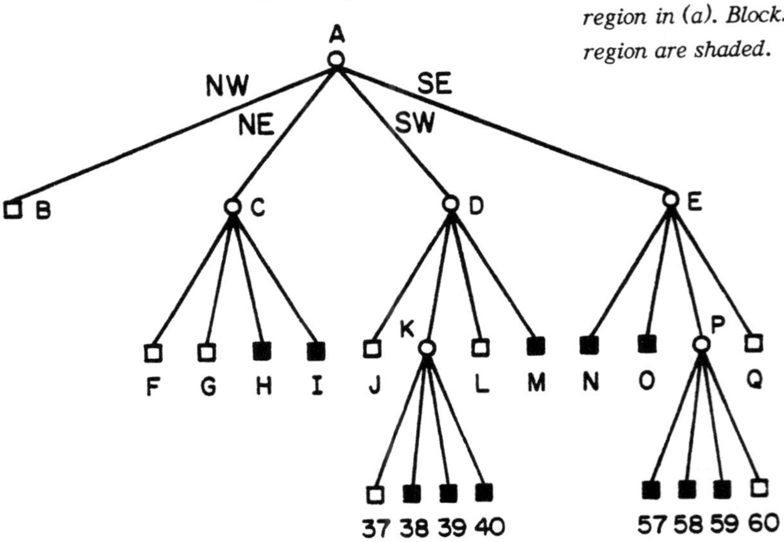

(d) Quadtree representation of the blocks in (c).

Figure 1. A region, its binary array, and its maximal blocks.

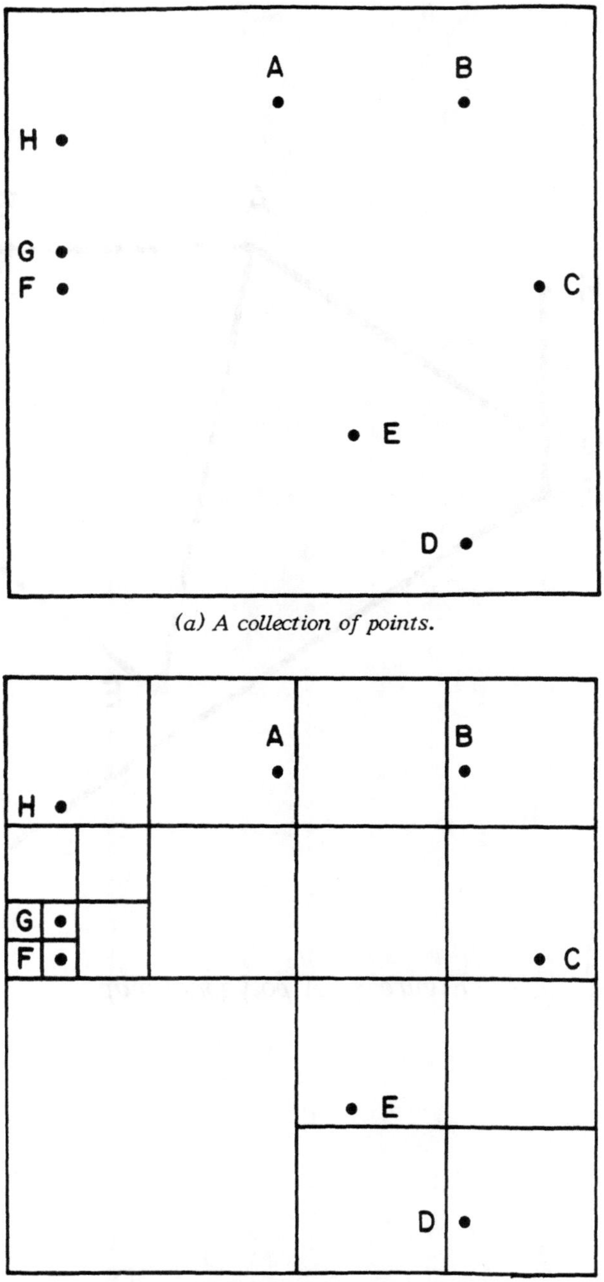

(a) A collection of points.

(b) The PR quadtree for the points of (a).

Figure 2. A collection of points and its PR quadtree.

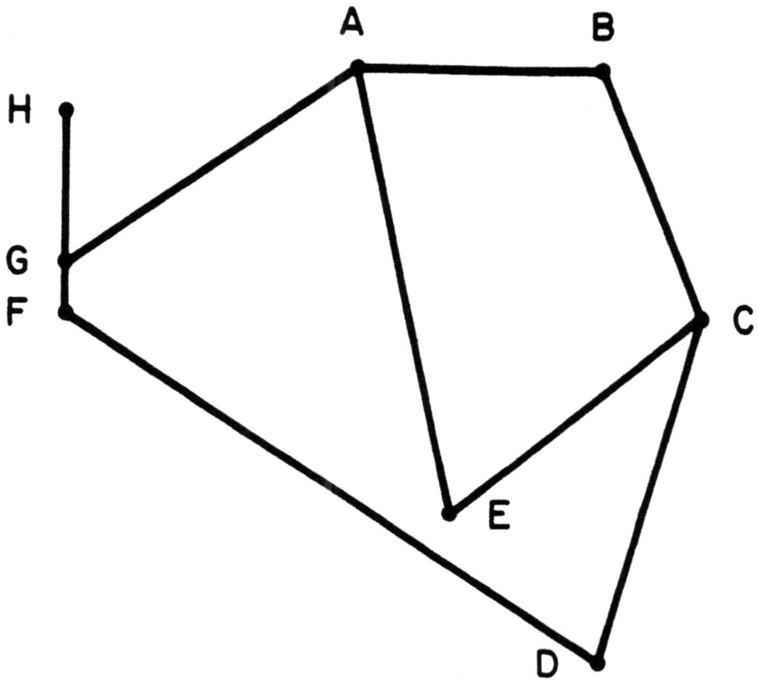

Figure 3. A polygonal map.

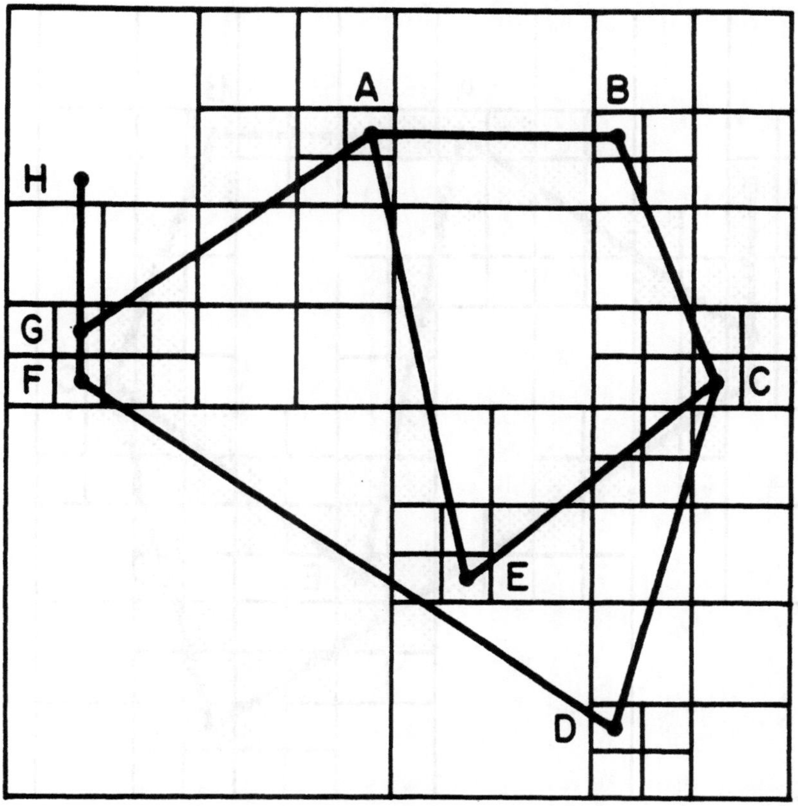

Figure 4. The edge quadtree for the polygonal map of Figure 3.

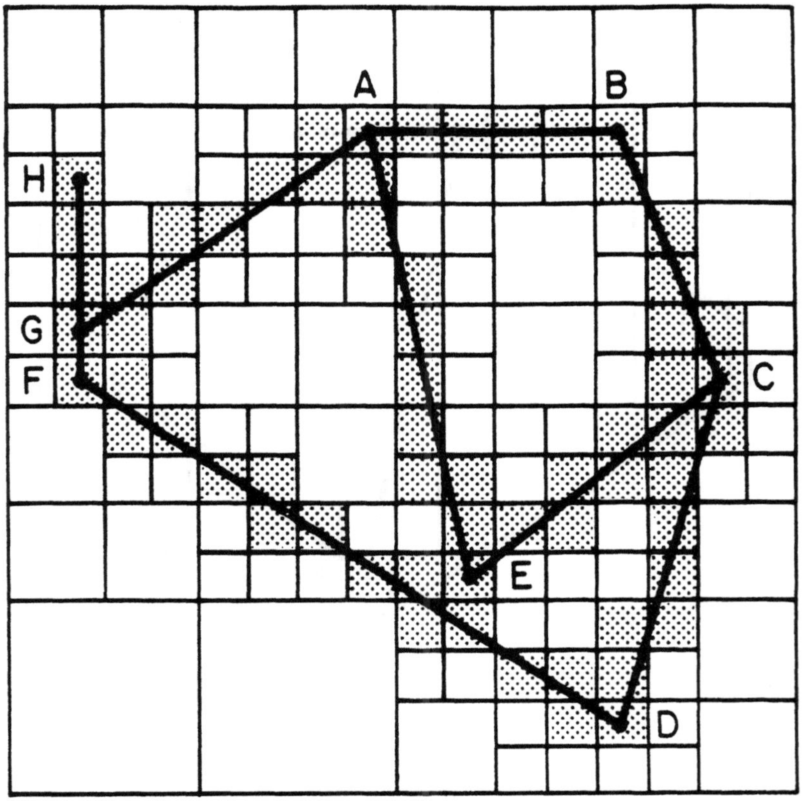

Figure 5. The MX quadtree for the polygonal map of Figure 3.

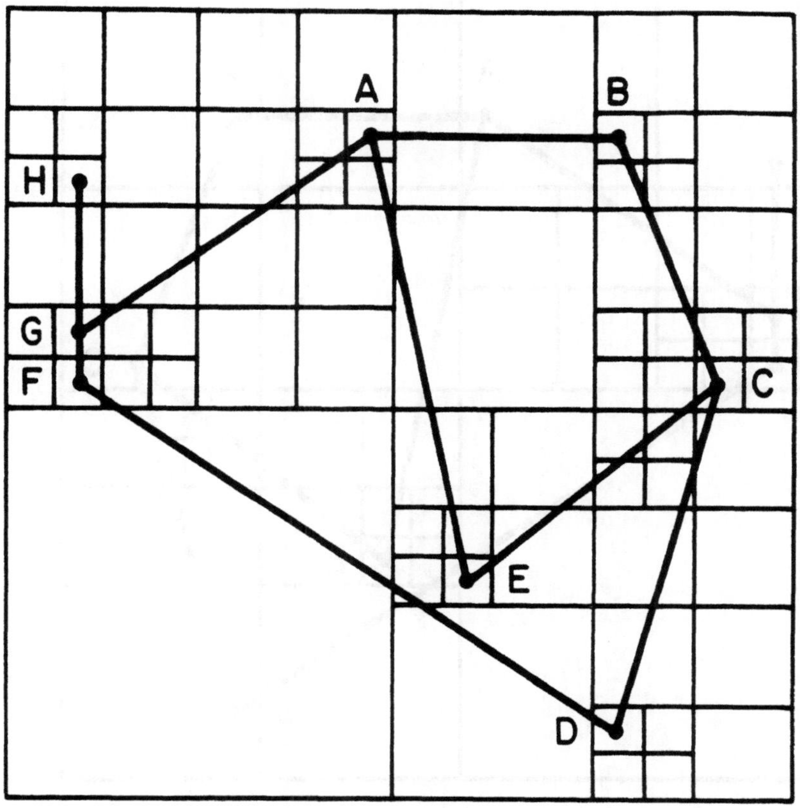

Figure 6. The linear edge quadtree for the polygonal map of Figure 3.

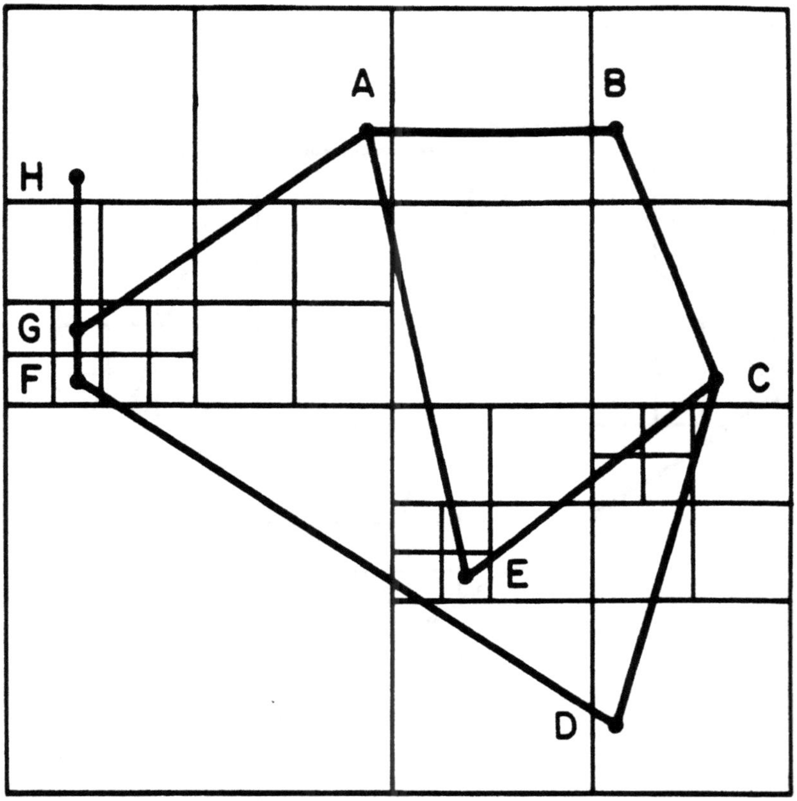

Figure 7. The PM_1 *quadtree for the polygonal map of Figure 3.*

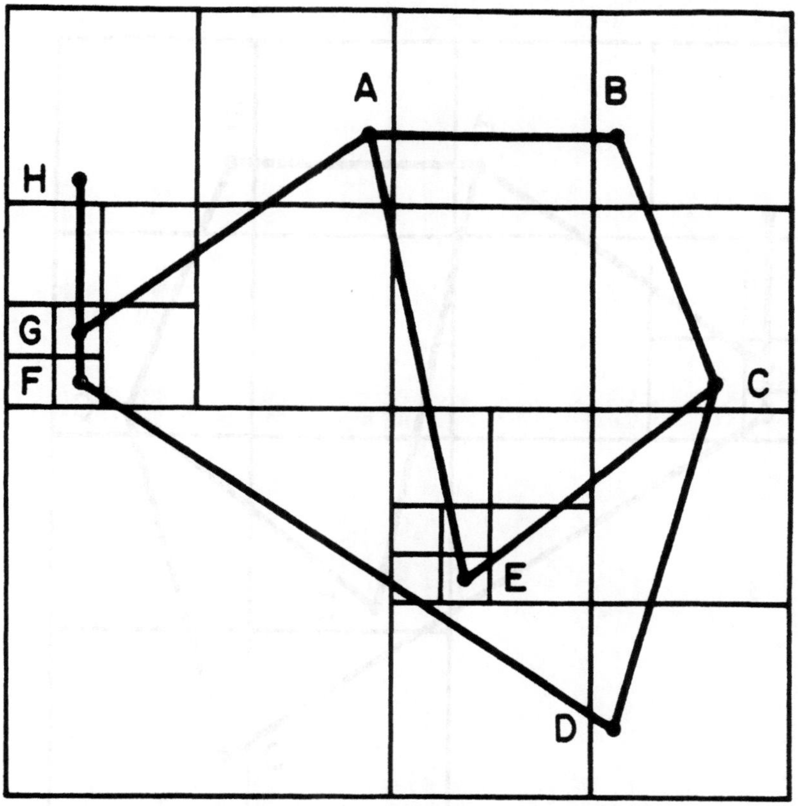

Figure 8. The PM_2 *quadtree for the polygonal map of Figure 3.*

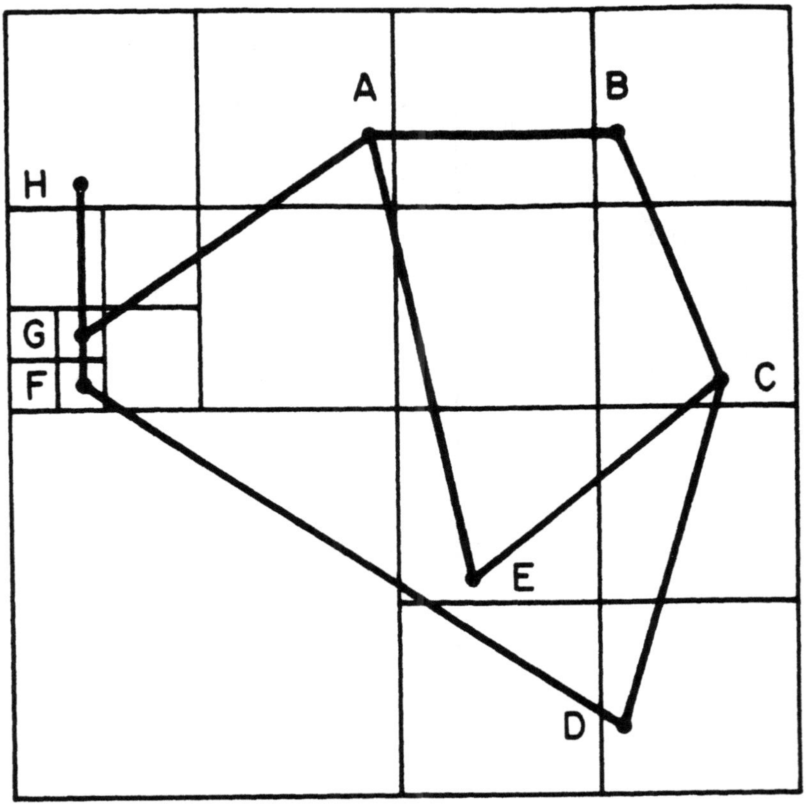

Figure 9. The PM_3 *quadtree for the polygonal map of Figure 3.*

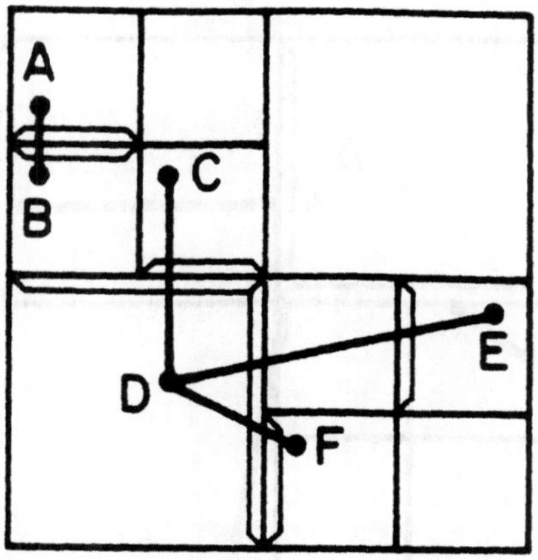

Figure 10.

The segment quadtree for a collection of line segments. Vertex nodes have exited edges marked by a bracket.

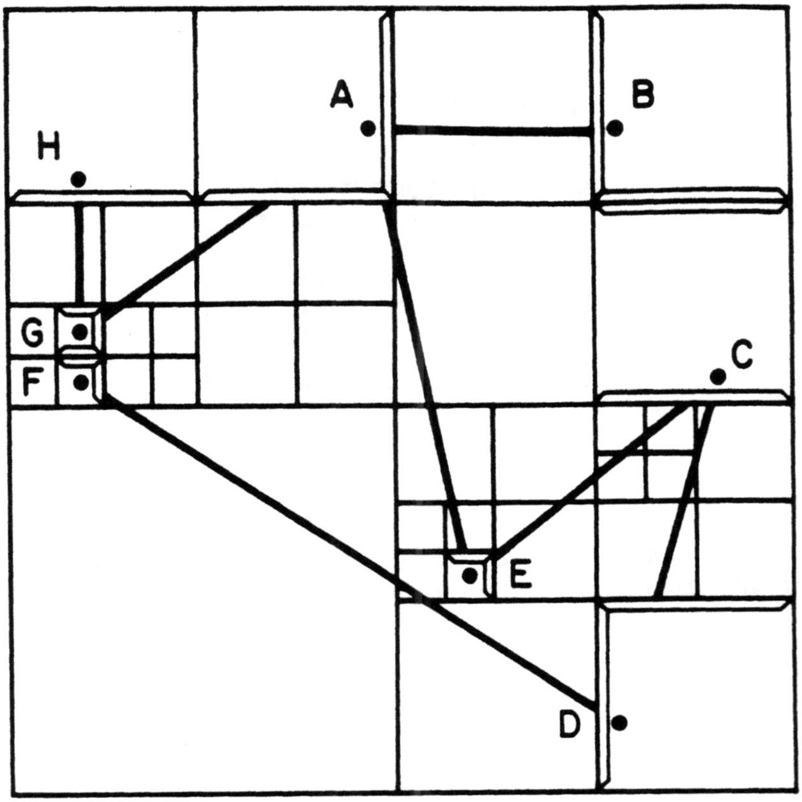

Figure 11. The segment quadtree for the polygonal map of Figure 3.

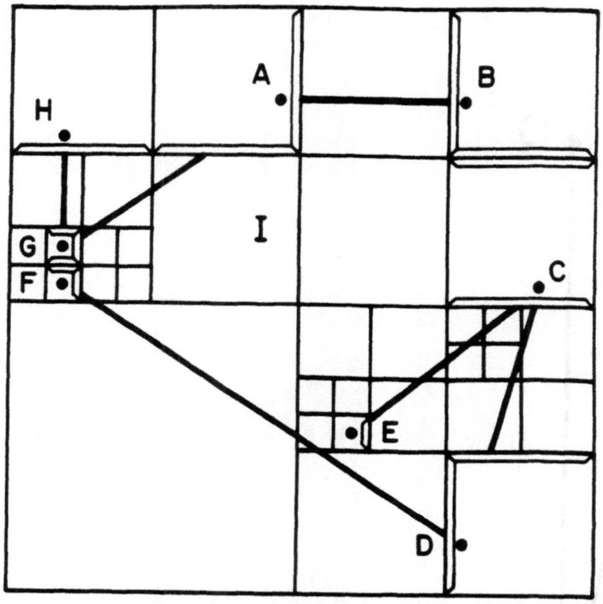

(a) The result of deleting segment AE from the segment quadtree of Figure 11.

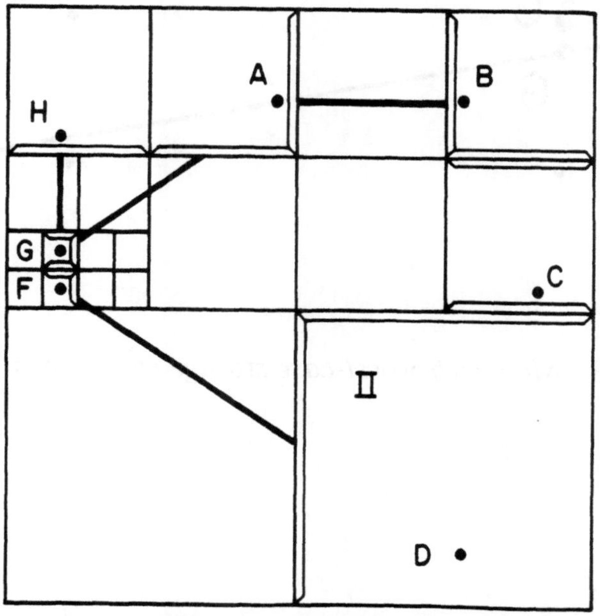

(b) The result of deleting segment CE from the segment quadtree of (a).

Figure 12. Examples of deletion of line segments from the segment quadtree.

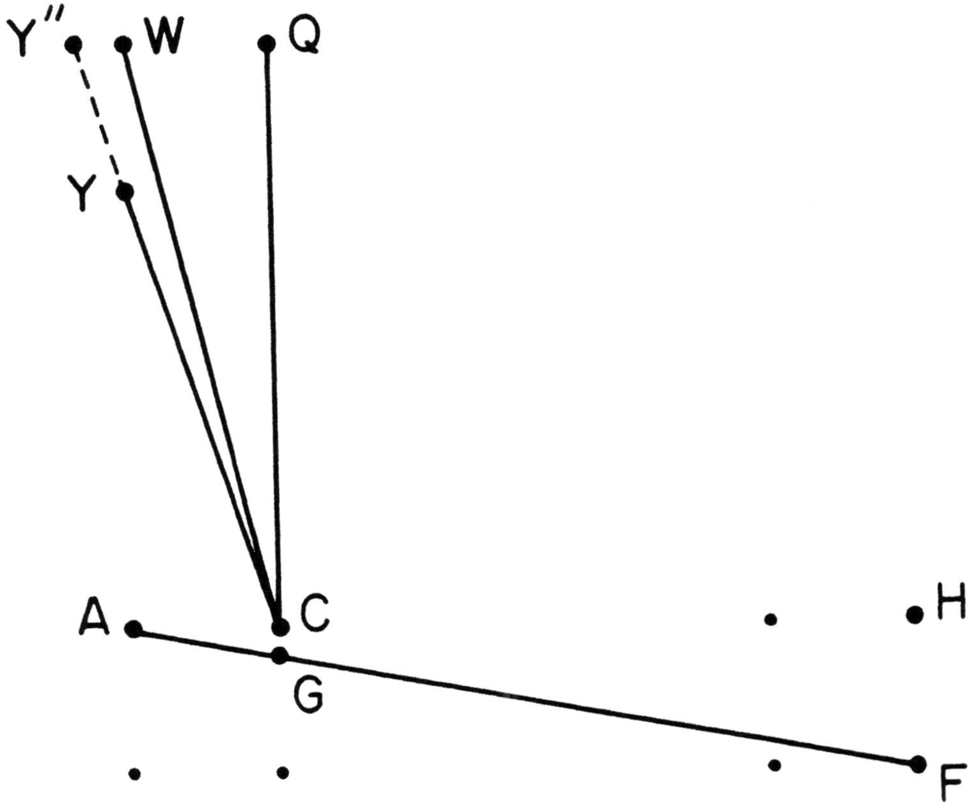

Figure 13. Map with worst-case storage requirements.

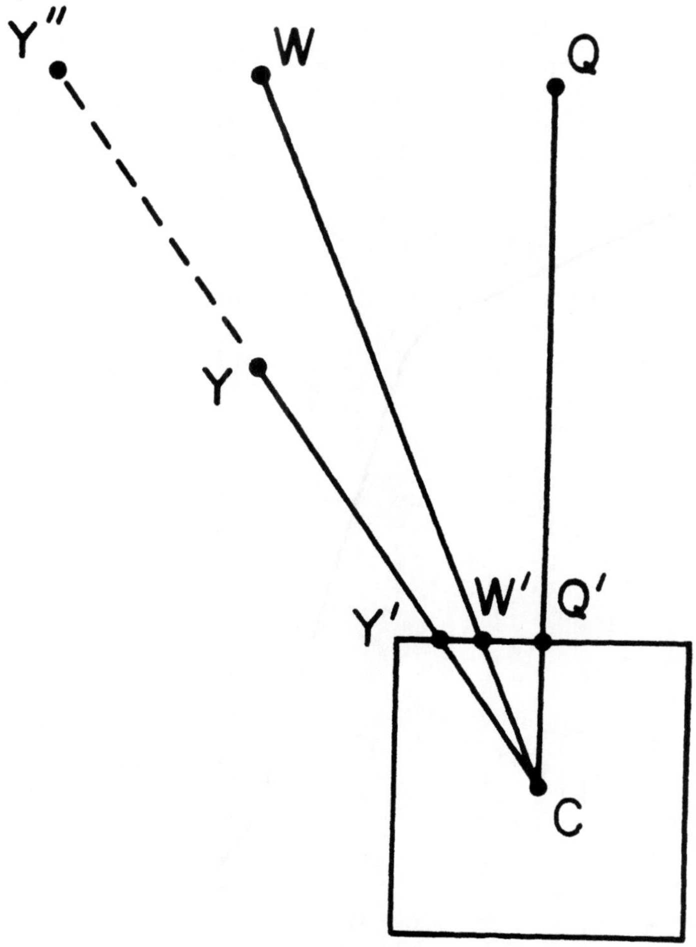

Figure 14. Detail of Figure 13 in the vicinity of point C.

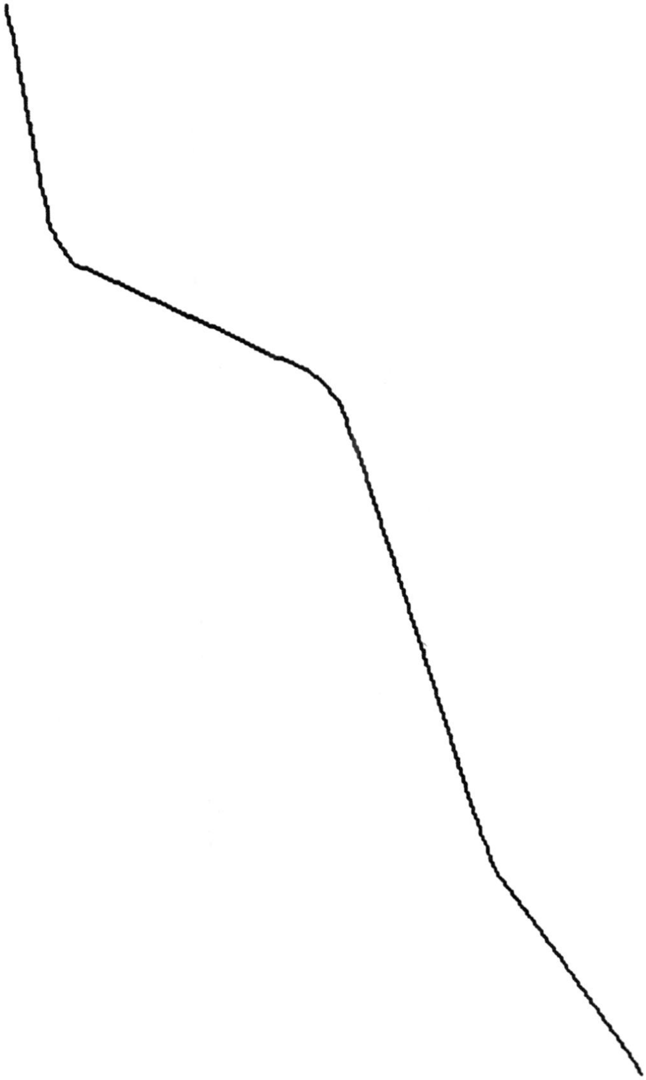

Figure 15. The Railline Map.

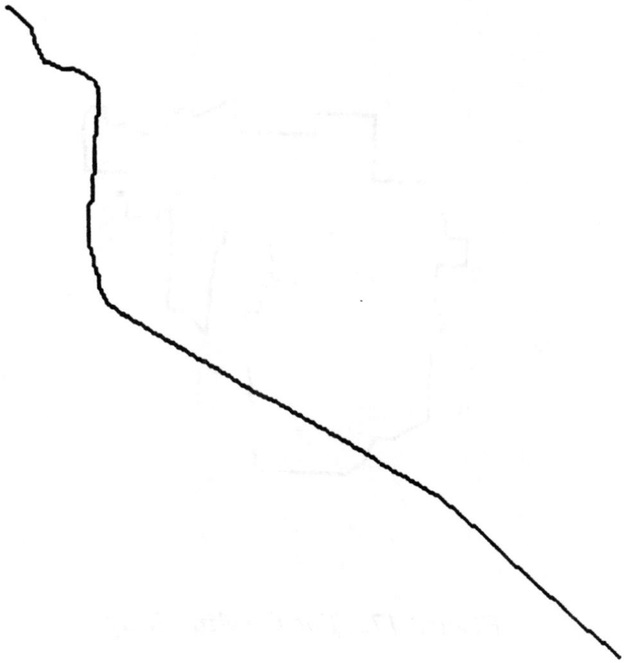

Figure 16. The Powerline Map.

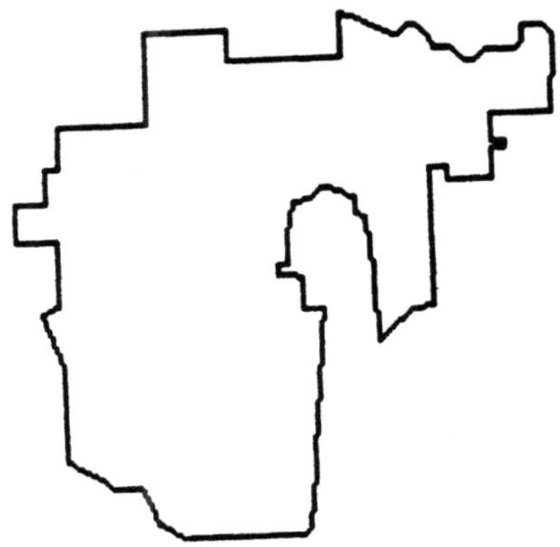

Figure 17. The Cityline Map.

Figure 18. The Roadline Map.

A model for raster graphics language primitives *

Wim J.M. Teunissen
Jan van den Bos

Department of Computer Science
University of Leiden
P.O. Box 9512
2300 RA Leiden
The Netherlands

ABSTRACT

Raster graphics systems are becoming increasingly popular due to improved technology and lower costs. However, this positive development has not had its follow-up in the software department: currently there is virtually no integrated raster graphics software available.

We propose a hierarchical model in which the applicability in raster graphics is of primary importance. The model is based upon a number of 0D, 1D and 2D primitives to generate graphical patterns. These patterns may also be formed by means of expressions over other patterns. They form the end-nodes of a data structure consisting of a directed, acyclic graph, the pattern graph, the nodes of which contain attributes. By using priority ordering in the graph '2.5D' pictures may be constructed. Attributes in the graph govern detectability, visibility, highlighting, level and graphical transformations. This two-stage approach to making pictures has been developed in order to achieve a model for raster graphics, catering for interaction.

1. Introduction

Most graphics software, as reflected in the current proposals for graphics standard specifications (GKS [1], PHIGS [2]), is based on line graphics, that is on 1D graphics primitives. The recent transition from vector graphics to raster graphics has led to little more than a few ad-hoc raster primitives in the standard proposals.

We propose a model in which 2D patterns play a basic role. These patterns are defined as colour functions over a domain of arbitrary shape. The domains are a subset of the 2D or 3D real space. The colour functions are defined in a RGB, HSV or HSI colour space and comprise constant, linear, repeating pattern, interpolation

* This research was supported by the Netherlands Foundation for Technical Research (STW).

and texture functions.

Patterns can be combined in expressions yielding a new pattern. Several operations are used: set-theoretic operations such as union, intersection and difference; domain transformations and colour transformations such as weighted mixing and interpolation.

At a higher level these patterns can be combined in a dynamic, hierarchic structure: the pattern graph, a directed acyclic graph the leaves of which are the patterns. The nodes in the graph contain the dynamically alterable attributes: geometric and graphic transformations, highlighting, visibility, detectability and level.

This two-stage approach, using expressions and graphs, has been followed in order to make *interactive* graphics possible, because only paths in the graph can be manipulated and no longer the constituent parts of patterns.

At display time the graph is interpreted, attributes are concatenated and/or applied, and the interpreted result is represented by a so-called fleck structure. Flecks are 2D virtual rasters, not necessarily rectangular. The flecks are arranged in a linked list and still contain the projected values of some attributes, but not those of the transformations. Again this organization caters to interaction. It is anticipated that the fleck chain forms the interface with the graphics hardware architecture.

In chapter 2 we will discuss the way graphical objects are built, and what role the datastructure plays. Chapter 3 will contain some remarks concerning the display of an object. In chapter 4 we will go into more detail on some of the information stored in the nodes of the graph. Some conclusions can be found in chapter 5.

2. The graphical objects and their representation

Composing a graphical object consists of putting together several basic primitives, and building a hierarchic data structure on top of it. For this purpose some operators and generators are provided.

2.1. Patterns

The basic graphical element is called a *pattern*. A pattern P is a pair (D, F), with D some subset of 2D real space, and F a function on D, with values in some colour space S. We call D the *domain* of P and F its *colour function*.

Contrary to most raster graphics software, where it is assumed that the user offers discrete data, the domain of a pattern can be a continuous subset of real space, e.g. $[0,1] \times [0,1]$. This will ease the use of the model, because the user will not be bothered with describing his object pixel by pixel. Because eventually discrete data is necessary for display, the model must take care of the conversion between the continuous and discrete representation. More on this in chapter 3.

Like the domain, the colour function is also specified in a continuous colour space, such as RGB or HSV [3].

The definition of a pattern consists of a description of both the domain and the colour function. Because we are trying to make full use of the fact that we are considering raster graphics applications, we included several domain primitives that generate 2D domains, such as a filled rectangle and polygon. Possible domain primitives are:

polymarker
polyline
polygon
ellipse
rectangle

The polygon, ellipse and rectangle primitives specify closed 2D domains of which the inside is coloured according to the given colour function. Primitives polymarker and polyline have been added to support some 0D and 1D graphics.

When specifying the colour function of a pattern, the user can choose from:

constant colour function
linear colour function
pattern-repeating colour function
texture generator
interpolation function

With the texture generating colour function, pseudo-random colours are generated, for example to display a forest seen from a large distance.

Using the pattern-repeating colour function results in a colour function that consists of a pattern (preferably rectangular) that is repeated over and over again (tiling).

Given a colour for a number of points, the interpolation colour function calculates a colour for every other point of the domain by interpolation.

It is not yet clear which primitives for defining domain and colour function should be part of the model. In particular the set of colour function primitives could change considerably. It is even possible that the set of primitives has to be extensible according to the user's wishes.

2.2. Pattern expressions

Because of the limited power of pattern definitions, we offer the possibility of constructing more complex patterns with *pattern expressions*. These are expressions on patterns, yielding a new pattern. Possible operations are [4,5]:

set operations:
- union
- difference
- intersection

domain transformations:
- scale
- translate
- rotate

colour transformations:
- weight
- translate
- intensify

The three set operations as well as the domain transformations are in principle operations on the domain of the pattern only. There are no problems but for union and intersection. Question is what colour the resulting pattern must receive on the intersection of the two domains. The answer is to add a dyadic colour operation when using one of these two operators. The colour operation will then be used to combine the two original colours into one for the resulting pattern, but only on the intersection of the domains.

The weight colour operation yields a colour function which assigns a colour to a point by weighting the two original colours according to some given weight factors. This is the only dyadic colour operation.

Using the translate colour transformation, one can 'add' some colour to the current value. The intensify colour transformation can be used to multiply the intensity by a given factor. These two transformations are in fact a translate and scale transformation within the 3D RGB colour space.

2.3. The pattern graph

Using the patterns as basic elements, a complete graphical object can be created by ordering and linking those elements in a hierarchical way: in a graph.

What we will call a *pattern graph* is an acyclic, directed graph with patterns in the leaves. An example is shown in figure 1. It is not permitted to have patterns in nodes of the graph other than leaf nodes.

The non-leaf nodes carry additional information, called *attributes*.

2.3.1. Attributes in the pattern graph

An attribute in the pattern graph is a domain or colour transformation, or it controls:

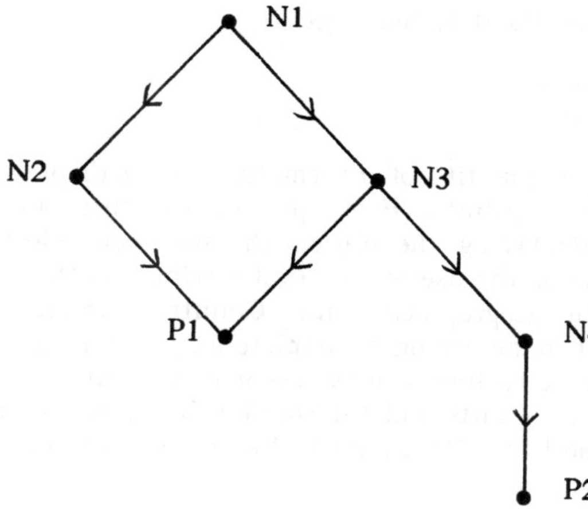

Figure 1.

An example of a pattern graph with nodes N1 .. N4, patterns P1 and P2.

- visibility
- detectability
- highlighting
- level
- transparency

The domain and colour transformations may be used to transform certain parts of an object into the desired shape or colour. The transformations that can be used here are the same as the ones that appear in the pattern expressions. In addition, at the pattern graph level, there is the attribute defining the window to viewport domain transformation.

The detection attribute can be used to declare a part of the object detectable, i.e. the program will notice the user pointing at that part of the picture with a pick device. After receiving the information that a detectable part of the picture was pointed at, the program may request the identification of the detected part. With this information the program can take appropriate action.

When pointing at some part of the picture with a light pen, the user may want some indication that the pen was noticed. One of the possibilities is to generate an echo with the help of the highlighting attribute. Possible implementations of highlighting may be:

- put a box around the detected object
- blink it
- intensify its colour
- change its colour

To be able to control the quantity of information on the display screen, the user is provided with the level attribute. Every part of a picture can be assigned one or more levels. When displaying the object, the user can select the levels to be displayed. An example of the use of the level attribute is the situation where one wants to display some geographical data. Country borders supply more than enough information when surveying a complete map of Europe. When zooming in on a specific country, city-limits may become interesting. After assigning a different level to the city-limits and the country borders, the only thing the user has to do in order to add the city-limits to the picture is to change the levels that must be displayed.

Visibility is an attribute that resembles level in that it also controls the visibility of parts of a picture. The main difference between these attributes lies in the locality of visibility (local to some node in the pattern graph), and the globality of level (global because the name of the level can be spread throughout the graph, cutting through the hierarchical structure).

Using the transparency attribute, the user can control the measure of transparency for every part of the picture, ranging from opaque to completely transparent. In calculating the resulting colour when some part P of the picture is partially transparent, P is taken as a filter, i.e. subtractive colour-mixing is applied.

The name attribute is used for identification purposes. This attribute was not included in the list of attributes because it is not a graphical attribute.

Another attribute that does not occur in the list is priority. It was not included because it is stored implicitly in the structure of the graph. This attribute controls the order in which the parts of a picture are drawn. This only has consequences when there exists overlap. In those cases the part with the highest priority comes on top of the other part(s) because it is drawn last, as in the Painter's algorithm. This priority order provides the extra 'half-dimension' in the 2.5D of the model. Priority is assigned by the user, when linking the nodes while creating the graph. By using priority the user can add some depth to a picture.

In chapter 4 we will discuss the way in which the attributes are concatenated and applied to the patterns.

2.3.2. Operations on the pattern graph

Because the pattern graph is intended to be a dynamic data structure, there are a number of operations with which the user can manipulate the pattern graph. These operations are:

- ADD *b* TO *a* BEHIND *p*
  As a result of this call, the node *b* will be added to the progeny of *a*. The additional information 'BEHIND *p*' is used to determine the priority of *b* as one lower than that of *p* (see Fig. 2a).

- ADD COPY OF *b* TO *a* BEHIND *p*
  A copy of the subgraph under *b* will be linked at *a*, with a priority one lower than that of *p* (see Fig. 2b).

- REMOVE *b* FROM *a*
  Removes the link between the nodes *a* and *b* (see Fig. 2c).

- REMOVE AND PRUNE *b* FROM *a*
  Removes the link between *a* and *b*, and additionally prunes the sub-graph under *b* where the removal has left it disjunct with the rest of the graph (see Fig. 2d).

One of the things we hope to achieve is the development of some language construct within which the operation on the graph comes naturally. The objective is to make the user think in terms of hierarchically structured objects, rather than in terms of building a graph.

2.4. Why pattern expressions as well as pattern graphs?

What we will try to explain in this section is the reason for having pattern expressions as well as pattern graphs, two ways of composing graphical objects into more complex ones.

The most important difference between the expressions and the graph, is the fact that combining patterns using expressions results in a pattern in which the substructure has vanished, while the elements from which a pattern graph is built, are still distinguishable in the graph, and can be operated on separately.

When our intention would be to display static graphical objects, we could suffice with only pattern expressions. Without having to deal with interaction, an important reason for having a pattern graph would disappear.

Alternatively, we could do without pattern expressions and leave the structure of the expressions in the graph. This would lead to a model like ILP [6]. However, it would have the disadvantage that, for every change in the graph, even the parts of which the user knows beforehand that they remain static, will have to be reinterpreted when generating a new picture. Due to this, response time could increase dramatically.

Another, minor, argument in favour of having both expressions and graphs, is that a pattern should be a 'finished' component of an object, while the graph should only serve as glue between these components.

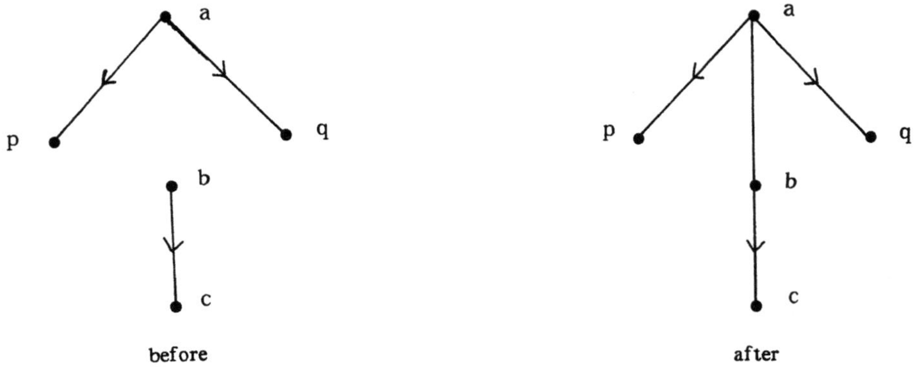

Figure 2a. ADD b TO a BEHIND p.

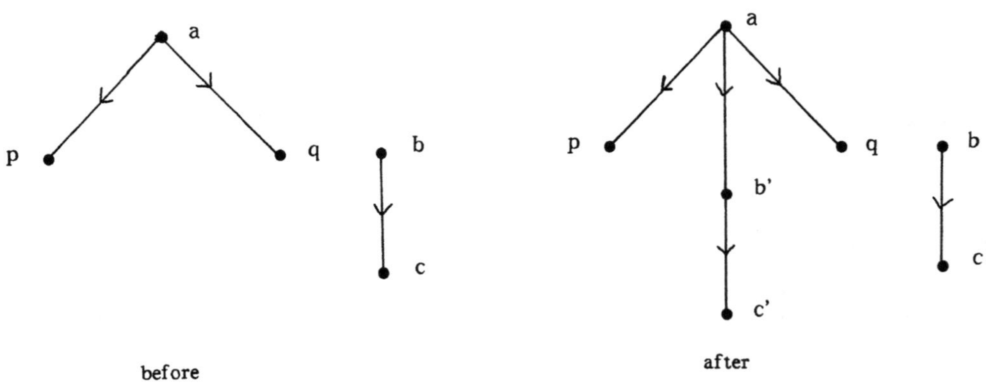

Figure 2b. ADD COPY OF b TO a BEHIND p.

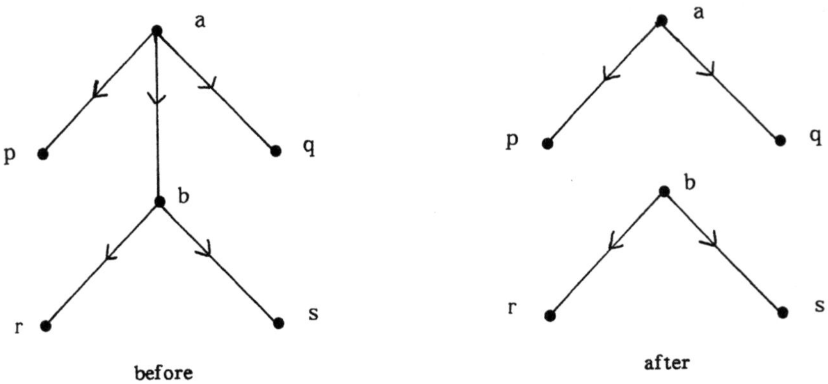

Figure 2c. REMOVE b FROM a.

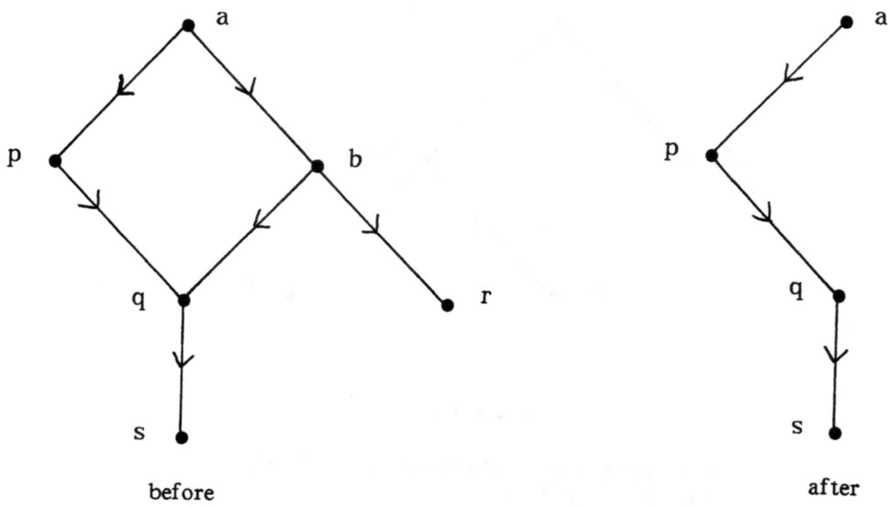

Figure 2d. REMOVE AND PRUNE b FROM a.

3. Displaying the pattern graph

After completing the description of an object, the user can display that object, or part of it. In this chapter we will describe how the graph is displayed.

3.1. Paths in the pattern graph: flecks

When parsing a graph in order to display it, the paths in the graph are traversed recursively, one by one. During this (pre-order) traversal all the attributes in the nodes are gathered and concatenated (rules governing the concatenation can be found in chapter 4). Arriving at a leaf containing a pattern, the concatenated attributes (like the domain and colour transformations) are applied to the pattern. The parsed structures resulting from this operation are called *flecks*. There is a one-to-one correspondence between paths in the graph ending in a pattern, and flecks.

An example is shown in figure 3; observe that N2 does not contain a pattern and therefore no fleck results from the path N1-N2. The paths N1-N3-P1 and N1-N3-P2 however do result in two flecks.

The reason we have flecks is to be able to react efficiently to changes in the graph and compute only those flecks that are new or have changed. Minimizing the number of fleck-computations is important because they involve converting data from a continuous into a discrete representation, and exactly this conversion is expected to be the most time-consuming process in the model.

The flecks are linked in the *fleck chain*. This list of flecks should reflect the status of the pattern graph at every moment.

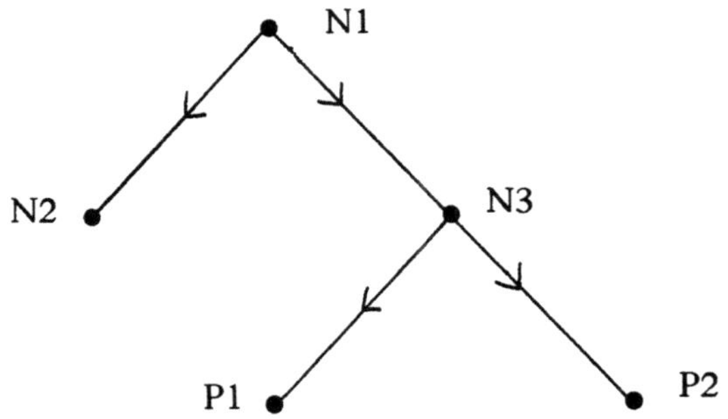

Figure 3

A pattern graph with nodes N1, N2, N3 and patterns P1, P2.

3.2. Computing a fleck

Consider the simple pattern graph of figure 4.

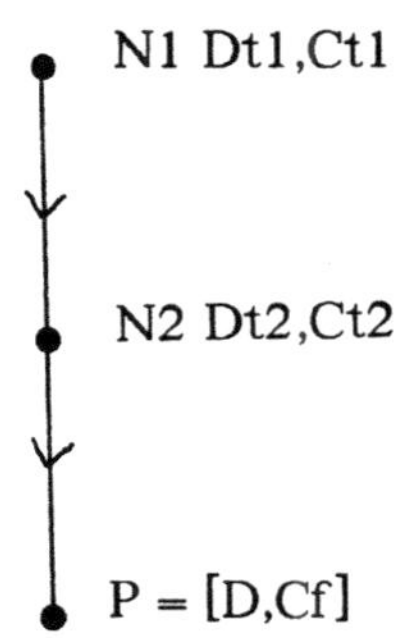

Figure 4

A pattern graph, with domain and colour transformations in the nodes.

With the domain transformations Dt1 and Dt2 and the domain D of P, the domain of the resulting fleck will be:

$$Dt1 (Dt2 (D)) = Dt1 \circ Dt2 (D) \qquad (3.1)$$

Its colour function can be obtained from the colour function Cf and the colour transformations Ct1 and Ct2 using the following formula:

$$Ct1 (Ct2 (Cf \circ Dt2^{-1} \circ Dt1^{-1})) = (Ct1 \circ Ct2) \circ Cf \circ (Dt1 \circ Dt2)^{-1} \qquad (3.2)$$

When the user issues the display command for this graph, the graph will be parsed, at the end of which, when reaching the pattern P, the composed domain transformation Dt1 o Dt2 is applied to the domain of P. Next step is to allocate enough space to contain the discrete data for the fleck. This data consists of the colour for every pixel in the fleck. This colour can subsequently be calculated from the colour function of P and the appropriate transformations, using equation (3.2).

3.3. Storing the pixel data of a fleck

The main problem with flecks is to find a suitable data representation. Because of the huge amount of data involved, this representation must be chosen with care, in order to minimize the demand for memory.

Some of the techniques used to represent pixel data are:

- 2D rectangular rasters.
  This is the most straightforward way to store pixel data: a two-dimensional array is declared in which the colour for every pixel can be stored.

- Run length encoding.
  With run length encoding an attempt is made to reduce the need for memory. This is achieved by taking together runs of pixels that have the same colour (a run consists of a number of consecutive pixels on a scan line).

- Binary and Quad trees [7].
  These methods try to exploit the fact that most pictures contain areas of the same colour. Taking these areas together can save memory. Main idea behind both the binary and quad trees is the divide and conquer principle: when an area is monochromic store the colour, when it is not, divide it into 2 or 4 pieces and try again. Using quad trees, the subdivision is in four equally shaped parts, whereas with binary trees the division is in two halves, alternately dividing horizontally and vertically.

In choosing between these storage techniques, the following arguments can be brought forward.

- The only method that takes no advantage of a possible simplicity of a picture is the one with the 2D rasters. Of course, this need not be a disadvantage, because the overhead that can be involved in space saving methods can be considerable. For pictures from fields like image-processing, 2D rasters are generally preferred because using some other technique is usually without any substantial gain, and can easily deteriorate in an amount of overhead that is much larger than the gain in data compaction.

- Run length encoding is especially useful when used with a hardware graphics device that accepts run length encoded data.

- Promising techniques seem to be the binary and quad trees. In spite of the considerable overhead, they exploit the 2D aspect of a picture fully. The main disadvantage of these representations is their inflexibility when it comes to transforming the picture they represent. For example, a translation can have substantial consequences for the tree representation. However, because the flecks are considered to be static during their lifetime, this disadvantage of tree coding will not cause any problem here.

3.4. Attributes of the flecks

Apart from the pixel data, a number of flags is kept in every fleck. These flags carry the value of the concatenated attributes for:

visibility
detectability
highlighting
level
transparency

These attributes have in common that they all control some aspect of the fleck status, rather than denoting geometric properties.

Visibility could be implemented by deleting or inserting the fleck in the fleck chain, but more efficient is to have a flag with every fleck indicating whether it is visible or not.

The priority attribute is an exception again: it is not kept as an explicit flag in the fleck, but it is used to determine the order in which the flecks occur in the fleck chain. This order will be used when displaying the flecks on some raster screen: lowest priority first (Painter's algorithm).

3.5. Operations on the fleck chain

Changes in the pattern graph are reflected in the fleck chain. In this paragraph the possible operations on a fleck or on the fleck chain are listed, together with the changes in the pattern graph that cause them:

- Adding a fleck to the fleck chain.
  This is a consequence of adding paths to the pattern graph by means of the ADD operation (see 2.3.2).

- Removing a fleck from the fleck chain.
  The deletion of a fleck can only be the result of a REMOVE operation on the pattern graph (see 2.3.2).

- Changing the pixel data of a fleck.
  Due to a change of a domain transformation in a node of the pattern graph, the flecks that correspond with a path through that node have to be recomputed.

- Changing an attribute of a fleck.
  Changing attributes other than the domain transformation in a node can result in a change of the corresponding attribute in a number of flecks.

As stated earlier, the fleck chain must reflect the status of the pattern graph at every moment. Keeping the attributes such as visibility, in the fleck, rather than deleting and recomputing the fleck with every change of the visibility of a fleck, helps to make this possible. However, in some cases it may be desirable to change the fleck chain in the foreground, and to update the pattern graph in the background.

4. Attributes in more detail

In this chapter we will study the window to viewport transformations and the attributes visibility, level and detectability in more detail. These attributes may be considered representative for all other attributes.

The following notation to identify flecks will be used. The fleck corresponding with the path N1-P1 in figure 5 will be denoted f11. Likewise the other flecks are f122 and f123, corresponding with N1-N2-P3 and N1-N2-P3 respectively. Furthermore, to indicate the value of some attribute within a node N, the notation 'N.V' will be used. It will mean that the attribute under consideration has the value V in node N.

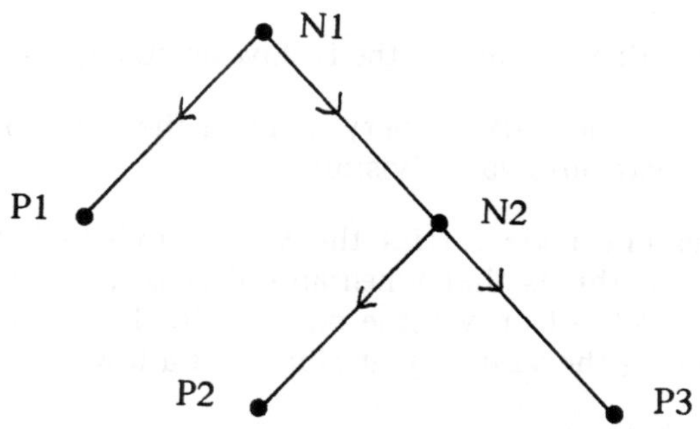

Figure 5.

4.1. The window to viewport transformations

The window to viewport transformations are a special set of domain transformations. They are special in two ways; their specification (using a window and a viewport), and the fact that not only an affine transformation is defined, but also some clipping has to be done.

When specifying a window to viewport transformation, both the window and the viewport have to be given. They are both defined in user (world) coordinates (there are no normalized device coordinates as in GKS)! This will enable the user to define more than one window to viewport transformation for a single path in the graph. The display screen will have some default dimensions in user coordinates.

Another important property will be explained using the pattern graph in figure 4. Let Dt2 be a window (W) to viewport (V) transformation (with affine transformation A, such that A(W) = V) and Dt1 some arbitrary transformation. Applying rule 3.1 to obtain the domain of the fleck, will result in:

$$Dt1\ (\ Dt2\ (\ D\ )\ ) = Dt1\ (\ A\ (\ W \cap D\ )\ ) =$$

$$Dt1\ (\ V \cap A\ (\ D\ )\ ) = Dt1\ (\ V\ ) \cap Dt1 \circ A\ (\ D\ )$$

In other words the viewport is transformed by Dt1. This is necessary because without transforming V, the application of a transformation like Dt1 can cause an empty intersection of the image of D with the viewport, which will prevent D from being displayed. This is undesirable because in this way Dt1 can have an effect on how Dt2 applies to D, despite the fact that the node N1 appears above N2 and P in the pattern graph.

4.2. The visibility attribute

When computing the visibility for flecks, the following rule is applied:

> A fleck V is visible, if and only if every node on the path corresponding with V has the visibility attribute value 'visible'.

Consequently, whenever one node carries the value 'invisible', the fleck will be invisible. The logic behind this is that when an object is made invisible, it should be completely invisible, and not only some parts of it. Partially invisible objects can be obtained by changing the visibility attributes at a lower level in the graph.

An example is shown in figure 6.

Only the fleck f11 is visible, the other flecks (f122, f123) will be invisible. Flecks that are invisible due to attributes like visibility (or level) are maintained within the fleck chain, but are skipped by the process that displays the flecks because of the internal attribute setting of the fleck.

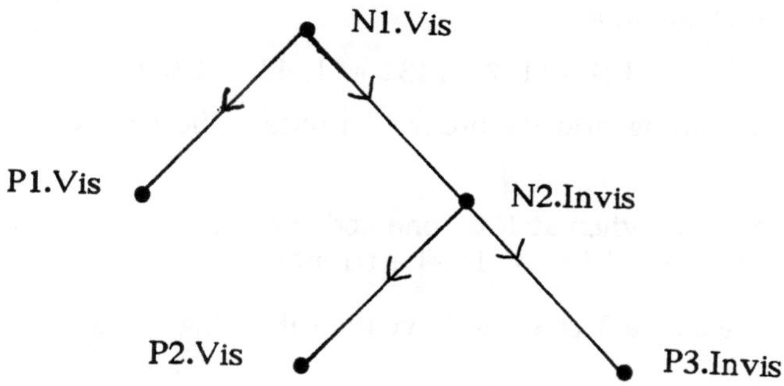

Figure 6

A pattern graph with the visibility attributes shown.

4.3. The level attribute

Suppose we have a pattern graph as shown in figure 7.

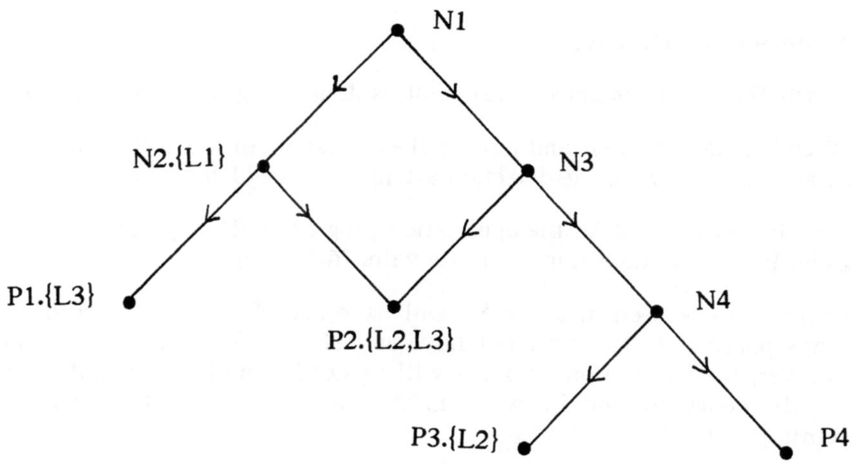

Figure 7

A pattern graph with the level attributes shown.

The corresponding fleck chain is:

f121 - f122 - f132 - f1343 - f1344

with the flecks in ascending priority order. To obtain the level of a fleck, we use the following rule:

> A fleck is of level Li, when at least one node on the corresponding path in the graph contains the level Li as its level attribute.

Thus, the flecks in the above fleck chain have the following levels:

f121	{ L1, L3 }
f122	{ L1, L2, L3 }
f132	{ L2, L3 }
f1343	{ L2 }
f1344	∅

Displaying level L1 means displaying the flecks f121 and f122. The fleck f1344, which does not belong to any user-defined level, is by default always displayed. Alternatively we could assign all flecks without a user-defined level, the level L0. Using this convention even the display of these flecks can be controlled using the level attribute.

4.4. The detection attribute

Deciding whether a fleck is detectable or not, is done using the following rule:

> A fleck V is detectable if and only if the corresponding path P in the graph has at least one node with the detection attribute value 'detectable'.

Following the detection of V, the application program will be given a set of names of nodes on P that had detection attribute value 'detectable'.

An example is to be seen in figure 8. Only the fleck f11 will not be detectable. This means pointing at f11 will not have any effect. When pointing at f122 or f123 however, the application program will be notified and additionally given the names of the nodes N2 and P2 when f122 was meant, or just the name of N2 when pointing at f123.

5. Conclusions

A model has been described directly oriented towards (2.5D) interactive raster graphics. This raster graphics orientation shows itself in the 2D primitives for defining patterns and in the specifically designed discrete representation of the flecks.

Interaction is provided by the ability to change the structure as well as the attributes in the pattern graph, an acyclic, directed graph. The leaves of a pattern graph are the patterns, which can be composed out of other patterns using pattern

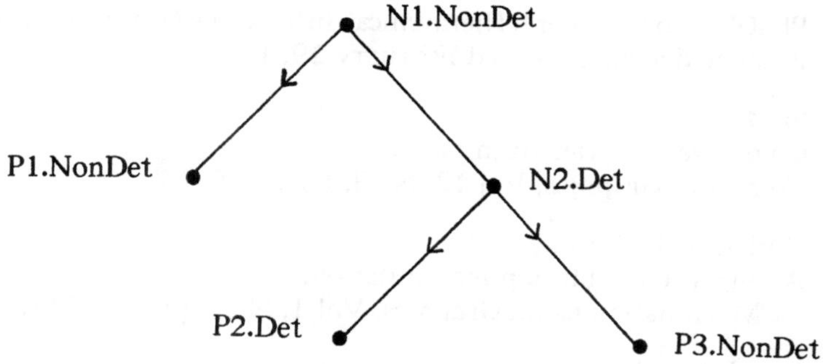

Figure 8

A pattern graph with the detectability attributes shown.

expressions. The graph and the expressions form two layers within the model: the graph being the dynamic layer, the expressions the static layer.

A preliminary implementation of the model has been completed recently [8]. First results indicate that the conversion from a continuous to a discrete representation while generating a chain of a considerable number of flecks, presents the bottleneck when displaying the graph. Improvements will have to be made to this implementation, in order to enhance interaction.

Another way to increase the performance is by adding special purpose hardware. Displaying the flecks is the first obvious place where such hardware could be used. Equipping the raster graphics station with intelligence to store, interpret and display the fleck chain, will no doubt decrease the response time when minor changes in the fleck chain (such as changing attributes) are required. In a further stage, hardware support for conversion from continuous representation to discrete flecks may be desired, especially to cope with pictures of complex structure (many flecks). This additional hardware will almost certainly mean moving the task of creating the flecks to the raster graphics station because the hardware will be located there. Consequently the interface with the hardware will move such that a suitable linear representation of the pattern graph will have to be handed to the hardware. Operations like domain and colour transformations are among the first tasks to be performed by that hardware, followed by the generation and display of the flecks.

References

[1] GKS, Draft international standard, ISO/DIS 7942 (November 1982)

[2] PHIGS: Programmer's Hierarchical Interactive Graphics System.
Baseline document, dated February 29, 1984.

[3] Smith, A.
Colour gamut transform pairs.
Computer Graphics, Vol 12, No 3, pp 12-19.

[4] Guibas, L.J., Stolfi, J.
A language for bitmap manipulation.
ACM Transactions on Graphics, Vol 1, No 3, pp 191-214.

[5] Bos, J. van den
Calculus for Operations on Graphics Colour Rasters.
Submitted for publication.

[6] Hagen, P.J.W., et al.
ILP: Intermediate Language for Pictures.
Mathematical Centre Tracts 130, Amsterdam 1980.

[7] Samet, H.
The Quadtree and Related Hierarchical Data Structures.
ACM Computing Surveys, Vol 16, No 2, pp 187-260.

[8] Evers, P., Vos, J.
Patroongraphen voor interactieve rastergrafiek (in Dutch).
Master thesis nr 1, 1985
University of Nijmegen, The Netherlands.

Pattern representation *

P.J.W. ten Hagen
and
C.G. Trienekens

CWI, Centre for Mathematics and Computer Science
Kruislaan 413
1098 SJ Amsterdam
The Netherlands

1. Introduction

This paper discusses the representation of patterns given certain requirements. Patterns are area oriented picture elements. The requirements are that the picture making devices can use raster technology and that the applications using the pictures are highly interactive, making intensive use of real-time picture change.

It is a well known fact that in the general case small picture changes require a complete regeneration of the raster image in order to make this change visible. This situation causes interaction on raster devices being either unacceptably slow or highly restricted because the kind of changes that can be efficiently supported is limited.

Recently introduced methods originating from image processing techniques have provided more elegant methods for raster image representation. Examples are quadtrees, octrees, run length encoding schemes, and other hierarchical representations. However, at this moment all of these methods are insufficient for interaction support.

Graphics devices using vector technology are essentially low quality devices for representing area-oriented pictures. Their ability to support real-time picture change and therefore interaction stems from the fact that they support a structured display file, which on the one hand can be changed locally and on the other hand can be traversed very efficiently generating the new screen image. Efficient picture change obviously can be realized by combining the ability to make local changes and the ability to quickly regenerate the image from the display file.

* These investigations were supported by the Netherlands Technology Foundation (STW)

The representation for area-oriented pictures proposed here on the one hand allows the primitives to be part of a structured display file, and on the other hand represents each picture primitive in such a way that fast rasterization (comparable to fast vector generation) is possible. Being part of a structured display file among other things requires that picture elements can be retransformed or differently coloured while being displayed. Fast rasterization requires that the individual picture elements can be scan converted quickly and in the right order. The most time consuming step in the rasterization process (2D or 3D) is the sorting of the points that make up an area. The strategy being followed to realize picture representation for interactive use on raster displays, includes a representation in a structured display file which has already performed most, if not all, of the sorting.

2. Primitive pattern representation

In ten Hagen, de Ruiter and Trienekens [1] a system for area-oriented picture elements, called *patterns* , is proposed. In this section we will summarise this proposal giving some emphasis on the aspects relevant for representation. The proposal defines the pattern functionality and its associated semantics for application programmers. As a result the notation in that paper is different from the one chosen here. In this paper implementation issues are discussed for which mathematical notation is more appropriate.

The representation issues and display list solution will be discussed for 2D primitives. The primitives in [1] are 3D primitives. In section 3 it will be pointed out how 2D and 3D primitives are related and what consequences this has for the implementation.

A pattern primitive P is a pair (D,C) where:

> D is a domain function, which specifies a 2D or 3D planar region, and
> C is a colour function, which assigns a colour to each point of the domain.

e.g.: P = (D,C).

Conceptually what will take place when P is visualized is that D is mapped onto the raster of the device. For each rasterpoint the colour of the corresponding point of D is calculated by C. This colour is assigned to the rasterpoint (pixel).

The system has a number of elementary domain functions, such as: POLYGON, PARALELLOGRAM, and a number of elementary colour functions, such as: SOLID_COLOUR, CELLS and INTERPOLATE. Any combination of domain and colour function is a picture primitive. Domains can have holes or consist of unconnected regions. However, domains are finite.

Pattern primitives can be operands in pattern expressions. The operators for these expressions are set theoretic operands, such as UNION, INTERSECTION, DIFFERENCE etc.. They are called pattern combining operators. These operators are affecting the interior of patterns. The result of, say, a union is a new domain which is the union of the interiors of the domains of the operands. The resulting colour function of the union for overlapping parts of the regions will be a new colour function which is somehow a mixture of the two original functions, and for non-overlapping regions it will be the original function of the corresponding pattern. How the colour function will mix colours is determined by a parameter attributed to the union function. This parameter is called the *mix-attribute* for pattern combining operators.

The representation needs to be concerned primarily with pattern representations *after* combining. This means that it is important to know how a representation is constructed for a given pattern expression. It is, however, not required that the representation accomodates fast (real-time) combining. The combining operator is for convenient pattern definition. Pattern manipulations for realizing picture changes in real time do not include combining.

A second category of operators are monadic operators for geometric and colour transformations of patterns. In as far as these are used in the pattern definition phase they have to fulfill similar requirements: support convenient pattern definition, be able to represent patterns after transformation which need not to be applied in real-time. These requirements are derived from the basic design principle for the area oriented primitives, namely that there will be a definition phase which is distinct from the presentation and manipulation phase.

During the manipulation phase complex patterns originating from a possibly complex pattern expression will be treated as a unit which does not change. For these complex patterns it is necessary to have a representation which allows all kinds of manipulations to support interaction such as: transformations (again!), blinking, removal, identification and grouping.

In the next paragraphs, the prerasterized representation will be described from two points of view. First, how to construct it from a pattern expression and second, how it can support interaction. The latter will only be done from the point of view of transformations. The other aspects will be dealt with in a future paper.

A representation function must store both domain- and colour function. These will be treated as separate components. The correspondence will be, that at all times, the colour function can supply the colour value of a point in the domain. This property must be maintained for complex patterns and under transformations.

Note that a geometric transformation can affect both domain and colour function. A colour transformation will only affect the colour function.

Eventually a rasterization is envisaged to take place as follows: the domain is mapped onto the raster. As a result all rasterpoints (pixels) belonging to the mapped domain can be associated with a point of the original domain. For each of these points the colour function will supply the value.

In scheme:

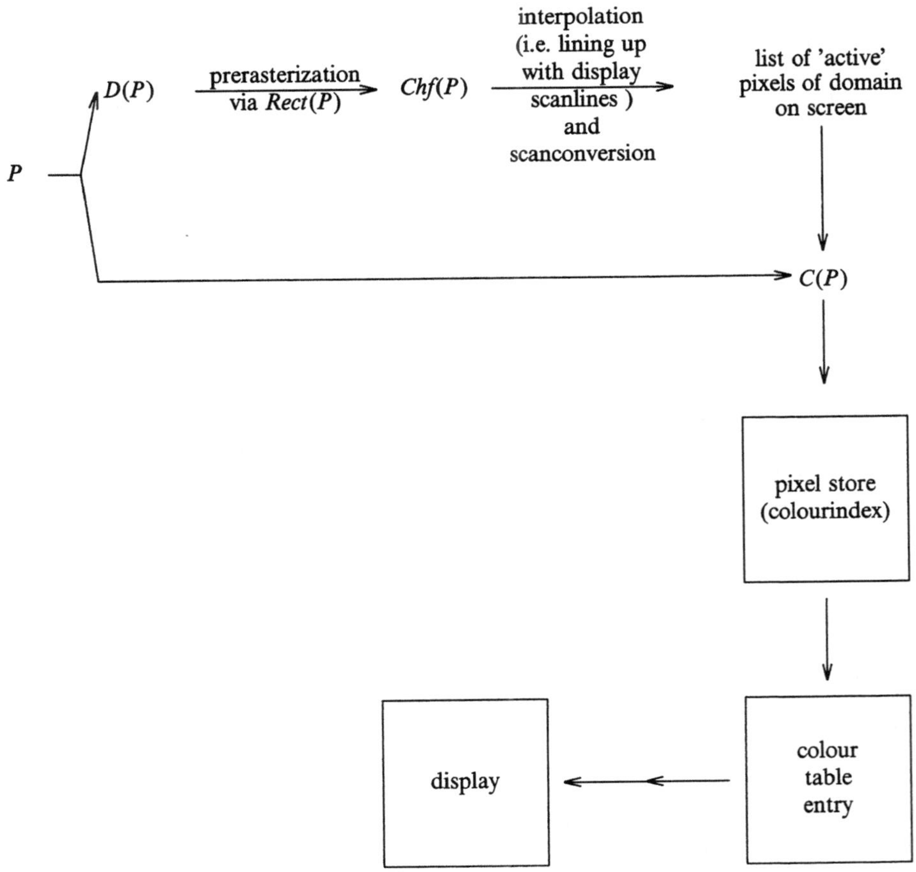

In order for the colour function to be a separate component in the representation it is necessary that the colour function is defined for all points in the domain. Moreover, the colour function must be independent of the domain. If, for instance, as a result of intersection the shape of the domain changes drastically, then the colour function still must be defined. This requirement can cause severe performance problems which must be solved by choosing an adequate representation. For instance, under union a colour function may look quite different depending on whether a point is in an overlapping part or not. Colour functions should preferably not have to reconstruct parts of the domains during their evaluation.

The prerasterization method that will be described anticipates that the primitives and the raster they will be mapped onto, will be oriented the same. The orientation is invariant under translation and scaling. This suggests that these operations can be carried out efficiently. Rotation requires a re-orientation and hence calculation of a completely new representation. However, the original representation will still be of some help when calculating the rotated one.

2.1. Domain representation

The first facility provided by the representation functions for domains is to define the smallest upright rectangle that contains the domain. This is the initial step for rasterization later on. All subsequent manipulations with the domain must keep the smallest rectangle associated with the domain updated.

This rectangle has on each side at least one intersection with the pattern. (See figure 1). Hence, one way to represent it could be storing the minimum and maximum pattern domain values in the axes directions in a 'lower-left' and an 'upper-right' rectangle point.

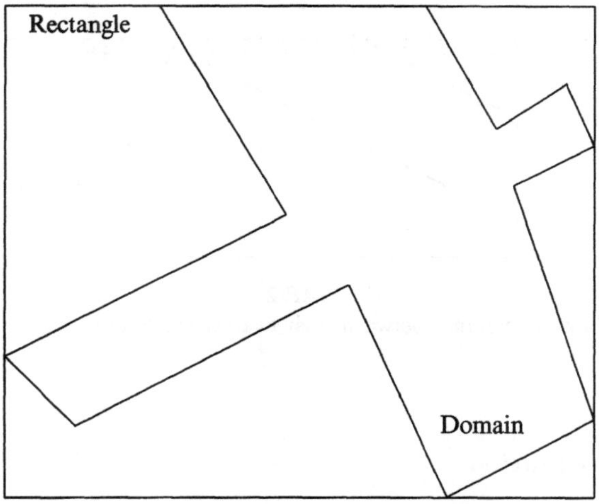

FIGURE 1
Smallest upright rectangle containing the domain

A further step in the direction of rasterization which is provided as part of the representation function is a characteristic function [1] over this smallest rectangle. The characteristic function is raster independent or (approximately) continuous. When final rasterization will take place, the characteristic function only needs to be evaluated on the rasterpoints. In particular, the colour function needs to be evaluated for those points.

The characteristic function can be stored using run-length-encoding (RLE) techniques. By applying linear interpolation techniques the RLE for an arbitrary scanline can be reconstructed from its nearest neighbours in the coding, provided that the precision along the scanline (real numbers) and the distance between the

[1] This characteristic function indicates whether or not an element is a member of the pattern. Its outcome only results in two values: 1 (or true) if that element is part of the pattern and 0 (or false) if it falls outside the pattern.

nearest neighbours is within the precision required for the approximation. Figure 2 gives an example of encoding, where coding lines (not all depicted) are chosen to have equal ∇ y separation.

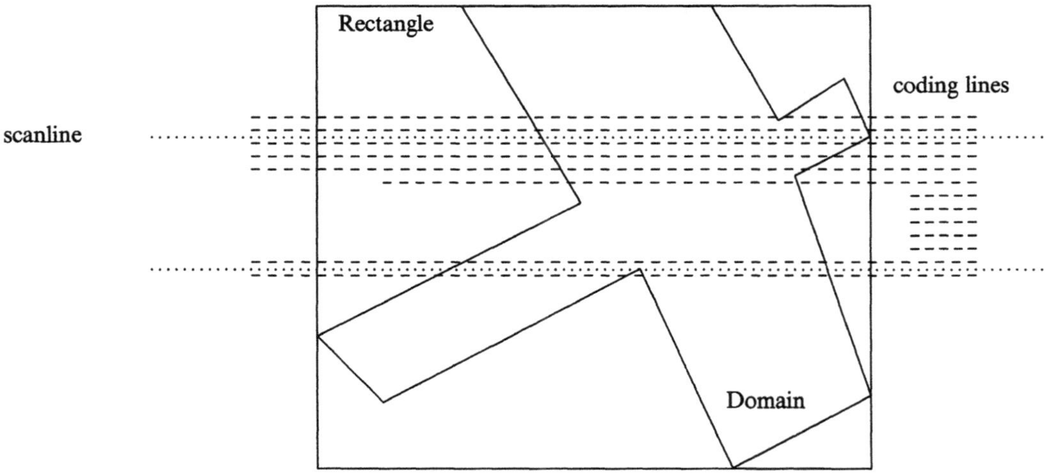

FIGURE 2
Some arbitrary scanlines between their nearest neighbour coding lines

2.2. Colour representation

Colour functions can work with true colours or with colour indices. In the latter case a colour table exists which defines a true colour for each valid index. A colour function has at all times access to the colour table. Hence, whenever a true colour is required rather than the index, it can be retrieved. This property will be used in cases of colour mixing, which is done with true colours.

Intermediate true colour values need not be mapped back into the (nearest) corresponding colour index, at least not until real rasterization takes place. This makes it possible to avoid propagation of rounding off errors of intermediate colour values.

Colour functions can be generators or pseudo-rasters. Generators are procedures yielding a colour for each point in a domain, pseudo-rasters are two-dimensional arrays of colour cells covering a domain. It is possible to rewrite a generator as a pseudo-raster, but the reverse is generally not the case. Examples of generators are SOLID and RANDOM (see [1]).

Combining patterns during pattern expression evaluation may require rewriting of generators or pseudo-rasters (as new pseudo-rasters) in order to have one colour function after mixing in cases of overlap.

2.3. Pattern expression representations

Pattern expressions are defined in more detail in [1]. They are built from operands (primitive patterns or pattern (sub)expressions) and operators. We will first discuss the representation requirements for the various operands assuming that the operands are primitive patterns. Subsequently the description of the representation functions will be extended to cover subexpressions as well.

It will turn out that two basic representation strategies can be followed. At this time no decision will be taken about which strategy has preference. However, properties that allow a comparison of the two will be highlighted.

A pattern can be written as

$$P = (D_p, C_p)$$

with

$$D(P) = D_p, \text{ the domain of P}$$

and

$$C(P) = C_p, \text{ the colourfunction of P.}$$

In the following we will point out that the quadruple

$$R\ (\ D_p, C_p, Rect_p, Chf_p\ )$$

where D, C are the primitive domain function and the colour function (C is not necessarily primitive), and Rect and Chf are the enclosing rectangle and characteristic function respectively providing redundant information, is the general form of representing a primitive pattern, which suits our purposes.

Depending on domain or colour functions these four elements are explicitly present or can be generated when needed. Hence, the system will interface to primitive pattern objects through four elementary functions:

Domain of P	$(D(P))$
Colourfunction of P	$(C(P))$
Rectangle of P	$(Rect(P))$
Characteristic function of P	$(Chf(P))$

2.3.1. Pattern intersection

Write $P_1 = (D_1, C_1)$ and $P_2 = (D_2, C_2)$.

A pattern expression of the form

$$P_1 \cap_{mix} P_2,$$

can yield a resulting pattern with the following properties:

By definition ($=_{def}$) : **Domain function**

$$D(P_1 \cap_{mix} P_2) =_{def} D(P_1) \cap D(P_2) \tag{1}$$

By definition : **Colour function**

$$C(P_1 \cap_{mix} P_2) =_{def} C(P_1)_{/D(P_1 \cap P_2)}\ \underline{mix}\ C(P_2)_{/D(P_1 \cap P_2)} \tag{2}$$

where $\underline{mix}$ or *mix* is used for 'specified colour mixing function'
and

$_{/D(P_1 \cap P_2)}$ for 'restricted to the domain of $P_1 \cap P_2$'.

From now on we will use the symbol " subscript / " in the special meaning of *restricted to* the then following domain.

Equation (2) can be further simplified to :

$$C(P_1 \cap_{mix} P_2) = (C(P_1)\ \underline{mix}\ C(P_2))_{/D(P_1 \cap P_2)} \tag{3}$$

By definition : **general pattern function**

$$P_1 \cap_{mix} P_2 =_{def} (D(P_1 \cap_{mix} P_2), C(P_1 \cap_{mix} P_2)) \tag{4}$$

Substituting equations (1) and (3) in (4) and using the property

$$(D, C_{/D}) = (D, C)$$

gives the **resulting pattern intersection equation** :

$$P_1 \cap_{mix} P_2 = (D(P_1) \cap D(P_2), C(P_1)\ \underline{mix}\ C(P_2)) \tag{5}$$

Based on these definitions and properties we can now formulate how both **enclosing rectangle** and **characteristic function** can be calculated for intersections.

Let Rect(P) be the function which yields the smallest enclosing rectangle of the domain D (of pattern P).

Let Chf(P) be the characteristic function of the domain D (of pattern P), restricted to the rectangle of P.

Then:

$$D(Chf(P)) = Rect(P) \tag{6}$$

For intersection of two primitive patterns the following properties are true:

$$Rect\,(P_1 \cap_{mix} P_2) = Rect\big(\,D(P_1) \cap D(P_2)\,\big) \tag{7}$$

with

$$Rect\,(P_1 \cap_{mix} P_2) \subseteq Rect\,(P_1) \cap Rect\,(P_2) \tag{8}$$

Note that the smallest enclosing intersection rectangle can be empty even if the enclosing rectangles intersect. See also figure 3.

$$Chf\ (P_1 \cap_{mix} P_2) = Chf\ (P_1)_{/Rect\,(P_1 \cap P_2)}\ \underline{and}\ Chf\ (P_2)_{/Rect\,(P_1 \cap P_2)} \tag{9}$$

This equation can be rewritten as

$$Chf\ (P_1 \cap_{mix} P_2) = \big(\,Chf\ (P_1)\ \underline{and}\ Chf\ (P_2)\,\big)_{/Rect\,(P_1 \cap P_2)} \tag{10}$$

The *and* function will be used as follows:

$$chf_1\ \underline{and}\ chf_2 =_{def} \Big\{\ \underline{A}\ x \in D(chf_1) \cap D(chf_2)\ \mid\ \underline{if}\ Chf_1(x) = Chf_2(x) = 1\ \underline{then}\ 1\ \underline{else}\ 0\ \Big\} \tag{11}$$

A schematic representation of $R(\,P_1 \cap_{mix} P_2\,)$ is now as follows:

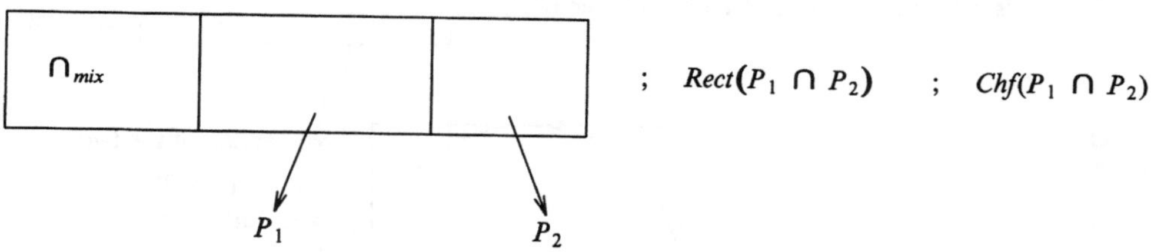

which can be further simplified to the **pattern intersection representation**

$$R(\,P_1 \cap_{mix} P_2\,) = \Big(\ D(P_1) \cap D(P_2),\ \ C(P_1)\ \underline{mix}\ C(P_2),\ \ Rect\big(\,D(P_1) \cap D(P_2)\,\big),\ \ Chf\ (P_1)\ \underline{and}\ Chf\ (P_2)\ \Big) \tag{12}$$

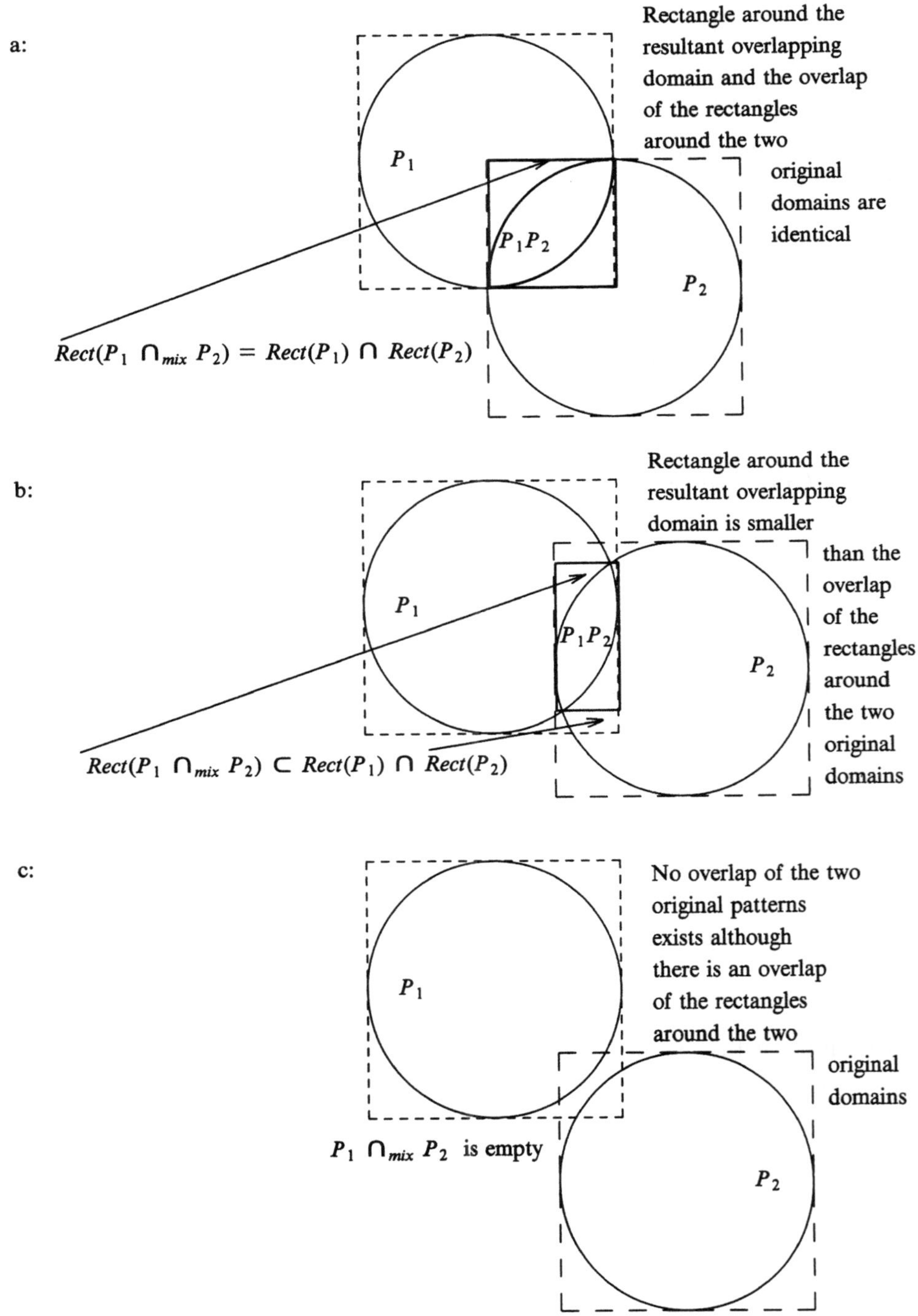

FIGURE 3
Examples of intersection of two patterns

2.3.2. Union of patterns

A pattern expression of the form

$$P_1 \cup_{mix} P_2$$

can yield a pattern with the following properties:

Domain function

$$D(P_1 \cup_{mix} P_2) =_{def} D(P_1) \cup D(P_2) \quad (1)$$

This can be rewritten in an **alternative way** as :

$$\begin{aligned} D(P_1 \cup_{mix} P_2) = \; & D(P_1) \neg (D(P_1) \cap D(P_2)) \cup \\ & D(P_2) \neg (D(P_1) \cap D(P_2)) \cup \\ & D(P_1) \cap D(P_2) \end{aligned} \quad (2)$$

The latter is a decomposition of the resulting domain in three disjunct subdomains, each with a different simple colour function. The symbol $\neg$ will be used for '*excluded* the following domain'.

In writing a shorthand for

$$D(P_1) \cap D(P_2)$$

as

$$D(P_1 P_2)$$

the equation can be simplified to

$$\begin{aligned} D(P_1 \cup_{mix} P_2) = \; & D(P_1) \neg D(P_1 P_2) \cup \\ & D(P_2) \neg D(P_1 P_2) \cup \\ & D(P_1 P_2) \end{aligned} \quad (2')$$

Using properties and definitions mentioned in this and the previous section the **resultant colourfunction** is :

$$\begin{aligned} C(P_1 \cup_{mix} P_2) = \; & C(P_1)_{/D(P_1) \neg D(P_1 P_2)} ; \\ & C(P_2)_{/D(P_2) \neg D(P_1 P_2)} ; \\ & (C(P_1) \, \underline{mix} \, C(P_2))_{/D(P_1 P_2)} \end{aligned} \quad (3)$$

Conclusion:
As a result a union of patterns can be written in two alternative ways:

- either as one primitive pattern having a fairly complex (three component) colour function, or
- as a sequence of three primitive patterns having a simple colour function.

We will first give the derivations of both alternative pattern representations. Following this we will compare the two on the basis of their rectangle and characteristic functions properties.

general pattern function

$$P_1 \cup_{mix} P_2 =_{def} \left(D(P_1 \cup_{mix} P_2), C(P_1 \cup_{mix} P_2) \right) \tag{4}$$

When substituting the first alternative domain description (equation (1)) and colour function (3) in this pattern equation (4) the

first pattern union equation yields :

$$P_1 \cup_{mix} P_2 =$$

$$\Big(\; D(P_1) \cup D(P_2), \; C(P_1)_{/D(P_1) \neg D(P_1P_2)}; C(P_2)_{/D(P_2) \neg D(P_1P_2)}; \left(C(P_1) \underline{mix} \; C(P_2) \right)_{/D(P_1P_2)} \; \Big) \tag{5}$$

However, when substituting the second alternative domain description (equation (2)) and colour function (3), together with using the property

$$(D, C_{/D}) = (D, C),$$

in the pattern equation (4) the alternative

second pattern union equation yields :

$$P_1 \cup_{mix} P_2 = \Big\{ \; \left(D(P_1) \neg D(P_1P_2), C(P_1) \right), \; \left(D(P_2) \neg D(P_1P_2), C(P_2) \right), \; \left(D(P_1P_2), C(P_1) \underline{mix} \; C(P_2) \right) \; \Big\} \tag{6}$$

The two alternative representations are depicted for one intersection in figure 4.

From now on we will use the terms case (1) and case (2) to point to alternative 1, respectively 2, of the pattern representation.
The rectangles associated with the resulting patterns have the following properties:

Case (1);

$$Rect(P_1 \cup_{mix} P_2) = Rect\left(D(P_1) \cup D(P_2) \right) \tag{7}$$

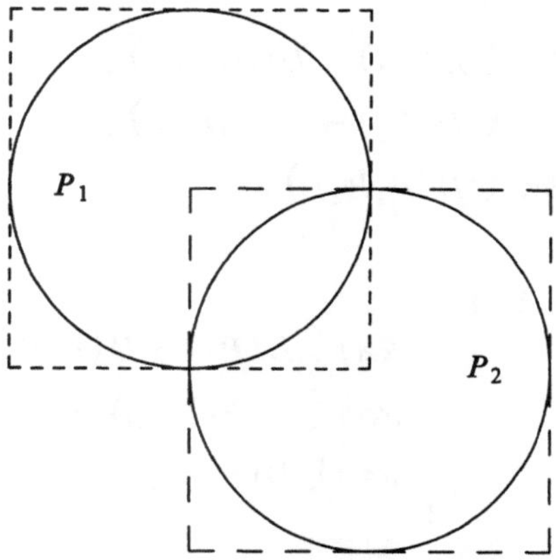

Two patterns P_1 and P_2 with their resp. enclosing rectangles

case (1):

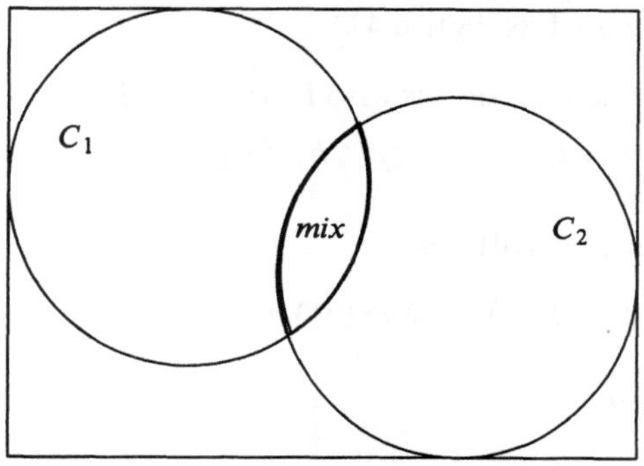

Union of the two patterns in case (1) : One pattern with 'growing' rectangle around one (larger) domain with one (three-component) colourfunction

case (2):

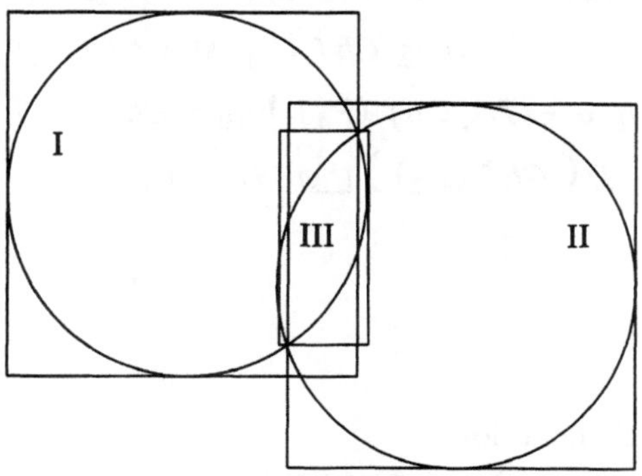

Union of the two patterns in case (2) : three disjunct patterns I, II, III, each with 'shrinking' rectangle and domain and one 'simple' colourfunction per pattern

FIGURE 4
Example of a union of two patterns

Case (2);

$$Rect(P_1 \cup_{mix} P_2) = \begin{array}{l} Rect(\, D(P_1) \neg D(P_1P_2)\,), \\ Rect(\, D(P_2) \neg D(P_1P_2)\,), \\ Rect(\, D(P_1P_2)\,) \end{array} \tag{8}$$

with

$$Rect(\, D(P_1) \cup D(P_2)\,) \supseteq (\; Rect(\, D(P_1) \neg D(P_1P_2)\,) \cup Rect(\, D(P_2) \neg D(P_1P_2)\,) \cup Rect(\, D(P_1P_2)\,) \;) \tag{9}$$

The second alternative's set of rectangles can be considerably smaller in area than the first alternative's rectangle (see figure 4).

For case (1) the characteristic function is also fairly complex:

$$Chf\,(P_1 \cup_{mix} P_2) = Chf\,(P_1) \underline{or}\; Chf\,(P_2) \tag{10}$$

The $\underline{or}$ function will be used as follows:

(Keep in mind that $D(\, Chf\,(P)\,) = Rect(P)$)

$Chf\,(P_1)\; \underline{or}\; Chf\,(P_2) =_{def}$

$$\left\{ \begin{array}{r} \underline{A}\; x \in Rect(\, D(\, Chf\,(P_1)\,) \cup D(\, Chf\,(P_2)\,)\,) \mid \\ \underline{if}\; x \in (\, D(\, Chf\,(P_1)\,) \cap D(\, Chf\,(P_2)\,)\,) \\ \underline{then}\; Chf\,(P_1) \vee^2 Chf\,(P_2) \\ \underline{else}\; \underline{if}\; x \in D(\, Chf\,(P_1)\,)\; \underline{then}\; Chf\,(P_1) \\ \underline{else}\; \underline{if}\; x \in D(\, Chf\,(P_2)\,)\; \underline{then}\; D(\, Chf\,(P_2)\,) \\ \underline{else}\; 0 \end{array} \right\} \tag{11}$$

In case (2) the characteristic function is

$$Chf\,(P_1 \cup_{mix} P_2) = \begin{array}{r} Chf\,(P_1)_{/Rect(\, D(P_1) \neg D(P_1P_2)\,)}\,; \\ Chf\,(P_2)_{/Rect(\, D(P_2) \neg D(P_1P_2)\,)}\,; \\ (\, Chf\,(P_1)\; \underline{and}\; Chf\,(P_2)\,)_{/Rect(\, D(P_1P_2)\,)} \end{array} \tag{12}$$

---

[2] $Chf\,(P_1)(x) \vee Chf\,(P_2)(x) =_{def}$
$\underline{if}\; Chf\,(P_1)(x) = Chf\,(P_2)(x) = 0\; \underline{then}\; 0\; \underline{else}\; 1$.

As a result the **pattern union representation** can be written as:

Case (1):

$$R(P_1 \cup_{mix} P_2) =$$

$$\Big(\quad D(P_1) \cup D(P_2)\ , \quad C(P_1)_{/D(P_1) \neg D(P_1P_2)} ; C(P_2)_{/D(P_2) \neg D(P_1P_2)} ; \big(C(P_1)\ \underline{mix}\ C(P_2) \big)_{/D(P_1P_2)} , \quad Rect\big(D(P_1) \cup D(P_2) \big), \quad Chf\ (P_1)\ \underline{or}\ Chf\ (P_2) \quad \Big) \tag{13}$$

Case (2):

$$R(P_1 \cup_{mix} P_2) = \tag{14}$$

$$\Big\{ \big(D(P_1) \neg D(P_1P_2), C(P_1), Rect\big(D(P_1) \neg D(P_1P_2) \big), Chf\ (P_1) \big),$$
$$\big(D(P_2) \neg D(P_1P_2), C(P_2), Rect\big(D(P_2) \neg D(P_1P_2) \big), Chf\ (P_2) \big),$$
$$\big(D(P_1P_2), C(P_1)\ \underline{mix}\ C(P_2), Rect\big(D(P_1P_2) \big), Chf\ (P_1)\ \underline{and}\ Chf\ (P_2) \big) \Big\}$$

$$= \{ R(P_1 \neg P_2), R(P_2 \neg P_1), R(P_1 \cap_{mix} P_2) \}$$

Note that the colour function only needs to be given for the pattern domain. Similarly, that the characteristic function only needs to be defined for the rectangle surrounding the domain. For instance, the first two characteristic functions in (14) are identical to the Chf for P_1 and P_2 respectively but they have smaller domains. This may lead to fewer storage locations for their representation.

Based on the observation that case (2) leads to smaller rectangles and simpler colour functions we give preference to case (2). However, this introduces the need for considering lists of primitive patterns as operands rather than single ones. We only need to consider lists containing disjunct patterns! All operations will have to maintain the disjunction property for lists of patterns.

2.3.3. Pattern reduction

The pattern reduction operator is used to maintain the disjunction property.

Let P, Q be patterns such that $P \supset Q$. Then

$$R\,(\,P\,\underline{r}\,Q\,) =_{def} \Big(D(P) \neg D(Q),\; C(P)_{/D(P)\neg D(Q)},\; Rect\big(D(P)\neg D(Q)\big),\; Chf\,(P)_{/D(P)\neg D(Q)} \Big) \tag{1}$$

(pronounce P reduced by Q)

This can be rewritten as:

$$R\,(\,P\,\underline{r}\,Q\,) = \big(\,D(P)\neg D(Q),\, C(P),\, Rect\big(\,D(P)\neg D(Q)\,\big),\, Chf\,(P)\,\big) \tag{2}$$

Hence, the reduction operator removes the domain of Q from the domain of P, called the reduced domain of P. The colour function, rectangle function and characteristic function now apply only to the reduced domain.

Using the reduction operator we can *reformulate* the union operation for patterns for case (2) as given in the previous section.

$$P_1 \cup_{mix} P_2 = \{\, (P_1P_2)_{\underline{mix}},\, P_1\,\underline{r}\,P_1P_2,\, P_2\,\underline{r}\,P_1P_2 \,\} \tag{3}$$

where P_1P_2 is a shorthand notation for $P_1 \cap P_2$.

This makes immediately clear what happens: the result is written in three disjunct patterns, the first one contains the domain for which colour function mixing has to be done. This domain is taken away from the two original domains.

Now the union of a list of disjunct patterns with a new one can proceed by calculating the union of the new pattern with each of the patterns from the list, thereby reducing the new pattern by the intersection of each pattern from the list:

$$\cup_{mix}(P_1, P_2, P_3) = \Big\{ (P_1P_2P_3)_{mix},\; \{\,(P_1P_2)_{mix}, (P_1P_3)_{mix}, (P_2P_3)_{mix}\,\}\,\underline{r}\,P_1P_2P_3,\; P_1\,\underline{r}\,(P_1P_2, P_1P_3),\; P_2\,\underline{r}\,(P_1P_2, P_2P_3),\; P_3\,\underline{r}\,(P_1P_3, P_2P_3) \Big\} \tag{4}$$

2.3.4. Run length encoding for the characteristic function

The representation of the domains in the prerasterized form is similar to run length encoding methods. The coding here however, must be raster independent. Differences are that the scan lines in our encoding can be on arbitrary y-values (but always in x-direction) and the number of scanlines used is minimal.

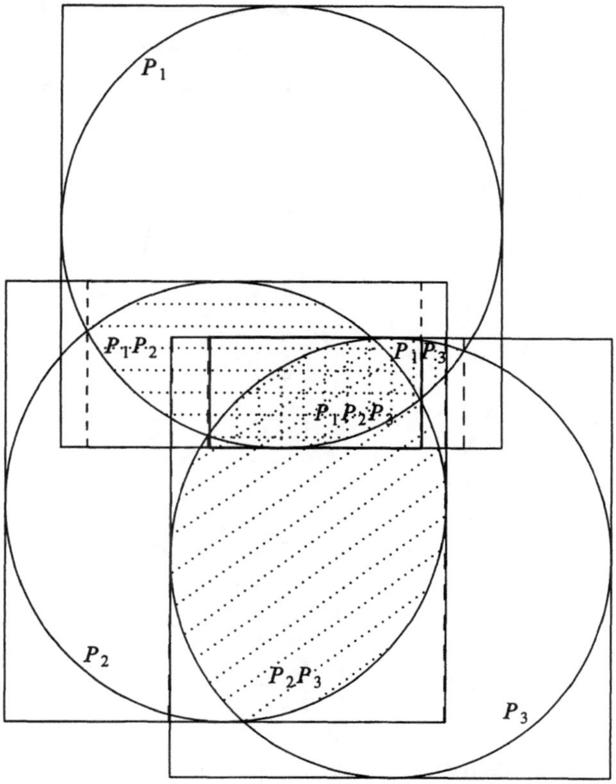

FIGURE 5
Union of three patterns, resulting in seven 'new' disjuncted patterns

For instance, a POLYGON primitive with n points (specifying the boundary) will have at most n scanlines represented in the encoding characteristic function. Hence, the coding skips over all scanlines which can be reconstructed unambiguously. In this way transformations can be applied and domains whose "rasters" are not lined up can be matched. The Chf provides a uniform representation for domains which can be taken instead of the domain itself when needed. An example is depicted in figure 6.

In order to be able to reconstruct the pattern lines from the Chf while interpolating or during display rasterization it is necessary to add more details to the coordinates of the rasterpoints, namely the 'type' of the intersecting line at each rasterpoint. The 'type' is indicated by means of letter symbols. The letter symbols and their meanings are the following:

c: intersection of a continuous polygon line, i.e. with same slope between its two nearest neighbour scanlines.

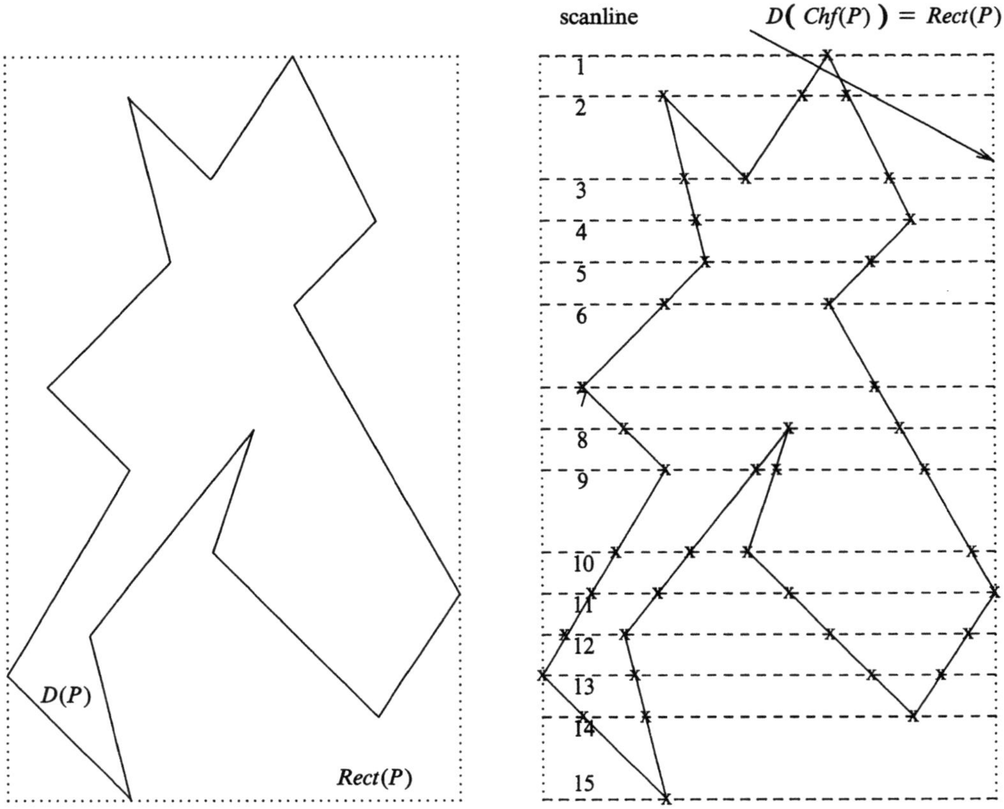

Polygon of 15 points
and its rectangle

Chf of the polygon:
15 scanlines, plus scanpoints x

FIGURE 6

C: intersection of a continuous polygon line, i.e. with different slopes from the previous scanline to the current one, and from the current one to the next scanline.

B: 'bottom' intersection point,
i.e. from here two connecting lines only exist with the previous scanline.

T: 'top' intersection point,
i.e. from here two connecting lines only exist with the next scanline.

H1 - H2: 'horizontal' intersection points. H1 can have a line
connected to either the previous or next scanline. The same is true for H2.

Note that for the types C, B, T, H1, H2 the intersection of the polygon and the scanline is a specified boundary point! The different intersection types are represented in figure 7.

By way of example the representation of POLYGONal domains will be specified. The treatment of most other domains is similar.

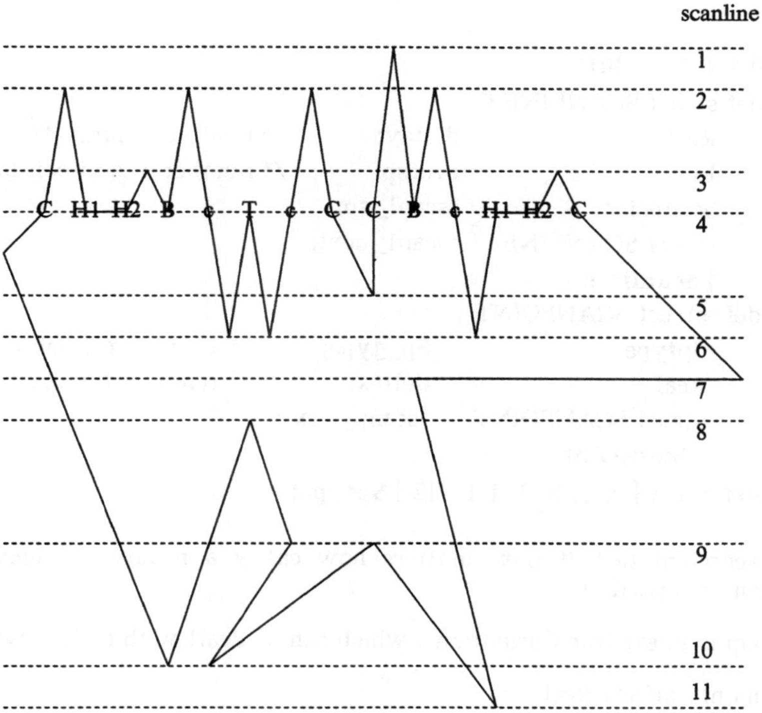

FIGURE 7
POLYGON of 31 points, only 11 scanlines.
Characteristic function needs extra 'type' information.
Different types of intersecting polygon lines are depicted in scanline 4.

First a rectangle is given by four real values:

minx, miny, ,maxx, maxy.

e.g. in C(GKS)-notation:

```
typedef float Real;
typedef   struct {
          Real      minx, miny, maxx, maxy;
          } Rectan;
```

Next a sequence of scanlines is given as follows:

```
typedef struct {
          Int        nrofsl;     /* number of scanlines */
          Scanline   *crle_sl;   /* list of scanlines */
          } Crle;                /* continuous run length encoding */
```

with

```
typedef int       Int;
typedef struct SCANLINE {
        Real              deltay;        /* relative to miny */
        Int               nrofsp;        /* number of scanpoints */
        Scanpoint         *scanl_sp;
        struct SCANLINE   *scanl_next;
        } Scanline;
typedef struct SCANPOINT {
        Sptype            Sp_type;       /* type of scanpoint */
        Real              deltax;        /* relative to minx */
        struct SCANPOINT  *scanp_next;
        } Scanpoint;
typedef enum { c, C, B, T, H1, H2 } Sptype;
```

Given this representation it now matters how easily a number of elementary operations can be carried out.

The first group is linear transformations, which can be dealt with as follows:

- translation only affects Rect
- scaling only affects all points of Chf, including the points defining the scanlines themselves
- rotation requires a complete new calculation of Chf and Rect, however, the current already scan converted representation can be dealt with more easily than the general case.

The second group is made up by the elementary actions used in intersection calculations, such as generating common scanlines and merging scanlines. The same elementary actions are used in conversion to discrete rasters.

An important strategic question is, to what extent pathological cases must be identified and possibly removed. Many applications would for instance become much more efficient if domains were guaranteed to be connected. Maintenance of this property under intersection is one of the cases to be studied.

3. Relation between 2D and 3D area's

The 3D primitives of [1] are all planar primitives. This means that the area's can be described as 2D area's relative to a local coordinate system in the plane. If a mapping from 3D to 2D is taken following the GKS-3D model (see [3]) there will be an intermediate representation where the x-y values under projection will not change. If the local coordinate system is chosen such that it coincides with x and y directions, they can be treated (but for z-values) as 2D area's.

In a future paper it will be described how it can be arranged that the pattern expression will be generated in this representation. This implies that the x-y part of the geometry can be described as for the 2D case. The z-value wil only affect the colour and mix functions.

As a result we only have to consider the 2D case for domains.

Projections, hidden surface effects and the like can be represented as part of the colour function expressions.

References

[1] P.J.W. ten Hagen, M.M. de Ruiter and C.G. Trienekens, Raster Graphics Facilities (RGF) in Programming Languages, Preliminary report CWI, department of Interactive Systems (1985).

[2] Information Processing - Graphical Kernel System (GKS) - Functional Description, ISO DIS 7942 (draft) (1984).

[3] Information Processing Systems - Computer Graphics - Graphical Kernel System for Three Dimensions (GKS-3D) - Functional Description, ISO/TC97/SC21/WG-2 N277 Rev (draft) (1985).

A 3D animation system

Pascal Leray

CCETT
35510 Cesson-Sevigne
France

ABSTRACT

A hardware architecture for image generation is described that allows the combination of polygon rendering and ray casting. Since special purpose hardware is used for both tasks, a considerable speed up is achieved.

1. Introduction

Usually large computation times are required for 3D raster graphics applications. Ray tracing 2000 polygons requires on a VAX 11 / 750 five to ten minutes of computation time. Therefore, 3D animation using ray tracing is very expensive: it costs between two and three thousand dollar to produce one second of ray traced animation.

In order to decrease those costs, we have designed the CUBI 7, a special purpose architecture, which reduces the computation time. To process 2000 polygons (with an unlimited number of vertices) about 40 milliseconds are needed.

In section 2 the architecture of the CUBI 7 is described. One of its main features is the possibility to choose between a Z-buffer algorithm operating on polygons, or a ray trace algorithm operating on either polygons or a CSG tree. Both algorithms use the same database, which is implemented using a new language, called NIAL, which is described in section 3. In section 4 can be found how a superset of PHIGS is embedded in NIAL. Section 5 contains some concluding remarks.

2. Ray casting and z-buffer algorithm for polygons

In this section the architecture of the CUBI 7 and some of its modules are described.

2.1. The CUBI 7 system

The system consists of (see Figure 1):

- An image memory with 40 bits for each pixel; 16 bits are used for depth values and 3 × 8 bits for RGB colors; the image format is dynamically programmable: 512 × 512, 576 × 720 or 1024 × 1024 pixels.

- Four slots for parallel processors, such as

  - a vector generator

  - a plane polygonal + facet module, which requires 0.1 microseconds per pixel to compute shading, colors and z-depth

  - a ray casting module to update the z-buffer with ray traced objects.

- One or more bit-slice microprocessors (AMD 2900 with a 4K × 112 bits memory for microprograms and 32K × 32 bits memory for data).

The CUBI 7 must be connected to a host computer, which may be a standard VAX (or Micro-Vax) or a SM90, a TELMAT designed multi-microprocessor system consisting of M68000 and floating point processors. The host computer contains the database for 3D animation and computes a superset of a PHIGS tree (see section 4).

The database consists of polygons (for a z-buffer algorithm) and a constructive solid geometry (CSG) tree (to be used for ray-casting computations). Data to be stored in the database is obtained from a modeling system running on the host. Presently two modeling systems are available, one implemented in APL and the other in FORTRAN.

Polygons have their own rotation and translation matrix associated with them, just like the objects to be ray traced. A global rotation and translation matrix is derived from the view point for perspective calculations.

The CUBI 7 system performs the following tasks:

- rotation and translation of objects

- shadow computations

- perspective transformation

- clipping

- polygon filling (at a rate of 0.1 microsecond per pixel)

- integer conversion of z-values in the range $[-2^{16}, +2^{16}]$

- update of image memory.

For some of these tasks the bit-slice processors are used. Simultaneously the ray casting module, called CRISTAL (see below), traverses the CSG tree.

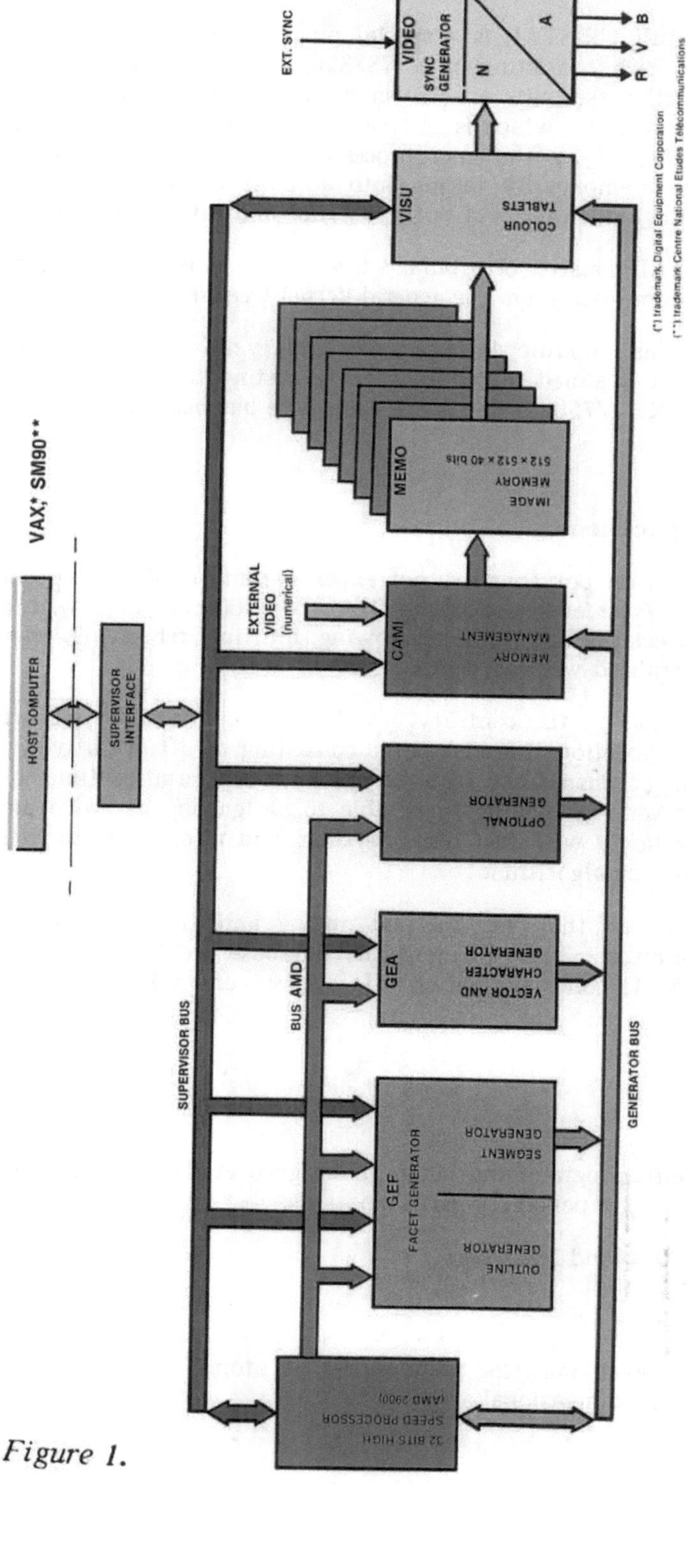
HOST COMPUTER
VAX,* SM90**
SUPERVISOR INTERFACE
SUPERVISOR BUS
BUS AMD
GENERATOR BUS
32 BITS HIGH SPEED PROCESSOR (AMD 2900)
GEF
FACET GENERATOR
OUTLINE GENERATOR
SEGMENT GENERATOR
GEA
VECTOR AND CHARACTER GENERATOR
OPTIONAL GENERATOR
CAMI
MEMORY MANAGEMENT
EXTERNAL VIDEO (numerical)
MEMO
IMAGE MEMORY
512 × 512 × 40 bits
VISU
COLOUR TABLETS
VIDEO
SYNC GENERATOR
N
A
EXT. SYNC
R V B
(*) trademark Digital Equipment Corporation
(**) trademark Centre National Etudes Télécommunications

Figure 1.

2.2. The ray casting module CRISTAL

The ray casting module CRISTAL is a special purpose architecture based on 16 microprocessor units each consisting of a NS 32032 processor and a NS 16081 floating point unit. All these units are driven by a same NS processor, called the supervisor processor. A drain, which is associated with the supervisor, receives all the pixel values generated by the microprocessor units. The drain sends these values to the image memory. By taking into account the z-values, the image memory eliminates the hidden parts of both polygons and ray traced objects.

The input for CRISTAL consists of a binary tree that is generated in the host. In the host that tree is computed from the general kernel tree (see section 4).

CRISTAL is an optional module; it is not available yet (delivery starts at the beginning of 1986). It is aimed to reduce the ray casting time with a factor 30 compared with a VAX 11/750. A hardware prototype has been realised with four M68000 processors.

2.3. Multimode applications

Z-buffer computations on polygons are not expensive and easily implemented in hardware. The CUBI 7 achieves a speed up factor of 1000 compared with a VAX 11/750. However, special effects - like shadowing, multiple reflections, refractions etc. - are not easily realized with polygons.

Ray tracing algorithms, on the contrary, yield extremely realistic pictures, but require excessive computation times. A scene consisting of 10 primitives, 2 light sources and containing transparency required one hour computation time to be ray traced. Hence, it is very interesting to be able to design objects and trajectories based on polygons quickly with fast response times and to compute the definitive images with a ray tracing algorithm.

Therefore, it is required that both the ray tracing and the z-buffer algorithm access the same database. To implement the database we have chosen a new language, called NIAL (a concatenation of NIL (a LISP concept) and APL). See the following section.

3. The NIAL system

NIAL is an interpreted programming language designed at the Queen's University, Kingston, Canada. Most importantly, NIAL contains:

- LISP primitives (and list trees)
- APL primitives
- nested arrays.

Scalars, vectors and even matrices may appear as atoms of a list. It may be accessed just like multi-dimensional array.

The NIAL interpreter is written in C and runs under

- VAX-VMS
- UNIX
- IBM PC.

NIAL programs may be linked with external subroutines written in C or FORTRAN. At the end of 1985 a NIAL compiler will be operational.

NIAL turned out to be very helpful in implementing the database residing in the host computer of the CUBI 7.

4. A superset of PHIGS in NIAL

PHIGS is FIXED, that is to say, PHIGS may be used to specify solid, but not articulated objects. For animation one needs transformation matrices that vary with time. Therefore our system contains:

- A KERNEL, which contains, on a certain moment, a PHIGS-like tree; this tree is obtained from a modeling system running on the host and may consist of polygons and CSG objects.
- The ray tracing process, which transforms the KERNEL data into a CSG binary tree.
- The z-buffer process, which transforms the KERNEL data into a set of polygons; this process evaluates dyadic operators on volumes, such as union, intersection, minus; moreover it generates polyhedrons for each elementary object - like cube, sphere, cylinder etc. - and it computes the polygonal intersections of polyhedrons.
- The trajectory process, which provides the main process - each time it is needed - with the values of the varying matrices.
- The main process, which processes the KERNEL data for each image again; processing of the KERNEL data results in a set of polygons with their associated matrices and a CSG tree; these results are sent to the CRISTAL module and the CUBI 7 system.

To represent the data four NIAL arrays are used:

- one array to store for each node (of the PHIGS-like tree) its name
- one array to store for each node the dyadic operator (such as union, intersection and difference) associated with it
- one array to store for each node its associated geometric operator (such as translation and rotation)
- one array to store for each node its surface parameters (such as shading law, color, fog).

The main process transforms the general kernel tree (consisting of polygon sets and CSG objects) such that it may be used as input for the CRISTAL module or for the facet generator and z-buffer algorithm. For the CRISTAL module the general kernel tree must be converted into a binary tree, for the facet generator it must be converted into a set of polygons.

5. Applications and conclusions

The data structure as it is described permits all kinds of animation, such as

- audiovisual broadcasting applications
- CAD-CAM and educational applications
- simulation.

It solves many 3D animation problems and can be built interactively in a modular way.

At the moment of writing of this paper the following has been implemented:

- the kernel
- the main process
- the z-buffer process for the union operator
- a sub-set of the trajectory process.

One of the interesting aspects is to have orthogonal relations between:

- the data structure in the kernel
- the trajectory process
- the two other processes
- man-machine interaction.

With this system we have designed a number of objects (see figures 2, 3, 4, and and 5). We hope to have the system fully implemented at the end of 1986.

Figure 2.

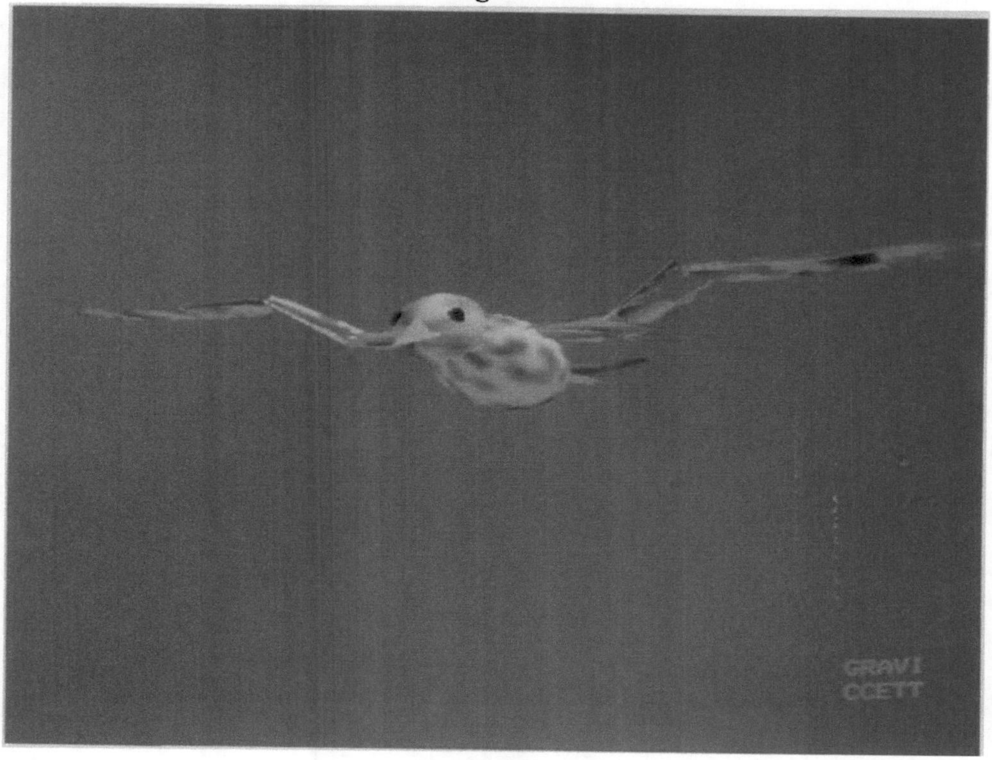

Figure 3.

Figure 4.

Figure 5.

Applications of the method of invariants in computer graphics

Kees van Overveld

Eindhoven University of Technology
Department of Mathematics and Computing Science
P.O.Box 513
5600 MB Eindhoven
The Netherlands

ABSTRACT

In order to evoke a discussion about possible future research themes for the Eindhoven Department of Mathematics and Computing Science, a small overview about the scientific background of the group is presented. We sketch the global framework of the method of invariants in deriving algorithms, and we apply this method to two well-known basic algorithms in computer graphics.

1. Introduction

At the Department of Mathematics and Computing Science of the Eindhoven University of Technology (EUT), up to now almost no experience in the field of computer graphics has been gained. We are intending, however, to change this situation drastically. To this aim, we are currently trying to get insight in the "hot topics" of the discipline, and, moreover, to isolate those topics which have a reasonable chance of success, given the background of our group.

To this respect, it is important to mention that Edsger W. Dijkstra used to be a professor at EUT. As is well known, he is an important propagator of formal methods in deriving fundamental algorithms [1,2]. The purpose of this talk therefore, is to present a few examples of formally derived algorithms as studied in our department, in order to give the participants of this workshop an idea of the kind of methods we apply, and which might be applied fruitfully in computer graphics. In return, we hope to receive some useful hints for future research, e.g. on (im)proving basic algorithms.

2. Some aspects of the method of invariants for deriving algorithms

When deriving a program within the framework of the method of invariants, the following points are of importance:

1) One starts by writing down a postcondition, which states precisely the desired relation between the relevant variables.

2) Statements are considered to be state transformers and as such they are formally derived in order to yield a sequence of variable states which eventually imply the postcondition in a logical way.

3) As each statement transforms the variable state, the actual variable state is written as an assertion between every two adjacent statements. (In trivial cases, however, this rule may be abandoned.)

4) A collection of state transformers, transforming the program's precondition (which should be chosen to be as weak as possible in order to make the program more widely applicable) into a state which logically implies the postcondition, has in a mathematical sense the status of a proven theorem and therefore needs no debugging.

A few small programming examples will elucidate the above features of the invariants method. First we present the usage of assertions. These are placed between curly brackets at the locations where they apply to.

{x < 2 <u>and</u> y = 3}	<---	the precondition of the program
‖[	<---	opening bracket
x := x + y ;	<---	statement 1
{x < 5 <u>and</u> y = 3}	<---	an intermediate state of the variables
y := y × x	<---	statement 2
]‖	<---	closing bracket
{x < 5 <u>and</u> y < 15}	<---	the postcondition of the program, comprising of ‖[statement 1 ; statement 2]‖

(Note that in order to fulfil the postcondition of the above program, given the same precondition, also the simpler algorithm consisting of only the one multiple assignment ‖[x,y := 0,0]‖ would have sufficed.)

The following example is less trivial; one can convince oneself that leaving out the intermediate assertions makes it a lot harder to understand the correctness of the algorithm.

{x = X <u>and</u> y = Y}
‖[
x := x + y ;
{x = X + Y <u>and</u> y = Y}
y := x - y ;
{x = X + Y <u>and</u> y = X}
x := x - y
]‖
{x = Y <u>and</u> y = X},

in other words: we have shown that the algorithm ‖[x:=x+y; y:=x-y; x:=x-y]‖ exchanges the contents of the integer variables x and y.

3. Concerning loops

The strength of algorithms that are to be implemented is, of course, the ability to repeat certain actions. In the language that we use to describe our algorithms, a repetition is denoted as follows:

{P}
do B → {P} S {P}
od
{P and not B}
{R}

In the above algorithm, B, P and R are boolean expressions which may or may not depend on the relevant variables. Their function is as follows. The boolean expression B is called the "guard" of the loop. As long as B is equivalent to "true", the statement S is executed, where S may be a compound statement. (Questions concerning the termination of loops will not be discussed in this talk.)

The boolean expression P, which should be true both before and after the execution of S, should be chosen such that R, i.e. the postcondition of the loop, is implied by P being true and B being false. P is usually called "the invariant" of the loop. A general method to formulate the invariant in case of a given postcondition is by replacing a well-chosen constant in the postcondition by a variable. This variable should be initiated such that the invariant holds upon entry of the loop. The expression of the guard, B, is easily seen to be the unequality of the values of the variable and the corresponding constant. Indeed: P being true and B being false then implies that the considered variable equals the value of the constant in the postcondition and therefore the truth of the postcondition.

We clarify this general strategy by a simple example. Suppose we have an array of N integers $X(i: 0 \leqslant i < N)$ where N is a given integer constant, greater than 0. Now we want to write a program which assigns to the integer r the value of the largest element of X. It goes without saying that we need a loop in order to fulfil this requirement. Conform the "rules" of the invariant method, we start by formulating the postcondition of the loop. It could be given by:

$$R:(\ \underline{A}\ i: 0 \leqslant i < N : X(i) \leqslant r)\ \underline{\text{and}}\ (\ \underline{E}\ i: 0 \leqslant i < N : X(i)=r)$$

The underlined A and E are the universal and existential quantifier, respectively. One way to formulate an invariant, corresponding to this postcondition, is by replacing the constant N at its first occurrence by a variable n where n is at least zero and at most N.

$$P(n):(\ \underline{A}\ i: 0 \leqslant i < n : X(i) \leqslant r)\ \underline{\text{and}}\ (\ \underline{E}\ i: 0 \leqslant i < N : X(i)=r)\ \underline{\text{and}}\ (0 \leqslant n \leqslant N)$$

It may be seen that the invariant holds for n=0 and r=X(0). Our initialisation therefore reads: n,r:= 0,X(0). The guard takes the form B: $n \neq N$. Since the termination of the loop occurs for n=N, we should find out by means of which statement(s) the invariant P holds with n replaced by n+1, so that the assignment n:=n+1 yields once more the validity of P. We do so by writing down P with all occurrences of n replaced by n+1 and subsequently reduce it to an expression in which we recognize the original P. The necessary reduction steps should be accomplished by appropriate statements in the program text under construction. As follows:

P(n+1):
(A i: 0 ⩽ i < n+1 : X(i) ⩽ r) and (E i: 0 ⩽ i < N : X(i)=r) and (0 ⩽ n+1 ⩽ N)

= {splitting the range 0 ⩽ i < n+1 into 0 ⩽ i < n and i=n}

(A i: 0 ⩽ i < n : X(i) ⩽ r) and (X(n) ⩽ r) and (E i: 0 ⩽ i < N : X(i)=r) and (0 ⩽ n+1 ⩽ N)

= {using that P(n) holds}

X(n) ⩽ r and n<N

At this instant, we "happen to remember" that the statement a := a max b is defined to have as a postcondition {b ⩽ a}. Since moreover n<N is guaranteed by the guard, we can conclude that, given P(n), executing the statement r := r max X(n) implies P(n+1). Our complete, annotated program therefore is:

```
|[n:int;
  n,r := 0,X(0) {here P(0) holds}
 ; do n ≠ N → {here we have P(n) and n ≠ N}
        r := r max X(n) {P(n+1) holds}
        ; n:=n+1 {P(n) holds}
 od {P(n) and n=N, hence R}
]|,
```

which is, of course, a not too unexpected result.

As to the choice of the invariant, we note that replacing the constant N at its second occurrence in the postcondition R instead of at the first occurrence would cause a much less attractive derivation. On the other hand, replacing the first 0 instead of the first N by a variable would yield a very similar algorithm.

4. Examples: two fundamental algorithms for computer graphics

The preceding two sections were intended to provide for at least a working knowledge of the invariants method for deriving algorithms, in order to appreciate the two examples from this section. The first example will be the formal derivation of a linear interpolation algorithm. As is well known, Bresenham [3], published in 1965 his algorithm which has been used throughout since. It is interesting to note (however not too surprisingly) that our algorithm turns out to be very similar to Bresenham's, be it that the initialisation is somewhat less involved.

Example 1:

"Generate the y-values of the points (x,y) in Z × Z which approximate best the straight line from (x_1 , y_1) to (x_2, y_2), assuming $x_2 \geqslant x_1$, $y_2 \geqslant y_1$ and ($x_2 - x_1$) $\geqslant$ ($y_2 - y_1$)".

We make this more precise by defining what we mean by "best approximation"; furthermore we demand that there are no "holes" between the interpolated points. We introduce as new variables Dx = ($x_2 - x_1$) and Dy = ($y_2 - y_1$). Then the formally stated problem reads:

|[x_1 , x_2, y_1 , y_2 :int;
y(x: $x_1 \leqslant x \leqslant x_2$): <u>array of</u> int;
    S;
{R:(<u>A</u> x: $x_1 \leqslant x \leqslant x_2$: | E(x) | is minimal) <u>and</u>
(<u>A</u> x: x_1 +1 $\leqslant x \leqslant x_2$: (y(x)-y(x-1)=0 <u>or</u> y(x)-y(x-1)=1))}
]|

The choice of our error term, E(x), is inspired by the equation of a straight line through two given points. Therefore, we define:

E(x)=(x - x_1)*Dy - Dx*(y(x) - y_1)

invariant: We construct the invariant by replacing all x_2 by n.

P(n):(<u>A</u> x: $x_1 \leqslant x \leqslant$ n: | E(x) | is minimal) <u>and</u>
    (<u>A</u> x: x_1 +1 $\leqslant$x $\leqslant$ n: (y(x)-y(x-1)=0 <u>or</u> y(x)-y(x-1)=1)<u>and</u> ($x_1 \leqslant n \leqslant x_2$)

init : n,y(x_1),E := x_1 , y_1 , 0 { P(x_1)}

guard : n< x_2

end : P(n) <u>and</u> n $\geqslant x_2$ <u>implies</u> R

note : We now derive the form of the repeatable statement.
Assume n< x_2, then:

{P(n) holds} P(n+1)=
| E(n+1) | is minimal <u>and</u> (y(n+1)-y(n)=0 <u>or</u> y(n+1)-y(n)=1)

case analysis :

{using the definition of E(n)} y(n+1)-y(n)=0: E(n+1)= E(n)+Dy

{using the definition of E(n)} y(n+1)-y(n)=1: E(n+1)= E(n)+Dy-Dx;

Using the fact that Dy $\leqslant$ Dx and some elementary algebra we find:
if E(n)< Dx/2 - Dy then | E(n)+Dy| < | E(n)+Dy-Dx|;

And similarly:
if E(n)> Dx/2 - Dy then | E(n)+Dy| > | E(n)+Dy-Dx|;

Now since we have to keep E(n+1) minimal, we learn from the above observations that the sign of E(n) - Dx/2 + Dy should be inspected in order to establish the value of y(n+1).

algorithm:

```
S = |[E,n: int;
n,y( x1 ),E := x1 , y1 ,0; {P( x1 )}
do n < x2 → {P(n)}
       if E - Dx/2 + Dy ≥0 → E,y(n+1):=E+ Dy -Dx,y(n)+1
       [] E - Dx/2 + Dy ≤ 0 → E,y(n+1):=E+ Dy,y(n)
       fi {P(n+1)}
       ; n:=n+1 {P(n)}
od {P(n) and n ≥ x2 implies R}
]|
```

In the above program, the symbol [] should be read as "else if" whereas the underlined fi-clause concludes the alternative guards for the if-statement. The introduction of a new variable, E', with E' = E - Dx/2 + Dy makes the algorithm somewhat more efficient.

Our second example concerns a circle-generation algorithm.

Example 2:

"Generate the y-values of the points (x,y) in $Z \times Z$ which approximate best the circle round (0,0) with radius r $\{r>0\}$, assuming $y>0$, $0 \leqslant x \leqslant x_2$ where $x_2 < r/\sqrt{2}$".

```
|[R, x2:int
y(x: 0 ≤ x ≤ x2): array of int;
     S;
{R:( A x: 0 ≤ x ≤ x2: | E(x) | is minimal) and ( A x :1 ≤ x ≤ x2: (y(x)-y(x-1)=0
or
y(x)-y(x-1)=-1))}
]|
```

Inspired by the equation for a circle round the origin with radius r, we define our error term:

$E(x) = x^2 + y^2(x) - r^2$

invariant :

P(n):(<u>A</u> x :0 ≤ x ≤ n: | E(x) | is minimal) <u>and</u>
(<u>A</u> x: 1 ≤ x ≤ n: (y(x)-y(x-1)=0 <u>or</u> y(x)-y(x-1)=-1)) <u>and</u> ($0 \leqslant n \leqslant x_2$)

init : n,y(0),E := 0, y_1 ,0 {P(n=0)}

guard: $n < x_2$

end : P(n) and $n \geqslant x_2$ implies R

note : assume $n < x_2$, then we have (using that P(n) holds):

P(n+1)= | E(n+1) | is minimal and (y(n+1)-y(n)=0 or y(n+1)-y(n)=-1)

case analysis:

{using the definition of E(n)} y(n+1)-y(n)=0: E(n+1)= E(n)+2n+1

and similarly

y(n+1)-y(n)=-1: E(n+1)= E(n)+2n+1-2y(n)+1 = E(n)+2(n-y(n)+1).

Using some elementary algebra we find:
if E(n) < y(n)-2n-3/2 then | E(n)+2n+1) | < | E(n)+2(n-y(n)+1) |;

and similarly:
if E(n) > y(n)-2n-3/2 then | E(n)+2n+1 | > | E(n)+2(n-y(n)+1) |

algorithm:

```
S = |[E,n: int;
      n,y(0),E := 0,R,0; {P(0) holds}
      do n <  x2 → {P(n) holds}
            if E-y(n)+2n+3/2 ⩾ 0 → E,y(n+1):=E+2(n-y(n)+1),y(n)-1
            [] E-y(n)+2n+3/2 ⩽ 0 → E,y(n+1):=E+2n+1,y(n)
            fi {P(n+1) holds}
            ; n:=n+1 {P(n) holds}
      od {P(n) and n ⩾  x2 implies R}
    ]|,
```

As with the algorithm of example 1, we can make this algorithm more efficient by introducing a variable E' where E' = E-y(n)+2n+3/2 in order to give the guards the very convenient form of E' ⩾ 0 and E' ⩽ 0, respectively. When doing so, we end up with an algorithm similar to that of Michener [4], based on Bresenham's methodoly. We stress the similarity between the circle algorithm and the straight line algorithm which essentially only differ in the definition of E.

4. Concluding remarks

In the preceding sections, we presented a small overview of the invariants method for deriving algorithms, together with a few examples taken from the field of computer graphics. We are very curious whether the method is applicable to less trivial problems in this field, such as the hidden surface or hidden line problems. In the stage of establishing our research subject, that we are in now, we are giving serious consideration to proceeding in this direction.

Acknowledgments

The author wishes to thank Rob Hoogerwoord of the Eindhoven University of Technology for his critical remarks during the preparation of the final version of this paper.

References

[1] Gries, D., 'The Science of Programming', Springer, New York, 1985.

[2] Dijkstra, E.W. and Feijen, W.H.J., 'Een methode van programmeren' (Dutch), Academic Service, The Hague, Holland, 1984.

[3] Bresenham, J.E., 'Algorithm for Computer Control of Digital Plotters', IBM Syst. J. 4(1)1965, pp 25-30.

[4] Foley, J.D. and Van Dam, A., 'Fundamentals of Interactive Computer Graphics', Adison-Wesley, Reading, 1982, pp 441-445.

Bibliography on quadtrees and related hierarchical data structures *

Hanan Samet

Computer Science Department
University of Maryland
College Park, Maryland 20742

ABSTRACT

This bibliography is an updated version of the one published in ACM Computing Surveys [214].

1. D.J. Abel, Comments on "detection of connectivity for regions represented by linear quadtrees", *Computers and Mathematics with Applications 10*, 2(1984), 167-170. [geometric property measurement]

2. D.J. Abel and J.L. Smith, A data structure and algorithm based on a linear key for a rectangle retrieval problem, *Computer Vision, Graphics, and Image Processing 24*, 1(October 1983), 1-13. [rectangles]

3. D.J. Abel and J.L. Smith, A simple approach to the nearest-neighbor problem, *The Australian Computer Journal 16*, 4(November 1984), 140-146. [point data]

4. D.J. Abel and J.L. Smith, A data structure and query algorithm for a database of areal entities, *The Australian Computer Journal 16*, 4(November 1984), 147-154. [region data]

5. N. Ahuja, On approaches to polygonal decomposition for hierarchical image representation, *Computer Vision, Graphics, and Image Processing 24*, 2(November 1983), 200-214. [region representation]

6. N. Ahuja and C. Nash, Octree representations of moving objects, *Computer Vision, Graphics, and Image Processing 26*, 2(May 1984), 207-216. [three-dimensional data]

* This work was supported in part by the National Science Foundation under Grant DCR-83-02118.

7. N. Alexandridis and A. Klinger, Picture decomposition, tree data-structures, and identifying directional symmetries as node combinations, *Computer Graphics, and Image Processing 8*, 1(August 1978), 43-77. [region representation]

8. V.V. Alexandrov and N.D. Grosky, Recursive approach to associative storage and search of information in data bases, *Proceedings of the Finnish-Soviet Symposium on Design and Application of Data Base Systems*, Turku, Finland, 1980, 271-284. [region representation]

9. V.V. Alexandrov, N.D. Grosky, and A.O. Polyakov, Recursive algorithms of data representation and processing, Academy of Sciences of the USSR, Leningrad Research Center, Leningrad, 1979. [region representation]

10. D.P. Anderson, Techniques for reducing pen plotting time, *ACM Transactions on Graphics 2*, 3(July 1983), 197-212. [computer graphics; point data]

11. F.P. Andresen, L.S. Davis, R.D. Eastman, and S. Kambhampati, Visual algorithms for autonomous navigation, *Proceedings of the International Conference on Robotics*, St. Louis, March 1985, 856-861. [three-dimensional data, path planning]

12. E. Artzy, G. Frieder, and G.T. Herman, The theory, design, implementation, and evaluation of a surface detection algorithm, *Computer Graphics and Image Processing 15*, 1(January 1981), 1-24. [three-dimensional data]

13. H.H. Atkinson, I. Gargantini, and T.R.S. Walsh, Counting regions, holes, and their nesting level in time proportional to their border, *Computer Vision, Graphics, and Image Processing 29*, 2(February 1985), 196-215. [geometric property measurement]

14. D. Avis, A survey of heuristics for the weighted matching problem, *Networks 13*, 4(1983), 475-493. [point data; Euclidean matching]

15. D.H. Ballard, Strip trees: A hierarchical representation for curves, *Communications of the ACM 24*, 5(May 1981), 310-321 (see also corrigendum, *Communications of the ACM 25*, 3(March 1982), 213). [line data]

16. R. Barera and A.M. Vazquez A hierarchical method for representing terrain relief, *Proceedings of the Pecora 9 Symposium on Spatial Information Technologies for Remote Sensing Today and Tomorrow*, Sioux Falls, South Dakota, October 1984, 87-92. [surface representation]

17. M.A. Bauer, Set operations in linear quadtrees, *Computer Vision, Graphics, and Image Processing 29*, 2(February 1985), 248-258. [region data]

18. S.B.M. Bell, B.M. Diaz, F. Holroyd, and M.J. Jackson, Spatially referenced methods of processing raster and vector data, *Image and Vision Computing 1*, 4(November 1983), 211-220. [region representation]

19. J.L. Bentley, A survey of techniques for fixed radius near neighbor searching, SLAC Report No. 186, Stanford Linear Accelerator Center, Stanford University, Stanford, CA, August 1975. [point data]

20. J.L. Bentley, Multidimensional binary search trees used for associative searching, *Communications of the ACM 18*, 9(September 1975), 509-517. [point data]

21. J.L. Bentley, Decomposable searching problems, *Information Processing Letters 8*, June 1979, 133-136. [point data]

22. J.L. Bentley, Multi-dimensional divide-and-conquer, *Communications of the ACM 23*, 4(April 1980), 214-229. [point data]

23. J.L. Bentley and J.H. Friedman, Data Structures for range searching, *ACM Computing Surveys 11*, 4(December 1979), 397-409. [point data]

24. J.L. Bentley and H.A. Maurer, A note on Euclidean near neighbor searching in the plane, *Information Processing Letters 8*, 3(March 1979), 133-136. [point data]

25. J.L. Bentley and H.A. Maurer, Efficient worst-case data structures for range searching, *Acta Informatica 13*, 2(1980), 155-168. [point data]

26. J.L. Bentley and J. Saxe, Decomposable searching problems I: static to dynamic transformations, *Journal of Algorithms 1*, (1980), 301-358. [point data]

27. J.L. Bentley and D.F. Stanat, Analysis of range searches in quad trees, *Information Processing Letters 3*, 6(July 1975), 170-173. [point data]

28. J.L. Bentley, D.F. Stanat, and E.H. Williams Jr., The complexity of fixed radius near neighbor searching, *Information Processing Letters 6*, December 1977, 209-212. [point data]

29. P.W. Besslich, Quadtree construction of binary images by dyadic array transformations, *Proceedings of the IEEE Conference on Pattern Recognition and Image Processing*, Las Vegas, 1982, 550-554. [hardware]

30. H. Blum, A transformation for extracting new descriptors of shape, in *Models for the Perception of Speech and Visual Form*, W. Wathen-Dunn, Ed., M.I.T. Press, Cambridge, MA, 1967, 362-380. [medial axis transforms]

31. A. Bolour, Optimality properties of multiple-key hashing functions, *Journal of the ACM 26*, 2(April 1979), 196-210. [point data]

32. R.A. Brooks and T. Lozano-Perez, A subdivision algorithm in configuration space for findpath with rotation, *Proceedings of the Seventh International Joint Conference on Artificial Intelligence*, Karlsruhe, West Germany, August 1983, 799-806. [three-dimensional data, path planning]

33. W.A. Burkhardt, Interpolation-based index maintenance, *BIT 23*, 3(1983), 274-294. [point data]

34. P.J. Burt, Tree and pyramid structures for coding hexagonally sampled binary images, *Computer Graphics and Image Processing 14*, 3(November 1980), 249-270. [pyramids]

35. P.J. Burt, T.H. Hong, and A. Rosenfeld, Segmentation and estimation of image region properties through cooperative hierarchical computation, *IEEE Transactions on Systems, Man, and Cybernetics 11*, 12(December 1981), 802-809. [pyramids]

36. F.W. Burton and J.G. Kollias, Comment on the explicit quadtree as a structure for computer graphics, *Computer Journal 26*, 2(May 1983), 188. [region representation]

37. F.W. Burton, V.J. Kollias, and J.G. Kollias, Expected and worst-case storage requirements for quadtrees, *Pattern Recognition Letters 3*, 2(March 1985), 131-135. [storage requirements]

38. F.W. Burton, J.G. Kollias, and N.A. Alexandridis, Implementation of the exponential pyramid data structure with application to determination of symmetries in pictures, *Computer Vision, Graphics, and Image Processing 25*, 2(February 1984), 218-225. [pyramids]

39. W. Burton, Representation of many-sided polygons and polygonal lines for rapid processing, *Communications of the ACM 20*, 3(March 1977), 166-171. [line data]

40. I. Carlbom, I. Chakravarty, and D. Vanderschel, A hierarchical data structure for representing the spatial decomposition of 3-D objects, *IEEE Computer Graphics and Applications 5*, 4(April 1985), 24-31. [three-dimensional data]

41. W.E. Carlson, An algorithm and data structure for 3D object synthesis using surface patch intersections, *Computer Graphics 16*, 3(July 1982), 255-264 (also *Proceedings of the SIGGRAPH'82 Conference*, Boston, July 1982). [surface representation]

42. C.H. Chien and J.K. Aggarwal, A normalized quadtree representation, *Computer Vision, Graphics, and Image Processing 26*, 3(June 1984), 331-346. [three-dimensional data]

43. E. Cohen, T. Lyche, and R. Riesenfeld, Discrete B-splines and subdivision techniques in computer-aided geometric design and computer graphics, *Computer Graphics and Image Processing 14*, 3(October 1980), 87-111. [computer graphics]

44. Y. Cohen, M.S. Landy, and M. Pavel, Hierarchical coding of binary images, *IEEE Transactions on Pattern Analysis and Machine Intelligence* 7, 3(May 1985), 284-298. [coding; approximation]

45. D. Comer, The Ubiquitous B-tree, *ACM Computing Surveys 11*, 2(June 1979), 121-137. [point data]

46. C.I. Connolly, Cumulative generation of octree models from range data, *Proceedings of the International Conference on Robotics*, Atlanta, March 1984, 25-32. [three-dimensional data]

47. B.G. Cook, The structural and algorithmic basis of a geographic data base, in *Proceedings of the First International Advanced Study Symposium on Topological Data Structures for Geographic Information Systems*, G. Dutton, Ed., Harvard Papers on Geographic Information Systems, 1978. [region representation]

48. E. Creutzburg, Complexities of quadtrees and the structure of pictures, Friedrich-Schiller University Technical Report N/81/74, Jena, East Germany, 1981. [storage requirements]

49. S.P. Dandamui and P.G. Sorenson, Performance of a modified k-tree, Department of Computational Science Report 84-10, University of Saskatchewan, Saskatoon, Canada, 1984. [point data]

50. S.P. Dandamui and P.G. Sorenson, Algorithms for the BD tree structure, Department of Computational Science Report 84-11, University of Saskatchewan, Saskatoon, Canada, 1984. [point data]

51. S.P. Dandamui and P.G. Sorenson, An empirical performance comparison of some variations of the k-d tree and BD tree, Department of Computational Science Report 84-13, University of Saskatchewan, Saskatoon, Canada, 1984. [point data]

52. E. Davis, Representing and acquiring geographic knowledge, Ph.D. dissertation, Department of Computer Science, Yale University, New Haven, Connecticut, 1984. [artificial intelligence; expert systems]

53. L.S. Davis and N. Roussopoulos, Approximate pattern matching in a pattern database system, *Information Systems 5*, 2(1980), 107-119. [image processing]

54. F. DeCoulon and U. Johnsen, Adaptive block schemes for source coding of black-and-white facsimile, *Electronics Letters 12*, 3(1976), 61-62 (see also erratum, *Electronics Letters 12*, 6(1976), 152). [coding; approximation]

55. L. DeFloriani, B. Falcidieno, G. Nagy, and C. Pienovi, Yet another method for triangulation and contouring for automated cartography. *Proceedings of the American Congress on Surveying and Mapping*, American Society of Photogrammetry, F.S. Cardwell, R. Black, and B.M. Cole, Eds., Hollywood, Florida, 1982, 101-110. [surface representation]

56. R.A. DeMillo, S.C. Eisenstat, and R.J. Lipton, Preserving average proximity in arrays, *Communications of the ACM 21*, 3(March 1978), 228-231. [point data]

57. D. Dobkin and R.J. Lipton, Some generalizations of binary search, *Proceedings of the Sixth SIGACT Symposium on Theory of Computing*, Seattle, April 1974, 310-316. [point data]

58. D. Dobkin and R.J. Lipton, Multidimensional searching problems, *SIAM Journal on Computing 5*, 2(June 1976), 181-186. [point data]

59. L.J. Doctor and J.G. Torborg, Display techniques for octree-encoded objects, *IEEE Computer Graphics and Applications 1*, 1(July 1981), 39-46. [region data]

60. L. Dorst and R.P.W. Duin, Spirograph theory: a framework for calculations on digitized straight lines, *IEEE Transactions on Pattern Analysis and Machine Intelligence 6*, 5(September 1984), 632-639. [line data; computer graphics; antialiasing]

61. L. Dorst and A.W.M. Smeulders, Discrete representation of straight lines, *IEEE Transactions on Pattern Analysis and Machine Intelligence 6*, 4(July 1984), 450-463. [line data; computer graphics; antialiasing]

62. R.O. Duda and P.E. Hart, *Pattern Classification and Scene Analysis*, Wiley Interscience, New York, 1973. [general]

63. C.R. Dyer, Computing the Euler number of an image from its quadtree, *Computer Graphics and Image Processing 13*, 3(July 1980), 270-276. [region data]

64. C.R. Dyer, A VLSI pyramid machine for parallel image processing, *Proceedings of the IEEE Conference on Pattern Recognition and Image Processing*, Dallas, 1981, 381-386. [hardware]

65. C.R. Dyer, The space efficiency of quadtrees, *Computer Graphics and Image Processing 19*, 4(August 1982), 335-348. [storage requirements]

66. C.R. Dyer, A. Rosenfeld, and H. Samet, Region representation: boundary codes from quadtrees, *Communications of the ACM 23*, 3(March 1980), 171-179. [region data]

67. C.M. Eastman, Representations for space planning, *Communications of the ACM 13*, 4(April 1970), 242-250. [region representation]

68. C.M. Eastman, Optimal bucket size for nearest neighbor searching in k-d trees, *Information Processing Letters 12*, 4(August 1981), 165-167. [point data]

69. C.M. Eastman and M. Zemankova, Partially specified nearest neighbor searches using k-d trees, *Information Processing Letters 15*, 2(September 1982), 53-56. [point data]

70. H. Edelsbrunner, Key-problems and key-methods in computational geometry, *Proceedings of the Symposium of Theoretical Aspects of Computer Science*, Paris, 1984, 1-13 (Lecture Notes in Computer Science 166, Springer-Verlag, New York, 1984). [general]

71. H. Edelsbrunner, L.J. Guibas, and J. Stolfi, Optimal point location in a monotone subdivision, to appear in *SIAM Journal on Computing*, 1984. [line data]

72. H. Edelsbrunner and J. van Leeuwen, Multidimensional data structures and algorithms: a bibliography, Institute for Information Processing Report F104, Technical University of Graz, Graz, Austria, January 1983. [general]

73. R. Fagin, J. Nievergelt, N. Pippenger, and H.R. Strong, Extendible hashing - a fast access method for dynamic files, *ACM Transactions on Database Systems 4*, 3(September 1979), 315-344. [point data]

74. O.D. Faugeras, M. Hebert, P. Mussi, and J.D. Boissonnat, Polyhedral approximation of 3-d objects without holes, *Computer Vision, Graphics, and Image Processing 25*, 2(February 1984), 169-183. [three-dimensional data]

75. O. D. Faugeras and J. Ponce, Prism trees: a hierarchical representation for 3-d objects, *Proceedings of the Eighth International Joint Conference on Artificial Intelligence*, Karlsruhe, West Germany, August 1983, 982-988. [surface representation]

76. B. Faverjon, Obstacle avoidance using an octree in the configuration space of a manipulator, *Proceedings of the International Conference on Robotics*, Atlanta, March 1984, 504-512. [three-dimensional data; path planning]

77. R.A. Finkel and J.L. Bentley, Quad trees: a data structure for retrieval on composite keys, *Acta Informatica 4*, 1(1974), 1-9. [point data]

78. P. Flajolet and C. Puech, Tree structures for partial match retrieval, *Proceedings of the Twenty-fourth Annual IEEE Symposium on the Foundations of Computer Science*, Tucson, November 1983, 282-288. [point data]

79. E. Fredkin, Trie memory, *Communications of the ACM 3*, 9(September 1960), 490-499. [point data]

80. H. Freeman, Computer processing of line-drawing images, *ACM Computing Surveys 6*, 1(March 1974), 57-97. [line data; region representation]

81. J.H. Friedman, F. Baskett, and L.J. Shustek, An algorithm for finding nearest neighbors, *IEEE Transactions on Computers 24*, 10(October 1975), 1000-1006. [point data]

82. J.H. Friedman, J.L. Bentley, and R.A. Finkel, An algorithm for finding best matches in logarithmic expected time, *ACM Transactions on Mathematical Software 3*, 3(September 1977), 209-226. [point data]

83. I. Gargantini, An effective way to represent quadtrees, *Communications of the ACM 25*, 12(December 1982), 905-910. [region representation]

84. I. Gargantini, Linear octtrees for fast processing of three dimensional objects, *Computer Graphics and Image Processing 20*, 4(December 1982), 365-374. [three-dimensional data]

85. I. Gargantini, Detection of connectivity for regions represented by linear quadtrees, *Computers and Mathematics with Applications 8*, 4(1982), 319-327. [geometric property measurement]

86. I. Gargantini, Translation, rotation, and superposition of linear quadtrees, *International Journal of Man-Machine Studies 18*, 3(March 1983), 253-263. [computer graphics]

87. P.C. Gaston and T. Lozano-Perez, Tactile recognition and localization using object models: the case of polyhedra on a plane, *IEEE Transactions on Pattern Analysis and Machine Intelligence 6*, 3(May 1984), 257-266. [three-dimensional data]

88. L. Gibson and D. Lucas, Vectorization of raster images using hierarchical methods, *Computer Graphics and Image Processing 20*, 1(September 1982), 82-89. [region representation]

89. R. Gillespie and W.A. Davis, Tree data structures for graphics and image processing, *Proceedings of the Seventh Conference of the Canadian Man-Computer Communications Society*, Waterloo, Canada, June 1981, 155-161. [region representation]

90. A.S. Glassner, Space subdivision for fast ray tracing, *IEEE Computer Graphics and Applications 4*, 10(October 1984), 15-22. [ray tracing; computer graphics]

91. D. Gomez and A. Guzman, Digital model for three-dimensional surface representation, *Geo-Processing*, 1(1979), 53-70. [surface representation]

92. W.I. Grosky, M. Li, and R. Jain, A bottom-up approach to constructing quadtrees from binary arrays, Computer Science Report CSC-81-011, Wayne State University, Detroit, MI, 1981. [region data]

93. W.I. Grosky and R. Jain, }iOptimal quadtrees for image segments, *IEEE Transactions on Pattern Analysis and Machine Intelligence* 5, 1(January 1983), 77-83. [storage requirements]

94. B. Grunbaum and G.C. Shephard, The eighty-one types of isohedral tilings in the plane, *Proceedings of the Cambridge Philosophical Society 82*, (1977), 177-196. [region representation]

95. H. Guting and H.P. Kriegel, Multidimensional B-tree: an efficient dynamic file structure for exact match queries, *Informatik Fachberichte 33*, (1980), 375-388. [point data]

96. H. Guting and H.P. Kriegel, Dynamic k-dimensional multiway search under time-varying access frequencies, Lecture Notes in Computer Science 104, (1981), 135-145. [point data]

97. R.M. Haralick, Some neighborhood operations, in *Real Time/Parallel Computing Image Analysis*, M. Onoe, K. Preston, and A. Rosenfeld, Eds., Plenum Press, New York, NY, 1981. [geometric property measurement]

98. D.M. Hardas and S.N. Srihari, Progressive refinement of 3-d images using coded binary trees: algorithms and architecture, *IEEE Transactions on Pattern Analysis and Machine Intelligence* 6, 6(November 1984), 748-757. [coding; approximation]

99. T.C. Henderson and E. Triendl, Storing feature descriptions as 2-d trees, *Proceedings of Pattern Recognition and Image Processing 82*, Las Vegas, Nevada, 1982, 555-556. [image processing]

100. K. Hinrichs and J. Nievergelt, The Grid File: a data structure to support proximity queries on spatial objects, Report 54, Institut fur Informatik, ETH, Zurich, July 1983. [point data]

101. D.S. Hirschberg, On the complexity of searching a set of vectors, *SIAM Journal on Computing* 9, 1(February 1980), 126-129. [line data]

102. C.A.R. Hoare, Notes on data structuring, in *Structured Programming*, O.J. Dahl, E.W. Dijkstra, and C.A.R. Hoare, Eds., Academic Press, London, 1972, 154. [general]

103. S.L. Horowitz and T. Pavlidis, Picture segmentation by a tree traversal algorithm, *Journal of the ACM 23*, 2(April 1976), 368-388. [image processing]

104. M. Hoshi and T. Yuba, A counter example to a monotonicity property of k-d trees, *Information Processing Letters 15*, 4(October 1982), 169-173. [point data]

105. D.A. Huffman, A method for the construction of minimum-redundancy codes, *Proceedings of the IRE 40*, 9(September 1952), 1098-1101. [coding]

106. G.M. Hunter, Efficient computation and data structures for graphics, Ph.D. dissertation, Department of Electrical Engineering and Computer Science, Princeton University, Princeton, NJ, 1978. [region representation; computer graphics]

107. G.M. Hunter and K. Steiglitz, Operations on images using quad trees, *IEEE Transactions on Pattern Analysis and Machine Intelligence 1*, 2(April 1979), 145-153. [region representation; computer graphics]

108. G.M. Hunter and K. Steiglitz, Linear transformation of pictures represented by quad trees, *Computer Graphics and Image Processing 10*, 3(July 1979), 289-296. [region representation; computer graphics]

109. H.A.H. Ibrahim, The connected component labeling algorithm on the NON-VON supercomputer, *Proceedings of the Workshop on Computer Vision: Representation and Control*, Annapolis, April 1984, 37-45. [hardware; geometric property measurement]

110. T. Ichikawa, A pyramidal representation of images and its feature extraction facility, *IEEE Transactions on Pattern Analysis and Machine Intelligence 3*, 3(May 1981), 257-264. [region representation]

111. M.G.B. Ismail and R. Steele, Adaptive pel location coding for bilevel facsimile signals, *Electronics Letters 16*, 10(May 8,1980), 361-363. [coding; approximation]

112. C.L. Jackins and S.L. Tanimoto, Oct-trees and their use in representing three-dimensional objects, *Computer Graphics and Image Processing 14*, 3(November 1980), 249-270. [three-dimensional data]

113. C. Jackins and S.L. Tanimoto, Quad-trees, oct-trees, and k-trees - a generalized approach to recursive decomposition of Euclidean space, *IEEE Transactions on Pattern Analysis and Machine Intelligence 5*, 5(September 1983), 533-539. [region representation]

114. L. Jones and S.S. Iyengar, Space and time efficient virtual quadtrees, *IEEE Transactions on Pattern Analysis and Machine Intelligence 6*, 2(March 1984), 244-247. [region representation]

115. E. Kawaguchi and T. Endo, On a method of binary picture representation and its application to data compression, *IEEE Transactions on Pattern Analysis and Machine Intelligence 2*, 1(January 1980), 27-35. [region representation]

116. E. Kawaguchi, T. Endo, and J. Matsunaga, Depth-first expression viewed from digital picture processing, *IEEE Transactions on Pattern Analysis and Machine Intelligence 5*, 4(July 1983), 373-384. [region representation]

117. E. Kawaguchi, T. Endo, and M. Yokota, DF-expression of binary-valued picture and its relation to other pyramidal representations, *Proceedings of the Fifth International Conference on Pattern Recognition*, Miami Beach, December 1980, 822-827. [region representation]

118. G. Kedem, The Quad-CIF tree: a data structure for hierarchical on-line algorithms, TR 91, Computer Science Department, The University of Rochester, Rochester, New York, September 1981. [rectangles]

119. M.D. Kelly, Edge detection in pictures by computer using planning, *Machine Intelligence* 6(1971), 397-409. [image processing]

120. D. Kirkpatrick, Optimal search in planar subdivisions, *SIAM Journal on Computing 12*, 1(February 1983), 28-35. [line data]

121. A. Klinger, Patterns and Search Statistics, in *Optimizing Methods in Statistics*, J.S. Rustagi, Ed., Academic Press, New York, 1971, 303-337. [region representation]

122. A. Klinger and C.R. Dyer, Experiments in picture representation using regular decomposition, *Computer Graphics and Image Processing 5*, 1(March 1976), 68-105. [region representation]

123. A. Klinger and M.L. Rhodes, Organization and access of image data by areas, *IEEE Transactions on Pattern Analysis and Machine Intelligence 1*, 1(January 1979), 50-60. [region representation]

124. G.D. Knott, Expandable open addressing hash table storage and retrieval, *Proceedings of SIGFIDET Workshop on Data Description, Access, and Control*, San Diego, November 1971, 187-206. [point data]

125. K. Knowlton, Progressive transmission of grey-scale and binary pictures by simple, efficient, and lossless encoding schemes, *Proceedings of the IEEE 68*, 7(July 1980), 885-896. [coding; approximation]

126. D.E. Knuth, *The Art of Computer Programming*, vol. 3, *Sorting and Searching*, Addison-Wesley, Reading, MA, 1973. [general]

127. P. Koistinen, M. Tamminen, and H. Samet, Viewing solid models by bintree conversion, *Proceedings of the EUROGRAPHICS'85 Conference*, Nice, September 1985. [CSG; three-dimensional data]

128. T.L. Kunii, T. Satoh, and K. Yamaguchi, Generation of topological boundary representations from octree encoding, *IEEE Computer Graphics and Applications 5*, 3(March 1985), 29-38. [three-dimensional data]

129. J.P. Lauzon, D.M. Mark, L. Kikuchi, and J.A. Guevara, Two-dimensional run-encoding for quadtree representation, *Computer Vision, Graphics, and Image Processing 30*, 1(April 1985), 56-69. [region representation]

130. D.T. Lee and B.J. Shacter, Two algorithms for constructing a Delaunay triangulation, *International Journal of Computer and Information Sciences 9*, 3(June 1980), 219-242. [point data]

131. D.T. Lee and C.K. Wong, Worst-case analysis for region and partial region searches in multidimensional binary search trees and quad trees, *Acta Informatica 9*, 1(1977), 23-29. [point data]

132. D.T. Lee and C.K. Wong, Quintary trees: a file structure for multidimensional database systems, *ACM Transactions on Database Systems 5*, 4(September 1980), 339-353. [point data]

133. P. Letelier, Transmission d'images à bas débit pour un système de communication téléphonique adapte aux sourds, Thèse de docteur-ingénieur, Université de Paris-Sud, Paris, September 1983. [region representation]

134. M. Li, W.I. Grosky, and R. Jain, Normalized quadtrees with respect to translations, *Computer Graphics and Image Processing 20*, 1(September 1982), 72-81. [storage requirements]

135. J. Linn, General methods for parallel searching, Technical Report 81, Digital Systems Laboratory, Stanford University, Stanford, CA, May 1973. [point data]

136. R.J. Lipton and R.E. Tarjan, Application of a planar separator theorem, *Proceedings of the Eighteenth Annual IEEE Symposium on the Foundations of Computer Science*, Providence, October 1977, 162-170. [point data]

137. W. Litwin, Linear hashing: a new tool for file and table addressing, *Proceedings of the Sixth International Conference on Very Large Data Bases*, Montreal, October 1980, 212-223. [point data]

138. T. Lozano-Perez, Automatic planning of manipulator transfer movements, *IEEE Transactions on Systems, Man, and Cybernetics 11*, 10(October 1981), 681-698. [three-dimensional data; path planning]

139. G. Lueker, A data structure for orthogonal range queries, *Proceedings 19th Symposium on Foundations of Computer Science*, IEEE, October 1978, 28-34. [point data]

140. V.Y. Lum, Multi-attribute retrieval with combined indexes, *Communications of the ACM 13*, 11(November 1970), 660-665. [point data]

141. R. Lumia, L.Shapiro, and O. Zuniga, A new connected components algorithm for virtual memory computers, *Computer Vision, Graphics, and Image Processing 22*, 2(May 1983), 287-300. [geometric property measurement]

142. R. Lumia, A new three-dimensional connected components algorithm, *Computer Vision, Graphics, and Image Processing 23*, 2(August 1983), 207-217. [geometric property measurement]

143. E.M. McCreight, Priority search trees, *SIAM Journal on Computing 14*, 2(May 1985), 257-276. [rectangles]

144. D.M. McKeown Jr. and J.L. Denlinger, Map-guided feature extraction from aerial imagery, *Proceedings of the Workshop on Computer Vision: Representation and Control*, Annapolis, April 1984, 205-213. [image processing]

145. D.M. Mark and D.J. Abel, Linear quadtrees from vector representations of polygons, *IEEE Transactions on Pattern Analysis and Machine Intelligence 7*, 3(May 1984), 344-349. [region data]

146. J.J. Martin, Organization of geographical data with quad trees and least square approximation, *Proceedings of the IEEE Conference on Pattern Recognition and Image Procesbmg*, Las Vegas, 1982, 458-463. [line data]

147. T. Matsuyama, L.V. Hao, and M. Nagao, A file organization for geographic information systems based on spatial proximity, *Computer Vision, Graphics, and Image Processing 26*, 3(June 1984), 303-318. [region data]

148. D. Meagher, Geometric modeling using octree encoding, *Computer Graphics and Image Processing 19*, 2(June 1982), 129-147. [three-dimensional data]

149. D. Meagher, The Solids engine: a processor for interactive solid modeling, *Proceedings of the NICOGRAPH '84 Conference*, Tokyo, November 1984. [three-dimensional data]

150. K. Mehlhorn, *Multi-dimensional Searching and Computational Geoemtry*, Springer-Verlag, Berlin, 1984. [point data]

151. T.H. Merrett, Multidimensional paging for efficient database querying, *Proceedings of the International Conference on Management of Data*, Milan, June 1978, 277-289. [point data]

152. T.H. Merrett and E.J. Otoo, Dynamic multipaging: a storage structure for large shared data banks, in *Improving Database Usability and Responsiveness*, P. Scheuermann, Ed., Academic Press, New York, 1982, 237-254. [point data]

153. R.D. Merrill, Representations of contours and regions for efficient computer search, *Communications of the ACM 16*, 2(February 1973), 69-82. [line data]

154. D.J. Milford and P.C. Willis, Quad encoded display, *IEE Proceedings 131*, E3(May 1984), 70-75. [hardware]

155. G.M. Morton, A computer oriented geodetic data base and a new technique in file sequencing, IBM Ltd., Ottawa, Canada, 1966. [region representation]

156. S.P. Mudur and P.A. Koparkar, Interval methods for processing geometric objects, *IEEE Computer Graphics and Applications 4*, 2(February 1984), 7-17. [general]

157. G. Nagy and S. Wagle, Geographic data processing, *ACM Computing Surveys 11*, 2(June 1979), 139-181. [line data]

158. J. Nievergelt, H. Hinterberger, and K.C. Sevcik, The Grid File: an adaptable, symmetric multikey file structure, *ACM Transactions on Database Systems 9*, 1(March 1984), 38-71. [point data]

159. J. Nievergelt and F.P. Preparata, Plane-sweep algorithms for intersecting geometric figures, *Communications of the ACM 25*, 10(October 1982), 739-746. [line data]

160. N.J. Nilsson, A mobile automaton: an application of artificial intelligence techniques, *Proceedings of the First International Joint Conference on Artificial Intelligence*, Washington D.C., 1969, 509-520. [artificial intelligence]

161. M.A. Oliver, Two display algorithms for octrees, in *Proceedings of the EUROGRAPHICS'84 Conference*, K. Bo and H.A. Tucker, Eds., North-Holland, 1984, 251-264. [three-dimensional data]

162. M.A. Oliver, T.R. King, and N.E. Wiseman, Quadtree scan conversion, in *Proceedings of the EUROGRAPHICS'84 Conference*, K. Bo and H.A. Tucker, Eds., North-Holland, 1984, 265-276. [region data]

163. M.A. Oliver and N.E. Wiseman, Operations on quadtree-encoded images, *Computer Journal 26*, 1(February 1983), 83-91. [region representation]

164. M.A. Oliver and N.E. Wiseman, Operations on quadtree leaves and related image areas, *Computer Journal 26*, 4(November 1983), 375-380. [region representation]

165. J.O. Omolayole and A. Klinger, A hierarchical data structure scheme for storing pictures, in *Pictorial Information Systems*, S.K. Chang and K.S. Fu, Eds., Springer-Verlag, 1980. [region representation]

166. J.A. Orenstein, Multidimensional tries used for associative searching, *Information Processing Letters 14*, 4(June 1982), 150-157. [point data]

167. J.A. Orenstein, A dynamic hash file for random and sequential accessing, *Proceedings of the Sixth International Conference on Very Large Data Bases*, Florence, October 1983, 132-141. [point data]

168. J.A. Orenstein and T.H. Merrett, A class of data structures for associative searching, *Proceedings of the Third ACM SIGACT-SIGMOD Symposium on Principles of Database Systems*, Waterloo, April 1984, 181-190. [point data]

169. J. O'Rourke, Dynamically quantized spaces for focusing the Hough Transform, *Proceedings of the Sixth International Joint Conference on Artificial Intelligence*, Vancouver, August 1981, 737-739. [point data]

170. J. O'Rourke and K.R. Sloan Jr., Dynamic quantization: two adaptive data structures for multidimensional squares, *IEEE Transactions on Pattern Analysis and Machine Intelligence 6*, 3(May 1984), 266-280. [point data]

171. T. Ottmann and D. Wood, 1-2 brother trees or AVL trees revisited, *The Computer Journal 23*, 3(August 1980), 248-255. [point data]

172. M. Ouksel and P. Scheuermann, Storage mappings for multidimensional linear dynamic hashing, *Proceedings of the Second ACM SIGACT-SIGMOD Symposium on Principles of Database Systems*, Atlanta, March 1983, 90-105. [point data]

173. M.H. Overmars, *The Design of Dynamic Data Structures*, Lecture Notes in Computer Science 156, Springer-Verlag, New York, 1983. [point data]

174. M.H. Overmars and J. van Leeuwen, Dynamic multi-dimensional data structures based on quad- and k-d trees, *Acta Informatica 17*, 3(1982), 267-285. [point data]

175. C.M. Park and A. Rosenfeld, Connectivity and genus in three dimensions, Computer Science TR-156, University of Maryland, College Park, MD, May 1971. [geometric property measurement]

176. F. Peters, An algorithm for transformations of pictures represented by quadtrees, to appear in *Computer Vision, Graphics, and Image Processing* (also Department of Mathematics and Computing Science, Eindhoven University of Technology, Eindhoven, The Netherlands, 1984). [region representation; computer graphics]

177. T. Peucker, A theory of the cartographic line, *International Yearbook of Cartography 16*, 1976, 134-143. [line data]

178. D.J. Peuquet, Raster processing: an alternative approach to automated cartographic data handling, *American Cartographer 6* 2(April 1979), 129-139. [region data]

179. D.J. Peuquet, A hybrid data structure for the storage and manipulation of very large spatial data sets, *Computer Vision, Graphics, and Image Processing 24*, 1(October 1983), 14-27. [region data]

180. J.L. Pfaltz and A. Rosenfeld, Computer representation of planar regions by their skeletons, *Communications of the ACM 10*, 2(February 1967), 119-122. [medial axis transforms]

181. M. Pietikainen, A. Rosenfeld, and I. Walter, Split-and-link algorithms for image segmentation, *Pattern Recognition 15*, 4(1982), 287-298. [pyramids]

182. C. Puech and H. Yahia, Quadtrees, octrees, hyperoctrees: a unified analytical approach to tree data structures used in graphics, geometric modeling, and image processing, *Proceedings of the Symposium on Computational Geometry*, Baltimore, June 1985, 272-280. [region data]

183. V.V. Raghvan and C.T. Yu, A note on a multidimensional searching problem, *Information Processing Letters 6*, 4(August 1977), 133-135. [point data]

184. V. Raman and S.S. Iyengar, Properties and applications of forests of quadtrees for pictorial data representation, *BIT 23*, 4(1983), 472-486. [region data]

185. S. Ranade, Use of quadtrees for edge enhancement, *IEEE Transactions on Systems, Man, and Cybernetics 11*, 5(May 1981), 370-373. [image processing]

186. S. Ranade, A. Rosenfeld, and J.M.S. Prewitt, Use of quadtrees for image segmentation, Computer Science TR-878, University of Maryland, College Park, MD, February 1980. [image processing]

187. S. Ranade, A. Rosenfeld, and H. Samet, Shape approximation using quadtrees, *Pattern Recognition 15*, 1(1982), 31-40. [image processing]

188. S. Ranade and M. Shneier, Using quadtrees to smooth images, *IEEE Transactions on Systems, Man, and Cybernetics 11*, 5(May 1981), 373-376. [image processing]

189. D.R. Reddy and S. Rubin, Representation of three-dimensional objects, CMU-CS-78-113, Computer Science Department, Carnegie-Mellon University, Pittsburgh, April 1978. [three-dimensional data]

190. E.M. Reingold and R.E. Tarjan, On the greedy heuristic for complete matching, *SIAM Journal on Computing 10*, 4(November 1981), 676-681. [point data; Euclidean matching]

191. A.A.G. Requicha, Representations of rigid solids: theory, methods, and systems, *ACM Computing Surveys 12*, 4(December 1980), 437-464. [three-dimensional data]

192. W.C. Rheinboldt and C.K. Mesztenyi, On a data structure for adaptive finite element mesh refinements, *ACM Transactions on Mathematical Software 6*, 2(June 1980), 166-187. [numerical analysis]

193. E.M. Riseman and M.A. Arbib, Computational techniques in the visual segmentation of static scenes, *Computer Graphics and Image Processing 6*, 3(June 1977), 221-276. [image processing]

194. J.T. Robinson, The k-d-B-tree: a search structure for large multidimensional dynamic indexes, *Proceedings of the SIGMOD Conference*, Ann Arbor, Michigan, April 1981, 10-18. [point data]

195. J.B. Rosenberg, Geographical data structures compared: a study of data structures supporting region queries, *IEEE Transactions on Computer-Aided Design 4*, 1(January 1985), 53-67. [rectangles]

196. A. Rosenfeld, Ed., *Multiresolution Image Processing and Analysis*, Springer-Verlag, Berlin, 1983. [general]

197. Rosenfeld, A., Picture processing 1984, *Computer Vision, Graphics, and Image Processing 26*, 3(June 1984), 347-384. [general]

198. A. Rosenfeld and A.C. Kak, *Digital Picture Processing*, Second Edition, Academic Press, New York, 1982. [general]

199. A. Rosenfeld and J.L. Pfaltz, Sequential operations in digital image processing, *Journal of the ACM 13*, 4(October 1966), 471-494. [image processing]

200. A. Rosenfeld, H. Samet, C. Shaffer, and R.E. Webber, Application of hierarchical data structures to geographical information systems, Computer Science TR-1197, University of Maryland, College Park, MD, June 1982. [geographic information systems]

201. A. Rosenfeld, H. Samet, C. Shaffer, and R.E. Webber, Application of hierarchical data structures to geographical information systems phase II, Computer Science TR 1327, University of Maryland, College Park, MD, September 1983. [geographic information systems]

202. S.D. Roth, Ray casting for modeling solids, *Computer Graphics and Image Processing 18*, 2(February 1982), 109-144. [computer graphics]

203. D. Rutovitz, Data structures for operations on digital images, in *Pictorial Pattern Recognition*, G.C. Cheng et al., Eds., Thompson Book Co., Washington D.C., 1968, 105-133. [region representation]

204. H. Samet, Region representation: quadtrees from boundary codes, *Communications of the ACM 23*, 3(March 1980), 163-170. [region data]

205. H. Samet, Region representation: quadtrees from binary arrays, *Computer Graphics and Image Processing 13*, 1(May 1980), 88-93. [region data]

206. H. Samet, Deletion in two-dimensional quad trees, *Communications of the ACM 23*, 12(December 1980), 703-710. [point data]

207. H. Samet, An algorithm for converting rasters to quadtrees, *IEEE Transactions on Pattern Analysis and Machine Intelligence 3*, 1(January 1981), 93-95. [region data]

208. H. Samet, Connected component labeling using quadtrees, *Journal of the ACM 28*, 3(July 1981), 487-501. [geometric property measurement]

209. H. Samet, Computing perimeters of images represented by quadtrees, *IEEE Transactions on Pattern Analysis and Machine Intelligence 3*, 6(November 1981), 683-687. [geometric property measurement]

210. H. Samet, Neighbor finding techniques for images represented by quadtrees, *Computer Graphics and Image Processing 18*, 1(January 1982), 37-57. [region data]

211. H. Samet, Distance transform for images represented by quadtrees, *IEEE Transactions on Pattern Analysis and Machine Intelligence 4*, 3(May 1982), 298-303. [medial axis transforms]

212. H. Samet, A quadtree medial axis transform, *Communications of the ACM 26*, 9(September 1983), 680-693 (see also corrigendum, *Communications of the ACM 27*, 2(February 1984), 151). [medial axis transforms]

213. H. Samet, Algorithms for the conversion of quadtrees to rasters, *Computer Vision, Graphics, and Image Processing 26*, 1(April 1984), 1-16. [region data]

214. H. Samet, The quadtree and related hierarchical data structures, *ACM Computing Surveys 16*, 2(June 1984), 187-260. [general]

215. H. Samet, A top-down quadtree traversal algorithm, *IEEE Transactions on Pattern Analysis and Machine Intelligence* 7, 1 (January 1985), 94-98 (also University of Maryland Computer Science TR-1237). [region data]

216. H. Samet, Reconstruction of quadtrees from quadtree medial axis transforms, *Computer Vision, Graphics, and Image Processing 29*, 3(March 1985), 311-328 (also University of Maryland Computer Science TR-1224). [medial axis transforms]

217. H. Samet, Data structures for quadtree approximation and compression, *Communications of the ACM 28*, 9(September 1985), 973-993 (also University of Maryland Computer Science TR-1209). [coding; approximation]

218. H. Samet and A. Rosenfeld, Quadtree structures for image processing, *Proceedings of the Fifth International Conference on Pattern Recognition*, Miami Beach, December 1980, 815-818. [region data]

219. H. Samet, A. Rosenfeld, C. Shaffer, and R.E. Webber, Quadtree region representation in cartography: experimental results, *IEEE Transactions on Systems, Man, and Cybernetics 13*, 6(November/December 1983), pp. 1148-1154. [geographic information systems]

220. H. Samet, A. Rosenfeld, C. Shaffer, and R.E. Webber, A geographic information system using quadtrees, *Pattern Recognition 17*, 6(November/December 1984), 647-656. [geographic information systems]

221. H. Samet, A. Rosenfeld, C.A. Shaffer, R.C. Nelson, and Y.G. Huang, Application of hierarchical data structures to geographical information systems Phase III, Computer Science TR 1457, University of Maryland, College Park, MD, November 1984. [geographic information systems]

222. H. Samet and C.A. Shaffer, A model for the analysis of neighbor finding in pointer-based quadtrees, *IEEE Transactions on Pattern Analysis and Machine Intelligence* 7, 6(November 1985) (also University of Maryland Computer Science TR-1432). [region data]

223. H. Samet, C.A. Shaffer, and R.E. Webber, The segment quadtree: a linear quadtree-based representation for linear features, *Proceedings of Computer Vision and Pattern Recognition 85*, San Francisco, June 1985, 385-389. [line data]

224. H. Samet and M. Tamminen, Efficient component labeling of images of arbitrary dimension, Computer Science TR-1480, University of Maryland, College Park, MD, February 1985 (subsumes TR-1420). [geometric property measurement]

225. H. Samet and M. Tamminen, Computing geometric properties of images represented by linear quadtrees, *IEEE Transactions on Pattern Analysis and Machine Intelligence* 7, 2(March 1985), 229-240 (also University of Maryland Computer Science TR 1359). [geometric property measurement]

226. H. Samet and M. Tamminen, Bintrees, CSG trees, and time, *Computer Graphics 19*, 3(July 1985), pp. 121-130 (also *Proceedings of the SIGGRAPH'85 Conference*, San Francisco, July 1985 and University of Maryland Computer Science TR-1472). [three-dimensional data]

227. H. Samet and R.E. Webber, On encoding boundaries with quadtrees, Computer Science TR-1162, University of Maryland, College Park, MD, February 1982. [line data]

228. H. Samet and R. E. Webber, Using quadtrees to represent polygonal maps, *Proceedings of Computer Vision and Pattern Recognition 83*, Washington, DC, June 1983, 127-132. [line data]

229. H. Samet and R.E. Webber, On encoding boundaries with quadtrees, *IEEE Transactions on Pattern Analysis and Machine Intelligence 6*, 3(May 1984), 365-369. [line data]

230. H. Samet and R.E. Webber, Storing a collection of polygons using quadtrees, to appear in *ACM Transactions on Graphics* (also University of Maryland Computer Science TR-1372). [line data]

231. J.B. Saxe, On the number of range queries in k-space, *Discrete Applied Math 1*, 3(1979), 217-225. [point data]

232. D.S. Scott and S.S. Iyengar, A new data structure for efficient storing of images, *Pattern Recognition Letters 3*, 3(May 1985), 211-214. [region representation]

233. M.I. Shamos, Computational geometry, Ph.D. dissertation, Department of Computer Science, Yale University, New Haven, Connecticut, 1978. [point data]

234. M.I. Shamos and D. Hoey, Closest-point problems, *Proceedings of the Sixteenth Annual IEEE Symposium on the Foundations of Computer Science*, Berkeley, October 1975, 151-162. [point data]

235. M. Shneier, Path-length distances for quadtrees, *Information Sciences 23*, 1(February 1981), 49-67. [region data]

236. M. Shneier, Calculations of geometric properties using quadtrees, *Computer Graphics and Image Processing 16*, 3(July 1981), 296-302. [region data]

237. M. Shneier, Two hierarchical linear feature representations: edge pyramids and edge quadtrees, *Computer Graphics and Image Processing 17*, 3(November 1981), 211-224. [line data]

238. Y.V. Silva Filho, Average case analysis of region search in balanced k-d trees, *Information Processing Letters 8*, 5(June 1979), 219-223. [point data]

239. Y.V. Silva Filho, Optimal choice of discriminators in a balanced k-d binary search tree, *Information Processing Letters 13*, 2(November 1981), 67-70. [point data]

240. K.R. Sloan Jr., Dynamically quantized pyramids, *Proceedings of the Sixth International Joint Conference on Artificial Intelligence*, Vancouver, August 1981, 734-736. [point data]

241. K.R. Sloan Jr. and S.L. Tanimoto, Progressive refinement of raster images, *IEEE Transactions on Computers 28*, 11(November 1979), 871-874. [coding; approximation]

242. N. Solntseff and D. Wood, Pyramids: A data type for matrix representation in PASCAL, *BIT 17*, (1977), 344-350. [point data; matrix representation]

243. S.N. Srihari, Representation of three-dimensional digital images, *ACM Computing Surveys 13*, 1(December 1981), 399-424. [three-dimensional data]

244. Q. Stout, Linear-time component labeling and distance transforms in quadtrees, University of Michigan, Ann Arbor, 1985. [geometric property measurement]

245. I.E. Sutherland, R.F. Sproull, and R.A. Schumacker, A characterization of ten hidden-surface algorithms, *ACM Computing Surveys 6*, 1(March 1974), 1-55. [computer graphics]

246. M. Tamminen, The EXCELL method for efficient geometric access to data, *Acta Polytechnica Scandinavica*, Mathematics and Computer Science Series No. 34, Helsinki, 1981. [point data]

247. M. Tamminen, Hidden lines using the EXCELL method, *Computer Graphics Forum 11*, No. 3, 1982, 96-105. [computer graphics]

248. M. Tamminen, Performance analysis of cell based geometric file organizations, *Computer Vision, Graphics, and Image Processing 24*, 2(November 1983), 168-181. [region data]

249. M. Tamminen, Comment on quad- and octtrees, *Communications of the ACM 27*, 3(March 1984), 248-249. [region data]

250. M. Tamminen, Encoding pixel trees, *Computer Vision, Graphics, and Image Processing 28*, 1(October 1984), 44-57. [region data]

251. M. Tamminen and H. Samet, Efficient octree conversion by connectivity labeling, *Computer Graphics 18*, 3(July 1984), pp. 43-51 (also *Proceedings of the SIGGRAPH'84 Conference*, Minneapolis, July 1984). [three-dimensional data]

252. S. Tanimoto, Pictorial feature distortion in a pyramid, *Computer Graphics and Image Processing 5*, 3(September 1976), 333-352. [pyramids]

253. S.L. Tanimoto, Image transmission with gross information first, *Computer Graphics and Image Processing 9*, 1(January 1979), 72-76. [coding; approximation]

254. S. Tanimoto and A. Klinger, Eds., *Structured Computer Vision*, Academic Press, New York, 1980. [general]

255. S. Tanimoto and T. Pavlidis, A hierarchical data structure for picture processing, *Computer Graphics and Image Processing 4*, 2(June 1975), 104-119. [image processing]

256. G.T. Toussaint, Pattern recognition and geometrical complexity, *Proceedings of the Fifth International Conference on Pattern Recognition*, Miami Beach, December 1980, 1324-1346. [general]

257. H. Tropf and H. Herzog, Multidimensional range search in dynamically balanced trees, *Angewandte Informatik*, 2(1981), 71-77. [point data]

258. L.W. Tucker, Control strategy for an expert vision system using quadtree refinement, *Proceedings of the Workshop on Computer Vision: Representation and Control*, Annapolis, April 1984, 214-218. [image processing]

259. L.W. Tucker, Computer vision using quadtree refinement, Ph.D. dissertation, Department of Electrical Engineering and Computer Science, Polytechnic Institute of New York, Brooklyn, NY, May 1984. [image processing]

260. L. Uhr, Layered "recognition cone" networks that preprocess, classify, and describe, *IEEE Transactions on Computers 21*, 7(July 1972), 758-768. [pyramids]

261. A. Unnikrishnan and Y.V. Venkatesh, On the conversion of raster to linear quadtrees, Department of Electrical Engineering, Indian Institute of Science, Bangalore, India, May 1984. [region data]

262. V.K. Vaishnavi, Multidimensional height-balanced trees, *IEEE Transactions on Computers 33*, 4(April 1984), 334-343. [point data]

263. V.K. Vaishnavi, H.P. Kriegel, and D. Wood, Space and time optimal algorithms for a class of rectangle intersection problems, *Information Sciences 21*, (1980), 59-67. [point data]

264. V. Vaishnavi and D. Wood, Data structures for the rectangle containment and enclosure problems, *Computer Graphics and Image Processing 13*, (1980) 372-384. [point data]

265. J. van Leeuwen and D. Wood, The measure problem for rectangular ranges in d-space, *Journal of Algorithms 2*, 3(September 1981), 282-300. [rectangles]

266. M.L.P. van Lierop, Transformations on pictures represented by leafcodes, Department of Mathematics and Computing Science, Eindhoven University of Technology, Eindhoven, The Netherlands, 1984. [region representation; computer graphics]

267. J. Veenstra and N. Ahuja, Octree generation from silhouette views of an object, *Proceedings of the International Conference on Robotics*, St. Louis, March 1985, 843-848. [three-dimensional data]

268. J.L. Warnock, A hidden surface algorithm for computer generated half tone pictures, Computer Science Department TR 4-15, University of Utah, Salt Lake City, June 1969. [computer graphics]

269. R.E. Webber, Analysis of quadtree algorithms, Ph.D. dissertation, Computer Science Department, University of Maryland, College Park, MD, March 1984 (also University of Maryland Computer Science TR-1376). [general]

270. W. Weber, Three types of map data structures, their ANDs and NOTs, and a possible OR, in *Proceedings of the First International Advanced Study Symposium on Topological Data Structures for Geographic Information Systems*, G. Dutton, Ed., Harvard Papers on Geographic Information Systems, 1978. [region representation]

271. M. White, N-trees: large ordered indexes for multi-dimensional space, U.S. Bureau of the Census, Statistical Research Division, 1982. [point data]

272. D.E. Willard, Balanced forests of #roman {k-d} sup *# trees as a dynamic data structure, Aiken Computation Lab TR-23-78, Harvard University, Cambridge, 1978. [point data]

273. D.E. Willard, Polygon retrieval, *SIAM Journal on Computing 11*, 1(February 1982), 149-165. [point data]

274. D.E. Willard, New data structures for orthogonal range queries, *SIAM Journal on Computing 14*, 1(February 1982), 232-253. [point data]

275. D.S. Wise, Representing matrices as quadtrees for parallel processors, *Information Processing Letters 20*, 4(May 1985), 195-199. [numerical analysis]

276. E.K. Wong and K.S. Fu, A hierarchical-orthogonal-space approach to collision-free path planning, *Proceedings of the International Conference on Robotics*, St. Louis, March 1985, 506-511. [three-dimensional data, path planning]

277. T.C. Woo, A combinatorial analysis of boundary data structure schemata, *IEEE Computer Graphics and Applications 5*, 3(March 1985), 19-27. [three-dimensional data]

278. J.R. Woodwark, The explicit quad tree as a structure for computer graphics, *Computer Journal 25*, 2(May 1982), 235-238. [region representation]

279. J.R. Woodwark, Compressed quad trees, *Computer Journal 27*, 3(August 1984), 225-229. [region representation]

280. A.Y. Wu, T.H. Hong, and A. Rosenfeld, Threshold selection using quadtrees, *IEEE Transactions on Pattern Analysis and Machine Intelligence 4*, 1(January 1982), 90-94. [image processing]

281. K. Yamaguchi, T.L. Kunii, K. Fujimura, and H. Toriya, Octree-related data structures and algorithms, *IEEE Computer Graphics and Applications 4*, 1(January 1984), 53-59. [three-dimensional data]

282. M. Yau, Generating quadtrees of cross-sections from octrees, *Computer Vision, Graphics, and Image Processing 27*, 2(August 1984), 211-238. [three-dimensional data]

283. M. Yau and S.N. Srihari, A hierarchical data structure for multidimensional digital images, *Communications of the ACM 26*, 7(July 1983), 504-515. [three-dimensional data]

284. M.A. Yerry and M.S. Shepard, A modified quadtree approach to finite element mesh generation, *IEEE Computer Graphics and Applications 3*, 1(January/February 1983), 39-46. [numerical analysis]

MIX
Papier aus verantwortungsvollen Quellen
Paper from responsible sources
FSC® C105338

If you have any concerns about our products,
you can contact us on
ProductSafety@springernature.com

In case Publisher is established outside the EU,
the EU authorized representative is:
Springer Nature Customer Service Center GmbH
Europaplatz 3, 69115 Heidelberg, Germany

Printed by Libri Plureos GmbH
in Hamburg, Germany